AF413764

AMERICAN CROWN

AMERICAN CROWN

FROM REVOLUTIONARIES TO ROYALTY:
The Story of Prince William's American Heritage

STEPHANIE GREEN

PEGASUS BOOKS

NEW YORK LONDON

AMERICAN CROWN

Pegasus Books, Ltd.
148 West 37th Street, 12th Floor
New York, NY 10018

First Pegasus Books cloth edition July 2026

Interior design by Maria Fernandez

Library of Congress Cataloging-in-Publication Data is available.

ISBN: 979-8-89710-105-4

10 9 8 7 6 5 4 3 2 1

Printed in the United States of America
Distributed by Simon & Schuster
www.pegasusbooks.com

For my mother and grandmother

CONTENTS

JOSEPH STRONG
b. 1701 - Northampton, MA
d. 1773 - Coventry, CT

BENAJAH STRONG
b. 1740 - Coventry, CT
d. 1809 - Coventry, CT

ELIZABETH STRONG HALE
Sister of Benajah Strong
b. 1727 - Coventry, CT
d. 1767 - Coventry, CT

DR. JOSEPH STRONG
b. 1770 - Coventry, CT
d. 1812 - Philadelphia, PA

NATHAN HALE
Nephew of Benajah Strong
b. 1755 - Coventry, CT
d. 1776 - New York, NY

ELLEN STRONG
b. 1803 - Philadelphia, PA
d. 1863 - New York, NY

ELLEN WOOD WORK
b. 1831 - Chillicothe, OH
d. 1877 - New York, NY

FRANK WORK
b. 1819 - Chillicothe, OH
d. 1911 - New York, NY

FRANCES WORK BURKE ROCHE
b. 1857 - New York, NY
d. 1947 - New York, NY

JAMES BURKE ROCHE, Third Baron Fermoy
b. 1851 - London
d. 1920 - London

MAURICE BURKE ROCHE, Fourth Baron Fermoy
b. 1885 - London
d. 1955 - Norfolk, UK

FRANCES BURKE ROCHE SHAND KYDD
b. 1936 - Norfolk, UK
d. 2004 - Scotland

DIANA, PRINCESS OF WALES
b. 1961 - Norfolk, UK
d. 1997 - Paris, France

WILLIAM, PRINCE OF WALES
b. 1982 - London, UK

"Happy families are all alike; every unhappy family is unhappy in its own way."

—Leo Tolstoy, *Anna Karenina*

FOREWORD
by Maurice Roche, sixth Baron Fermoy

My family has its own special relationship with America. My great-grandmother Frances Burke Roche was a Manhattan heiress who brought her American spirit into the Fermoy clan, which is still deeply felt today, especially as the world marks two hundred and fifty years since American independence from Great Britain. Fanny, as she was known, gave us a Patriot bloodline that dates back to the beginning of the Republic. These ancestors were outstanding American heroes, innovators, entrepreneurs, and leaders of society. A common denominator among them was their dedication to country and a sense of service to their fellow man, qualities I still admire in my grandfather, Maurice, the fourth Baron Fermoy, whose title I inherited and whose name I proudly carry as my own. Maurice and his twin brother, Francis, served in World War I; Maurice in the US Army and Francis in the US Navy. I continued this legacy by serving as an officer in the Blues and Royals, a cavalry regiment of the British Army and part of the Household Cavalry, the monarch's official bodyguard.

Maurice went on to become a respected member of Parliament and friend of King George VI. His humility and decency made him a beloved figure among the elite and among the less fortunate members of his community whom he never forgot.

I have observed these traits in Maurice's great-grandson His Royal Highness Prince William, who as king will make the Fermoy family very proud and whose American forbears will look on bemusedly at the twists and turns their family have made from being at the heart of rebellion to having one of their own as the heir to the throne.

I hope these pages enlighten us on our shared history and values and inspire others to serve their country, however they can.

Two hundred and fifty years later, we are, in the end, one big family.

ACKNOWLEDGMENTS

The writing of this book has been a journey best measured in friends, rather than miles or pages. Many of my friendships have been imaginary. As I've gotten to know some of the characters in *American Crown*, I've longed for their companionship and have tried to emulate their qualities and avoid the various pitfalls that derailed their lives.

How I would have adored an afternoon in a horse drawn carriage with the irrepressible Fanny Roche, or a fireside chat with her father Frank. I'm sure the two of them would have given me some (probably unsolicited) advice, timeless in its wisdom.

While Nathan Hale is not regarded as a Founding Father, after studying him, I think he should be: few in our country possessed his courage, innate goodness, and utter belief in our country than he did. His life, and ultimate sacrifice, is something every patriot should cling to as an example of brotherly love.

Perhaps nobody would have made a better dinner party guest list than Jennie Jerome, her son Winston Churchill (maybe you've heard of him) or the equally glamorous Georgiana, Duchess of Devonshire. All of these are exponents of style—not just in the sartorial sense, but in their wit, charm, and ability to own a room. Of course, a few royal friends always come in handy, and I've grown in my admiration for Diana, Princess of Wales, which started in my eighties childhood when I would grasp any magazine with her on the cover. It is she who holds this book together, with her son William, whom I have not met, but hold in high esteem. It is unlikely he will ever be a friend of mine in the literal sense, but I hope he understands the affection for his family this book seeks to convey.

Now I get to tell you about my real friends, new and old. First, to my friends Catherine Timbers and Laura Rodriguez for being among the first to read my proposal. They are old friends through the Daughters of the American Revolution, and the support and encouragement I have received from my chapter and from members all over the country are indeed heartening.

A special thank you to Ed and Eve Lemon for introducing me to my agent, Dylan Colligan, with my agency, Javelin. He has been a stalwart supporter of this project from the moment I told him about it. Likewise, my publisher, Jessica Case at Pegasus Books, whose steadfast kindness and attention has guided me through the labor pains of producing my first book. Thanks to Nicole Maher for her wonderful promotion.

Amy Argetsinger, Ryan Bacic, and Aaron Wiener at *The Washington Post* all gave life to this project by paving a path for me to publish a story on William's American roots back in 2023. Without that article, it is unlikely this book would be here. Thank you all.

Thomas Lannon was a study in hospitality by allowing me to use the reading room at The Society of the Cincinnati's Anderson House where I hovered over my laptop beneath a bronze statue of Nathan Hale. Thank you also to Rachel Nellis and Andy Morse at the society for their support too. Many of the sources in this book were provided by their library.

In Coventry, Connecticut, I must thank John Holmy for being the ultimate city guide, and to Matthew Phelps for providing great insights into the life of Nathan Hale whose homestead I toured thanks to the staff there supervised by the lovely Ann Marie Charland.

In Chillicothe, Ohio, thank you to Pat Medert and the staff at the Ross County Historical Society for providing key insights into the hometown of Frank Work. At Mount Vernon, thank you very much indeed Dr. and Mrs. Douglas Bradburn for your support and friendship.

At Sulgrave Manor, I extend transatlantic gratitude to curator Dr. Gabriella de la Rosa and historian Dr. Sam Edwards.

In Newport, I must thank Guy Van Pelt, who opened the elegant doors of Elm Court and showed me the place where Fanny dined, danced, and called home for decades. I am immensely grateful to Mr. Van Pelt and Lord Fermoy, who has become a pen pal from London. Lord Fermoy provided Fanny's diaries to me, transcribed by her granddaughter Mary Burke Roche. I believe I am the only one outside the family to have access to these diaries, and for this, I will be forever grateful. At Sulgrave Manor, I must Dr. Sam Edwards, and to all my friends in the Colonial Dames who have offered such enthusiasm for the book's success.

The work of Mary Burke Roche is one of many on which I leaned for literary support. So many books and authors have provided the historical sustenance I needed to put this book together. First, I must thank Gary Boyd Roberts and William Addam Reitwasner for their seminal genealogical book on Diana's American ancestors. To Dr. Amanda Foreman, thank you for your dazzling work on Georgiana, and the film on which it is based. To Lord Roberts, thank you for coming off your perch as king of all historians to assist me. Your personal insights and your masterwork on King George III were perspective-shifting, especially for us Americans. To my old chum Dr. Douglas Brinkley, thank you for your encouragement and faith-based pats on the back when I really need them.

Finally, to my close friends and family, including Art Spitzer, my faith community, and my other friends who have lifted me up with so many prayers and in countless ways, thank you.

And to all the friends I have yet to meet on this journey, thank you and enjoy the ride with me.

1

LIEGE MAN OF LIFE AND LIMB

In December of 2024, world leaders gathered at Notre Dame Cathedral in Paris to celebrate the world landmark's great comeback after a devastating fire in 2019. But a different resurgence was on the mind of most who gathered under the sweeping rebuilt vaulted ceilings. In the front row was US President-Elect Donald Trump, who just weeks before had pulled off the greatest political comeback in modern history by winning the popular and Electoral College votes to secure a second term in the White House. Trump, who was personally invited by French president Emmanuel Macron, made what the *New York Times* called "a splashy re-entry onto the global stage" as world leaders lined up to pay their respects to someone they never expected—or perhaps never hoped—to greet in official capacity again. But the warm greeting of one of those leaders, at least, appeared genuine.[1] The United Kingdom had sent Prince William—the Prince of Wales and future King William V—as its official representative to Notre Dame, rather than its democratically elected but embattled prime minister, Sir Keir Starmer.

This was a strategic choice. Trump may have been the most powerful man in the cathedral that day, and Elon Musk may have been the wealthiest, but Prince William was the most beloved—a king of hearts for his fellow Britons, and to most Americans, who, despite their history with the Mother Country, still admire its royal family with great affection.

In short, Britain could have had no greater emissary. William cut a young, elegant, and enthusiastic figure, shaking the president-elect's hand and meeting with him privately later at the British ambassador's Paris residence. The chemistry between the two men—one old enough to be the other's father—was palpable and their affinity is personal. Trump's connection to the United Kingdom was more direct than that of most recent presidents. His mother Mary Anne MacLeod was born in Scotland on the Isle of Lewis. Her son Donald made no secret of his pride in his Scottish heritage and often plays golf at his resort along the Ayrshire coast. His respect and admiration for the royal family, especially the late Queen Elizabeth II, had been a constant in his political career. Decades earlier, Trump had been friendly with William's mother, the late Diana, Princess of Wales. One wonders if that friendship came up in his conversation with William, as Trump is fond of name-dropping, especially where celebrities and glamorous women are concerned. It's unlikely, however, that either man was aware of the astounding twist of fate that, courtesy of Diana's ancestry, made this meeting of a future president and future king unique in history. Through Diana, William is one sixteenth American—descended from an American family that goes back to the epicenter of the American Revolution and includes some of the most heroic figures of the time, including the martyred spy Nathan Hale, the nephew of William's patriot ancestor Benajah Strong of Coventry, Connecticut, a hotbed of American rebellion in the 1700s.[2]

Who would have thought that on that rainy day in Paris the future king of the United Kingdom had deeper American roots than the future president of the United States?

When Diana's American great-grandmother Frances Work married James Boothby Burke Roche, third Baron Fermoy, she set the stage for the Work-Strong bloodline to merge with the Spencer family, creating an Anglo-American alliance like none other.

As United States celebrates its 250th birthday in 2026, William's family celebrates coming full circle—from fighting the British monarchy to embodying it. As the United Kingdom struggles with internal political strife and replaces one inept prime minister after another, while William's father, the present King Charles III, struggles to manage the fallout from his younger brother Andrew's disgrace while trying to toe the line on his distant relationship with his own son Prince Harry, Prince William has emerged as the next best hope for international relationships and the monarchy itself.

His life over the past few years has been as tumultuous as the American Revolution itself with personal battles, triumphs, blood, sweat, tears, and the seizure of his destiny.

On May 6, 2023, William, Prince of Wales, knelt before his father, King Charles III, and took an oath of fealty with the eyes of the world watching. Cloaked in ceremonial velvet, he made a medieval pledge as a representative of the "Royal Blood." *"I, William, Prince of Wales, pledge my loyalty to you and faith and truth I will bear unto you, as your liege man of life and limb. So help me God."* The kiss on his father's cheek as he finished his oath provided a touching moment amid the rigid formality at Westminster Abbey. This was an occasion he had been pondering since the death of his grandmother Queen Elizabeth II, and indeed his whole life, which began on June 21, 1982, when he was born the first child of Charles, Prince of Wales and the former Lady Diana Spencer, who had stepped into what she hoped would be her Cinderella slippers and became the Princess of Wales less than a year earlier in the world's most-watched wedding at St. Paul's Cathedral.

As she sailed down the aisle that summer day, she wore the Spencer Tiara, a reminder that although she was marrying into world's most prestigious family, her own blood was thick with English—and American—history too. The Spencers were, in fact, more English than the Windsors and had produced some of England's most illustrious figures, including none other than Sir Winston Churchill, whose dazzling American mother, Jennie Jerome, gave Winston his inimitable charisma. Another Spencer ancestress, Georgiana, Duchess of Devonshire, used her fame and influence to support the American rebels and became a forerunner for women's involvement in British politics.

When William knelt that day in 2023, he was one step closer to achieving an American dream—one that his mother, who was fond of America and was planning to move there before her death in 1997, had put in motion. Although the future King William is and always will be British, and America is and likely always will be a republic, his connection to the nation of his mother's forbears will give the future of the so-called Special Relationship an even greater significance. As William contemplates his Yankee roots, so too will Americans have an opportunity to reexamine our own connection to his country and reassess the monarchy we ousted. As William Shakespeare said, "Uneasy lies the head that wears a crown." As we celebrate our 250th birthday as a nation, we must confront our past leaders—whether they be kings or patriots—as people with flaws and virtues, because patriotism is shared by kings and patriots alike. And their fates and families are linked much closer than most of us imagine.

2

A TALE OF
TWO GEORGES

When the late Queen Elizabeth II visited Philadelphia in 1976 to mark America's bicentennial, she said that Independence Day "should be celebrated as much in Britain as in America. Not in rejoicing at the separation of the American Colonists from the British Crown, but in sincere gratitude to the Founding Fathers of this great Republic for having taught Britain a very valuable lesson."[1]

Prince William's familial lesson from America begins in the 1730s with the birth of two men named George: George Washington and King George III. George Washington was born into the Virginia gentry in 1732. His great-grandfather Colonel John Washington had arrived on Virginian shores in the mid-1650s angling for a new life in the New World. The Washington family seat Sulgrave Manor, in Northampton, England, was just a short distance from Althorp, the far grander seat of the far grander Spencer family. Robert Washington, the son of Sulgrave Manor's builder, had sold the home to Lawrence Makepeace, his nephew. Makepeace's son, Abel, sold Sulgrave out of the family in 1659. The last Washington born at Sulgrave was the builder's grandson, Lawrence, born in 1568. The Spencer and Washington families, before being separated by the Atlantic after Colonel John's voyage, had been friends for years. Indeed, to this day some of the Spencers and Washingtons lie together in the Great Brington churchyard, two miles from Althorp.[2]

According to the current Lord Spencer in his family history *The Spencers*, this familial bond started with Lady Penelope Spencer, who made it her mission to make Althorp a mecca of hospitality, not just for the great and glamorous, but for everyone. This included their neighbors the Washington family, who had fallen on hard times after what appeared to be a steady social climb.[3]

Like the Spencers, Washington forbear Lawrence Washington made a fortune in the woolstapling business. In the process, he had amassed enough influence to become mayor of Northhampton by 1532, and with the help of Henry VIII purchased the manor and lands of Sulgrave for just over £324, which had been a monastery, for his own. Some would say his seizure of God's property cursed him, because by 1616 Sulgrave Manor had to be sold.

The first Lord Spencer lent a helping hand to the beleaguered Washingtons, giving them a small house in Brington. The next generation of Washingtons, Robert and his wife Elizabeth, were taken under the wing of Lady Penelope, who frequently mentions their adopted little girl Amy in her diaries. For their part, the Washingtons tried to repay her kindness with gifts of chicken and bacon during Christmastide, generous gifts in proportion to their income at the time.

Under the reign of James I, the Washington family saw a rise in stature. William and John, Robert's nephews, were elevated to Sir William and Sir John, thanks to finding favor with the monarch. Sir William and his family, especially, became fixtures at Althorp during the 1620s—this time not as pitiful neighbors, but as peers and playmates of Lord and Lady Spencer and their children.

When Spencer heir Henry needed military tutoring on his charger, it was Sir John who provided it. His sister Lucy Washington became a governess of the household. Their friendship was sealed in war as Sir John, Henry Spencer, and another Washington nephew fought side by side for the Royalists during the English Civil War, losing to the Parliamentarians.

Fleeing to Virginia, as did many loyal Englishmen fearing the depredations of Oliver Cromwell, Sir John would never forget the dazzling Spencer clan. In the years to come his great-grandson George Washington would mount a charger, too, and fight to prove himself in war—but this time against a king, not for one.

A young George Washington never knew his great-grandfather, but he likely heard about the proud family origins at Sulgrave Manor, which George would one day try to replicate at his plantation, Mount Vernon.

By 1755, then-Major George Washington was an aide-de-camp to General Edward Braddock in the British Army stationed in the American colonies. As they battled the French and Native Americans in Pennsylvania, George narrowly escaped death when two of his horses were shot while he was riding them. At the time George was risking his life for his king, George II. The Prince of Wales, heir to the British throne, was Prince George, the future George III. Prince George was born just six years after George Washington, and the two young boys lost their fathers during their most formative years. Augustine Washington had died suddenly from a chill in 1743, when George was eleven, and Frederick, Prince of Wales, died an equally untimely death at the age of forty-four, two months before his son's thirteenth birthday, moving young George one place higher in the line of succession.[4]

A portrait of George Washington as a British serving officer painted by Charles Williams Peale shows a confident young man in his colonial military uniform. It conveys the regality and elegant masculinity that would mark Washington's bearing for the rest of his life. Meanwhile, Prince George cut an equally striking figure as he entered manhood. Horace Walpole described the future king as "tall and full of dignity; his countenance florid and good-natured; his manner graceful and obliging."[5]

While both were good dancers and attractive to women, they both adopted codes of morality and propriety early in life, rooted in their strong Christian faith. When George III became king he was one of the first monarchs in Britain and one of few in the world to not have a mistress, a stark contrast to his predecessor whose extramarital affairs were well-known and accepted.

This reliance on faith was born out of early loss. Not only did they see the early deaths of their fathers, but they would also outlive most of their siblings. In 1752, George Washington saw his older brother Lawrence die of tuberculosis in his early thirties. Brushes with mortality at a young age often instill lessons in fortitude, and this was evident in the personal conduct of both Georges.

In 1760, after his succession to the throne, George III issued a proclamation "for the encouragement of piety and virtue, and for the preventing and punishing of vice, profaneness and immorality." George Washington's *Rules of Civility and Decent Behaviour in Company and Conversation*, a list of dos and don'ts, is still a popular read for the aspiring lady or gentleman. Both men sought to champion and embody humility and moral uprightness, sometimes to the point of austerity.[6]

The king not only abstained from alcohol but deemed it improper to play cards on Sundays and high holidays. He gave few dinner parties, preferring to entertain—when he had to—on a smaller scale. George III opted to shave himself and write his own letters, despite these mundane tasks being executed by servants for previous monarchs. When he received communion, he removed his crown, symbolizing his belief that he knelt before the altar as a lowly sinner just like every other supplicant before God.

His only indulgence was his bibliomania, solidifying his reputation as one of the most intellectually dexterous monarchs in British history. His library included some three hundred books on the American colonies, which continued to fascinate him even after the American Revolution, according to his biographer Andrew Roberts. Enlightenment writers whose ideas led to the overthrow of monarchies like Voltaire, Jean-Jacques Rousseau, and Edmund Burke also found a place on his shelves. Music was a close second in his passions. He could play several instruments and enjoyed the friendship of George Frideric Handel, who said of King George, "While that boy lives, my music will never want a protector."[7]

By the time of his 1761 coronation, attended by Benjamin Franklin, then Deputy Postmaster-General in the American colonies, George was a Renaissance man with an equally cultivated woman at his side: Queen Charlotte, whom he had married shortly after acceding to the throne in 1760. Although the two had virtually no courtship and married under political pressure, their common interest in music and culture begat a loving, fruitful, and faithful marriage. They would eventually produce fifteen children. George built Buckingham House, now Buckingham Palace, for Charlotte.[8]

George Washington was not as fortunate in his fecundity. He married the wealthy widow Martha Custis in 1759, and although they, too, had a faithful and harmonious life together, George Washington never sired any children of his own. But he adopted many children, including treating his young comrade in arms the Marquis de Lafayette as if he were his own son.

Indeed, both Georges were more comfortable with their identity as "Farmer George." They preferred being ensconced in nature, boots covered in manure, or reading and spending quiet time with their wives, rather than being the leaders of two warring nations. Fate, however, had other plans. The French and Indian War, in which George had served as a British officer, would necessitate new taxes to pay for the protection of the thirteen colonies, whose population was growing faster than that of population of England.[9]

Although the French and Indian War had been successful, its financing had left Britain in serious debt. George III's biographer explains that the king's ministers had estimated it would cost over 20,000 pounds in eighteenth-century money to maintain a peacetime military presence. The British taxpayer, they reasoned, should not be paying the whole of the bill, an idea that was lost on the colonists and their colonial governors. "Not a penny of any of George III's taxes on Americans was ever spent on anyone except Americans—this did not occur to civil servants until far too late," Andrew Roberts explains.[10]

George III's reluctance to travel, locally or long distances, may have had geopolitical consequences. During the whole of his reign, he never stepped foot in Scotland or Ireland, and he was the first monarch since Elizabeth I not to visit continental Europe. In *The Last King of America*, Roberts suggests that had he made a state visit to the colonies "to gain an inkling of America's potential and her discontents, the story of the next twenty years might well have been very different."[11]

Like most Americans, a young George Washington revered his king as a man and a monarch, but by 1763 His Majesty's policies began to encumber the Virginian. A Virginian who was ambitious to acquire more land. That October, Lord Halifax issued a proclamation prohibiting westward settlements and expansions by the colonists, mostly to appease Native American tribes who were loyal to British interests during the French and Indian War and wanted recompense for their efforts. Colonists who had already moved along the slopes of the Appalachian Mountains would be required to return eastward.

This policy was in direct opposition to the land speculation efforts of many of the key Founding Fathers such as Thomas Jefferson, the Lee family, and most notably, George Washington, who had started the Mississippi Land Company to cultivate land in the Ohio Valley, comprising what is now Ohio, Tennessee, Indiana, Kentucky, and Illinois. The historian Ron Chernow called this decision a "catastrophic blunder," which was the turning point in the way George Washington viewed his king.[12]

When it was revealed that in 1770 this policy was exempted for British investors, Washington bitterly noted that it was an example of the British "malignant disposition towards Americans."

As tensions with America became more fractious, especially after the Stamp Act—another means of increasing national revenue for Britain—George III and his government knew that concessions had to be made, demonstrating that the king was a flexible and understanding statesman, not the bullying tyrant he was later characterized as being. George was willing to moderate the tax, then reduce the tax, and finally push for a repeal of the act, a virtual volte-face, to save his relationship with the colonists.

"I thought the modifying of the Stamp Act the wisest and most efficacious manner of proceeding," he wrote. "I thought repealing infinitely more eligible than enforcing, which could only tend to widen the breach between this country and America."[13]

But, by 1769, rebel uprisings in Boston necessitated two British regiments of some four thousand troops to police a city of fifteen thousand. Rebels such as Samuel Adams considered the British presence in his hometown surveillance, not the protection that the king insisted was his intention. The king maintained he was not a warmonger with a virtual stick keeping his subjects in line, but a benevolent father looking out for the physical welfare of his people.

A grateful flock gathered in New York in April 1770 for the unveiling of a mammoth statue to King George on Bowling Green. The monument had been started four years earlier in response to the king's repeal of the Stamp Act with "the deep sense this colony has of the eminent and singular blessings received from him during his most auspicious reign." The new statue, weighing two tons of lead and much larger than life-size, was greeted with revelry and cheers, even though just weeks earlier the Boston Massacre, which resulted in British soldiers shooting five Bostonians, exacerbated the London-Boston acrimony.[14]

"While we are declining the usurped authority of Parliament," wrote Benjamin Franklin, "I wish to see a steady dutiful attachment to the king and his family maintained among us." This was the general feeling among all the Founding Fathers, including Adams and Jefferson, in the years leading up to 1776. The scheming politicians in Parliament were the tyrants, and the king was an ally, was the prevailing opinion at the time in the colonies.[15]

After the Boston Tea Party in December 1773, Parliament wanted retribution after what they perceived as excessive provocations. The legendary tossing of tea into the harbor had been preceded by acts of brutal violence, including the tarring and feathering of British officials in Massachusetts. The Coercive Acts, known in America as Intolerable Acts, shut down Boston Harbor until the cost of the lost tea was repaid, and effectively nullified the Massachusetts Charter of 1691. This act was one of several that the king did not direct Prime Minister Lord North to enact. The king, however, loyal to his constitutional responsibilities, supported the decisions of his ministers.[16]

If the British government thought the Coercive Acts would whip the colonies into submission, they were dead wrong. If anything, they provided the motivation for other colonies to support Massachusetts, and to organize their own provocations against Parliament.

Speaking in the House of Commons, Lord North came out swinging in defense of the Coercive Acts, saying Americans had physically attacked subjects, "burnt ships, denied all obedience to your laws and authority . . . so long forbearing has our conduct been that it is incumbent on us now to take a different course. Whatever may be the consequences, we must risk something; if we do not, all is over."[17]

Meanwhile in Virginia, the lawyer Thomas Jefferson anonymously published *A Summary View of the Rights of British America* in which he pleaded with the king to stand up to Lord North and side with his subjects in the colonies, a foreshadowing of the declaration he would pen two years later. "Let not the name of George the Third be a blot in the page of history," he wrote. While these words evidently fell on deaf ears, King George did include *Summary View* in his massive book collection.[18]

On September 5, 1774, the first Continental Congress met in Philadelphia to organize against the Coercive Acts. George Washington was there, having completed his transition from British country gentleman to fully paid-up patriot rebel. It is important to note that the British regulars did not interrupt or shut down these proceedings, further evidence of the king's "forbearance" of what would later be known as "free speech" and open debate, even when it decried him. Note, too, that George

Washington did not represent a majority; patriots comprised a third of the population during this time and throughout the Revolutionary War, while another third remained loyal to the Crown, and another third were indifferent.[19]

Slavery was practiced in all thirteen colonies, especially in the southern colonies where Loyalist support was high. Roughly twenty percent of the American population was enslaved before the Revolution, to whom George III promised freedom in exchange for their loyalty to the Crown. As a younger man, George III wrote about slavery's repugnance, and eventually acted on his conviction, ultimately assenting to the 1807 abolition of the slave trade in the British Empire. It would take America until 1860 to do the same, with a second war in the interregnum to make that happen. While George III never owned slaves as George Washington and many of the other Founding Fathers did, his navy did capture a French slave-hub in 1779, indicating an economic interest in maintaining the slave trade. Historians differ on his exact views on slavery, but the scourge of its institution in Britain and in America has had lasting effects, as we will see later.

While the Continental Congress passed the Declaration of Rights and Resolves listing a vast number of grievances, including the Coercive Acts, General Gage, now the king's commander in chief in Massachusetts, pushed for more troops to quell the uprisings. Gage lobbied for hiring foreign troops as the colonist aggression expanded from Massachusetts to neighboring states. Parliament and the king's advisers never anticipated an all-out war. Still arrogant following their victory in the French and Indian War, thought they could suppress any rebel rabble quickly and easily.

On April 18, 1775, at around eight o'clock in the evening, Gage sent several hundred of his men to confiscate arms and ammunition the rebels were stockpiling near Concord, northwest of Boston. Before Paul Revere could mount his horse on that fateful night, the world had turned upside down, and the two Georges, and the countries they loved, would never be the same.

3

FOOD FOR WORMS

The town of Coventry, Connecticut, founded in 1712, is today a community of around twelve thousand citizens, most of whom commute to nearby Hartford for work. There are no hotels, only a few restaurants, and no Starbucks in sight. Coventry Lake, the town's favorite watering hole, has provided recreation for the town for centuries, and is the perfect setting to enjoy their fireworks around the Fourth of July.[1] They are a proud community of New Englanders, humble and down-to-earth, and prouder still of their place in the country's early history as over one hundred of their men answered the call to arms as revolutionary fervor was spreading from neighboring Massachusetts in the 1770s. British law required all men in Coventry and throughout the colonies to join a militia when they turned eighteen. Benajah Strong signed on as a private in the Connecticut Militia, joining forces with his friend from Coventry, Captain Elias Buell.[2] In 1775, these militias would be fighting against, not for, the country that had required their formation. The "rally rock" in front of Coventry High School marks the alleged location where the Lexington Alarm men gathered when they heard the news the war against Britian had started. Benajah Strong, born a British subject in a town named for a British city, was one of those men. He had no inkling that his sixth great-grandson would one day sit on the British throne. Coventry seems the most unlikely of hometowns for a future king, but this is where William's American story begins.

For Benajah and Coventry, the mid-eighteenth century was an era of rebellion not just politically, but culturally. Connecticut was once known as the "land of steady habits" thanks to its self-containment and state charter, which gave independence to its citizens, mostly landowners who worked in farming and land development. God, family, and farm were the pillars of life to which Benajah's ilk clung for inspiration and sustenance. It had been this way since 1635 when the Strong family reached the New World through Elder John Strong, who came from Kent, England, and would go on to establish the towns of Dorchester and Northampton, Massachusetts, in the 1650s. The family would disperse throughout New England, establishing a reputation for godly, civic, and scholarly pursuits.[3]

Benajah, born in 1740, belonged to the first generation of the Strong clan to be raised in Coventry after his father, Joseph Strong Jr., settled there after moving from Northampton. Benajah would eventually serve as justice of the peace, leading townsman, and treasurer, and represent Coventry in the Connecticut General Assembly for sixty-five sessions.[4]

But by the 1770s, Connecticut and the established order were changing rapidly. New England's reliance on Puritanism and Calvinist virtues of modesty and moderation was slipping away, along with the Church of England's stronghold in Connecticut. Anything related to England, or the "Tories" who supported her, was losing appeal. The church and mother country were no longer worshipped and glorified, replaced by French philosophers and their liberal teachings. The new religion, which had washed ashore in the late eighteenth century, was personal freedom. The frequent use of intoxicants, swearing in public, and even "night walking" were de rigueur. The local authorities in Coventry accepted these changing times with nonchalance—even violations on the Sabbath went unsanctioned.[5]

By the time Benajah was twenty years old, Connecticut's population had tripled and "the land of steady habits" was a land of political upheaval. The Sons of Liberty and their radical agitations had taken hold in Connecticut to protest the Stamp Act of 1765. Eastern Connecticut towns near Coventry became centers of anti-British sentiment when locals refused to import or sell British goods. Committees of Inspection were formed to harangue merchants to join the boycott. Business owners who did not bow to the pressure were outed in newspapers and decried at public meetings.

It was an aspiring poet from Connecticut who penned the following jingle to keep Boston in line:

> *Parliament an Act has made*
> *That will distress and ruin trade*
> *To raise a Tax as we are told,*
> *That will enslave both young and old;*
> *Look out poor Boston, make a stand,*
> *Don't suffer any Tea to land.*[6]

Unfortunately, the witty pen of a patriot and the machinations of the colonists did nothing to quell the British government's agenda, and Connecticut was soon as aggressive in its anti-British sentiments as its neighbor. The Sons of Liberty had branched out from Boston and taken root in Connecticut. Across the state, angry mobs hunted down uncooperative Tory loyalists, wreaking havoc and violence. Coventry and her eastern Connecticut towns were hotbeds of the American cause, and Benajah was ready for the fight.

He had enlisted in the Lexington Alarm, a volunteer militia ready to spread the word of imminent British invasion. Since the Boston Tea Party in 1773, Connecticut and her neighboring states had been under the surveillance, or in King George's view the protection, of British regulars.

Paul Revere, thanks to Longfellow's rousing poem, made the Lexington Alarm famous as he embarked on that iconic midnight ride, but there were countless men, like Benajah, who had been providing necessary communication for the colonists, a vital means of neighborly protection. When Americans arrived in New England, they had developed their own alarm systems to warn of Indian attacks or other dangers.

But by 1772, these countryside watches took on heavier responsibilities when Samuel Adams in Boston organized "Committees of Correspondence" to publish and communicate infringements of rights or aggressions by the British. In short order, most towns had these committees to not only communicate with their citizens about possible British violations, but, more importantly, to share and collate the intelligence they gathered. The scholar E. D. Collins says this communication system was the lifeblood of the Revolution. "Its importance as a piece of Revolutionary machinery can hardly be overestimated. It was correspondence, with cooperation at the terminal points, which brought about the Revolution."[7]

The meetinghouse where Coventry's committee was likely formed—several men elected at a town meeting and a chairman selected from among them—is no longer standing, but its location is marked today with a plaque. Benajah is listed along with two Hale brothers, John and Joseph, his nephews through his sister Elizabeth. The committee's primary responsibility would have been to receive and report news to the de facto central command of the Revolution in Boston.[8]

On the evening of April 18, Revere and the Boston committee noticed movements by the British. Committee member Dr. Joseph Warren asked Revere that evening to ride to Lexington to warn Adams and Hancock that the British were on the march. As Revere rode that night, he saw prearranged lantern signals that lit up the frosty air as he crossed the Charles River. He alerted every house he passed before finally reaching Adams and Hancock. After years of meetings and contingency planning, the Lexington Alarm, or Operation British Invasion, had begun.

Revere was on his way to Concord to continue his alarms but was turned back toward Lexington by British officers under General Gage, whose plan was to confiscate munitions and, if lucky, snatch Hancock and Samuel Adams, who would be tried for treason in England if Gage had his way. (Adams and Hancock now rest peacefully on American soil in Boston's Granary Burying Ground.)

When the British troops reached Lexington, halfway to Concord, they saw in the ghostly morning mist some seventy armed colonists lined up across the common. After the shock of confrontation with the impertinent rebels, the troops opened fire. The rebels returned the volley, then scattered, leaving eight of their own on the cold April ground. The seizure of Hancock, Adams, and military supplies had failed, yet many military assets had been destroyed. Gage counted 273 British casualties of the Lexington and Concord skirmishes out of 1,800 men engaged; American casualties numbered ninety-five men. Through their deaths, America's first patriots were born that morning. The shots heard around the world had been gloriously fired, and the American War of Independence was officially underway.

We do not know when precisely the news of the shots reached Coventry, but we do know that Benajah would have been involved in receiving the news and disseminating it to his neighbors. Benajah would have gotten an official announcement from a messenger rider named Israel Bissell. A letter from one Joseph Palmer, a firsthand witness at Lexington, exists today that provides physical evidence of a document being passed from town to town by Bissell with the news of the war's commencement. The idea was that when Bissell arrived in a town the letter would be endorsed—signed off by a member of the local committee—and then taken to the next town.

One can only imagine Palmer's panic as he tried to write the message: "Pray let the delegates of this colony to Connecticut see this. They know." It is likely he is using shorthand here in the interest of brevity. Based on the signatures and dates of this surviving document, we know that the letter was received in Norwich, and then went to New London, Lyme, and Saybrook in the days following April 18. Bissell's intrepid riding adventure through Connecticut is not as famous as Revere's, but it is no less heroic. "To arms! To arms! The war has begun," was his rallying cry.

Some legends say that his poor horse fell dead from fatigue from Bissell's whiplash speed and enthusiasm.[9]

By the time Bissell reached New York on April 23, some five days after the first shots were fired, the people were in a fury. When General Alexander McDougall endorsed the letter, he noticed British sloops unloading provisions clearly undeterred by the patriot intimidation. The New York City patriot contingent soon barged into City Hall and "took out the City Arms."

The last endorsement was signed in South Carolina in mid-May, and by that point all the major newspapers from Philadelphia to Williamsburg were printing details provided by Palmer's original message. The war had proceeded from an abstract discussion of human rights to a grassroots community uprising, thanks to a gunshot, a piece of paper, and a couple of horsemen.

On July 2, Colonel George Washington reported for duty at Cambridge Common ready to assume responsibility of the newly formed Continental Army, which Lin-Manuel Miranda, creator of the Broadway smash *Hamilton*, would later aptly describe as "a ragtag volunteer army in need of a shower." The Second Continental Congress met that December and while condemning Parliament and extricating itself from their clutches, still clung to its loyalty to King George III. "What allegiance is that we forget?" the Congress asked. "Allegiance to Parliament? We never owed—we never owned it. Allegiance to our King? Our words have ever avowed it—our conduct has been ever consistent with it."

The year 1775 ended disastrously for King George as his generals had failed to crush the rabble, as they had anticipated. The following year would be the worst in his life, and the year America and George Washington would fly like an eagle.

On July 4 of that year, Congress, presided over by John Hancock, released the Declaration of Independence, a 1,458-word document, authored by Thomas Jefferson. By this time the British Army was now out of Boston and every British official had been removed, achieving a quasi-independence for the colonists. The animus turned from Parliament to the king in the Declaration, which levelled twenty-eight charges against him, most of which, according to the king's biographer, were patently false.

John Adams, who would later become the second president and launch a political dynasty, had his own reservations. "There were other expressions which I would not have inserted if I had drawn it up, particularly that which called the King a tyrant. I thought this too personal, for I never believed George to be a tyrant in disposition and nature. I thought the expression too passionate and too much like scolding, for so grave and solemn a document."

The king's biographer also points out that forty-one of the fifty-six signers were slave owners, despite their platitudes about liberty and the pursuit of happiness. King George decried slavery as early as the 1750s as "repugnant to the Laws of Nature," although Britain would not formally ban participation in the slave trade for another fifty years.[10]

The Declaration was published and read not only in the colonies, but all over London, and the king remained regally silent on the document and its charges. In the king's vast correspondence, the prolific letter writer never put pen to paper about the most famous, and contentious, event of his reign.

The colonists, however, made their views heard in massive destruction of the king's image and coat of arms on storefronts, on churches, and government buildings. Streets and colleges were renamed. Boston's King Street became State Street and King's College in Manhattan became Columbia. Georgetown, in what would later be Washington, DC, has, of course, survived, as did King, Queen, and other royal and nobly-named streets in Alexandria, Virginia, just downriver. But the Declaration had awakened hearts, minds, and fire. The king was burned in riotous effigies. One was hung on a scaffold and burnt to ashes in a gruesome faux crucifixion.

The statue to a loving king that had been erected with affection in New York just six years earlier was yanked down by an angry mob of soldiers and civilians. Not ones for subtlety, the rioters cut off the statue's head and nose and fired a musket ball into its torso. The head was placed on a stake near a tavern, and the four thousand pounds of lead of the statue was melted to make musket balls for the Continental Army. The king's "head" was later rescued and sent back to London while the tail of the statue's horse is today being safeguarded by the New York Historical.[11]

During the terrors of 1776, there emerged the noblest of patriots who, like many on both sides of the war, met the saddest of fates. Nathan Hale, another Coventry man, was the nephew of Benajah Strong and thereby a relation of William, Prince of Wales. Hale gained an immortal place in history when he was hanged by the British as an American spy, as recounted by M. William Phelps in his recent biography of the young hero.[12]

In September of 1776, Captain Nathan Hale possessed all the key ingredients of an eighteenth-century gentleman: looks, intellect, charm, and, most importantly, the right provenance. Both of his parents were the products of old New England stock, and Nathan was known as one of the "Hales of Connecticut," which gave him the patina of an aristocrat. Although the aristocracy and the privileges of lineage were becoming things of the past, Nathan had another advantage: He was a young man living in "interesting times," as the Chinese blessing (or curse) goes. Perhaps no place on earth personified these changing times quite like New York City in 1776, which was invaded and captured by the British in mid-September under the command of General Sir William Howe. Within days of this seismic event, Captain Hale was having dinner in a tavern, behind enemy lines, not far from the center of the escalating war, taking some momentary peace in the candlelit milieu. He may have caught a glimpse of himself in the mirror as he removed his hat to dine, a custom of the day. While catching his reflection was always a pleasant experience as Nathan was known for his striking handsomeness, it was also a reminder of a blight on his very comfortable existence, something that had haunted him since his boyhood in Coventry: a pockmark, or mole, depending on whom you asked, on his neck. He was often teased about it by classmates, and told it was the harbinger of doom.[13]

But Nathan let this unpleasant memory pass, and settled into his meal and spirits, which he was known to enjoy, and used as an elixir to banish his occasional dark thoughts. As taverns of the day were places of conversation with strangers, much like a pub or bar is today, Nathan struck up a chat with Robert Rogers, who described himself as a fellow American and patriot. The two men had nothing in common—Hale was a devout Christian, studious and polite, whereas Rogers was known to be a scoundrel who would do anything for a quick buck. But the two had everything to talk about—the invasion of New York, and their pasts and uncertain futures. Thanks to Hale's easy charm, incessant curiosity, and the steady presence of spirits, their conversation flowed like the Hudson River.

Rogers would have learned the following about this lad from Coventry with more than a tinge of envy: A top scholar at Yale, where his uncle Benajah and other Strong and Hale men had matriculated before him, he was from an affluent background with a radiant confidence that youth and a solid upbringing bestow. But there was one thing that always tethered Nathan to the harsh realities of life: that hairy mole on his neck. "In his boyhood, playmates sometimes twitted him about it, telling him he would be hanged," recalled one of his boyhood chums, Asher Wright. Despite this "mark of the devil," Nathan held his head up high and was determined to live a life of purpose and achievement.[14] His mother, Elizabeth Strong Hale, was the sister of Benajah and instilled in her son a pride in their Strong family heritage. Nathan's namesake, the Reverend Nathan Strong, Elizabeth's cousin, was the Puritan meetinghouse clergyman for five decades who "espoused the cause of his country, in the War of Revolution" in his sermons, many times taking jabs at King George from the pulpit.

At the time of his birth on June 6, 1755, Nathan Hale was the sixth child born to Elizabeth and Richard Hale, whose family had also arrived in New England in the fifteenth century, becoming some of the original members of the First Church of Boston. Richard Hale, who was known as Rich, was a prosperous farmer and a pious, dedicated family man. A stalwart supporter of the American cause, he bucked the expectation that he would only buy and sell British products for his home and business. According to the historian Margaret Ellen Newell, he went out of his way to harvest extra crops of flax for the Continental Army

He did not allow his work ethic to distract him from the birth of his son Nathan, however. "The Lord be praised for the mother and child. Let him be a worthy servant," he is said to have told his men in the middle of their workday on hearing the news of the boy's arrival. Richard was so overcome with joy he allowed the men to take the rest of the day off. This was a day of celebration, for another Hale had arrived to make his mark on the world.[15] Nathan enjoyed a bucolic boyhood, ensconced in a loving community and family. But it would not last. As the mark on his neck reminded him, misfortune can be right around the corner. When Nathan turned twelve in 1767, Elizabeth died after suffering complications from delivering her twelfth child, Susannah, who had also died within a month of her birth. Now Nathan and Richard were left without a wife and mother, and Richard had his farm and eight other children to look after. This was a deeply transformative time for a young Nathan as he learned two of life's hardest lessons: the inevitability of death and the inescapable responsibilities of manhood.

His faith in God was a constant in his life. His strict Congregationalist upbringing required praying three times a day, attending two services on Sunday, and deifying members of the clergy, like his grandfather John Hale, a Harvard graduate and Calvinist preacher who was involved in the witch trials in Salem. The Strong family also had many men of the cloth in their clan, so Nathan was encircled by religion, and considered the clergy as a career for himself. He balanced his religious education with philosophical texts from Cicero, Horace, and Cato the Younger under the ministrations of the Reverend Dr. Huntington, who was keen to point out to his students the inequities of British rule. (Huntington's house is still standing in Coventry today, and is marked with an historical plaque to entertain Nathan's many fans.) This was, after all, the late 1760s, when the Revolution was in its nascent period, attracting open-minded youths.

While Nathan dealt with the loss of his mother through his faith and by preparing for college, Rich found comfort in a more traditional way. Within two years of Elizabeth's death, Rich married a young widow named Abigail Adams from Canterbury, a neighboring town. This was not at all surprising, as Rich Hale was a prosperous man of good family. Abigail (no relation to the future First Lady) was bright and beautiful and immediately built a bond with Nathan, who left for Yale with his brother Enoch as his father was settling down with his new bride.

In 1769, Enoch and Nathan were in a class of only thirty-six students. At that time, higher education was a luxury, not the entitlement it is today. The Hale family was unusual in that it was able to send two sons to Yale at the same time, but Nathan proved that they he would get their father's money's worth. "Carefully mind your studies that your time be not lost," his father paternally advised him.[16]

He excelled in academics, secret societies, wrestling, and being a red-blooded teenager, was filled with raging hormones. One night, Nathan, Enoch, and Benjamin Tallmadge, who would later recruit Nathan as a spy, worked off their masculine energy by breaking windows around campus. His other extracurriculars included cards, drinking, and pursuing the fairer sex.

Nathan accumulated demerits for missing chapel and playing cards, resulting in fines his father grudgingly paid. "Shun all vice—especially card playing," he wrote to Nathan, as gambling was strictly prohibited at Yale, and would result in expulsion if a student was found to be a repeat offender.

One of his card-playing buddies was Tallmadge, who became a lifelong confidante. The two bonded over their mutual love of classic philosophy and poetry, even dabbling in rhyme and verse in their correspondence with one another. They also had a common adoration of the spoken word as members of the school's debating society, Linonia, where unorthodox views about all manner of subjects were aired. The ladies who attended a debate about women's education, for which Nathan and Benjamin advocated, were particularly impressed. Whether they were taken by the strong oratory skills of the men, or their dashing good looks, is unknown to history.

What is clear is that from a young age Nathan possessed undeniable charisma. From his letters to his speeches, to his performances in school's theatrical productions, Nathan Hale was charm personified and was singled out by his peers as a rising star. "Possessing genius, taste, and order, he became distinguished as a scholar; and endowed in an eminent degree with those graces and gifts of Nature which add charm to youthful excellence, he gained universal esteem and confidence," recalled biographer Jared Sparks.[17]

Rather like the Yale of today, the Yale of the 1770s was a cradle of progressive sentiment. Although Benjamin and Enoch were from traditional families with strong Christian bents, they, and the Yale campus around them, agitated for change. "I consider our country, a land flowing as it were with milk and honey, holding open her arms & demanding assistance from all who can assist her in her sore distress. We should all be ready to step forth in the common cause," Benjamin wrote.[18]

The class boycotted British products and insisted on wearing American-made gowns for their graduation ceremony in 1773. One Loyalist alumnus wrote that his school had turned into "a nursery of sedition, faction, and republicanism."[19] Even Thomas Gage, commander of the British forces in North America, branded Yale "a seminary of democracy," a description its alumni, faculty, and students can rightly claim as a badge of honor.[20]

It is with this patriot fervor that Enoch, Nathan, and Benjamin left New Haven, Nathan and Benjamin having decided to take jobs as schoolmasters, plum positions for men of their day. Nathan settled in

East Haddam, Connecticut, while Benjamin taught in Wethersfield. The two men never lost their affection for one another, as expressed in their frequent missives. "I remain your constant friend" was their usual way of signing off.

These letters were heartening for Nathan as he found East Haddam boring and isolating. By 1774, he had transferred to the Union School in New London, where he taught mainly the wealthy boys in the community, but Nathan sneaked female students in the schoolhouse for instruction during a time when educating girls was forbidden.

His heart found a special friend in Alice Adams, his stepsister, who was married to a much older man, Elijah Ripley. Mr. Ripley died in December of 1774, and within weeks Nathan was wooing the young widow with his poetry. *Alicia, born with every striking charm, The eye to ravish or the heart to warm*, opens one such letter.

That autumn, as Nathan was teaching and keeping a wishful eye on Alice, and as the Grim Reaper was eyeing Mr. Ripley, the country was moving closer to its destiny. As the first Continental Congress convened that autumn, Nathan and all his boyhood friends, those who stayed behind in Coventry, and those who went to Yale and Harvard, were confronted with profound questions of life and death, country and loyalty.

"Liberty is our reigning topic, which loudly calls upon everyone to exert his talents and abilities to the utmost in defending of it—now is the time for heroes—now is the time for great men to immortalize their names in the deliverance of their country, and grace the annals of America with their glorious deeds," wrote James Hillhouse, in one of his letters to Nathan.[21]

These ideas of liberty and questions of loyalty came to a head on April 20, 1775, when Uncle Benajah sounded the alarm in Coventry that the "shot heard round the world" had officially started the war in Lexington and Concord. Immediately, 116 men and boys from Coventry, including most of Nathan's siblings, went to Boston where the rebels were building their army.

It is likely the news of war did not get to Nathan until the afternoon of April 22 as he was winding down his teaching day. A messenger had stopped in New London and a crowd quickly gathered. Nathan made his way out of the schoolhouse to see what was going on. By 7:00 P.M., the town of New London, under the guidance of Judge Richard Law, was organizing in Miner's Tavern.

With one of his pupils at his side, Nathan addressed the crowd, saying, "Let us march immediately and never lay down our arms until we obtain our independence." The pupil, Law's son, also named Richard, later remembered that moment and how struck he was "by the noble demeanor of his teacher, and the emphasis with which he addressed the assembly."

The next morning in class, Nathan brought reassurance to the young minds before him, who must have been deeply fearful of what was in store, and how the war might take away their fathers, brothers, and teachers. Hale talked to every student personally, easing their weary souls, but bucking up their courage with a firm handshake goodbye; he would be leaving to join Colonel Charles Webb's Connecticut Seventh Regiment.[22]

Like his fellow Connecticut soldiers commissioned by the Hartford General Assembly, Nathan waited for his orders as Washington organized his men and supplies. He spent the summer of 1775 watching New London's coastline for British ships or suspicious activity, but finally on September 1, Nathan was promoted to captain of the Seventh Regiment's Third Company, as second in command under Major Jonathan Lattimore. By the end of the month, the regiment was ordered by Washington to march toward camp near Boston.[23]

As the regiment made their way to Cambridge, Nathan was responsible for their safe passage and for keeping his men in line. This included enforcing army protocols and stopping unruly behavior like drunkenness. "What are you doing?" he snapped at a group of men playing cards, an activity as forbidden in the army as it was back at Yale. "This won't do!" Hale exclaimed, before ripping the cards to shreds.

These occasional shenanigans did not prevent the regiment from reaching their destination near Bunker Hill without any casualties or injuries, having narrowly avoided heavy firing en route through Roxbury.[24]

Nathan settled at the army's newly established camp on the outskirts of Boston called Winter Hill, but if he and his fellow men were gunning for action, they were told to hurry up and wait. As the fall of 1775 wore on, Nathan's days consisted of a rather boring, but civilized army officer's existence—exercising and drilling his regiment, dining with higher-ranking military leaders, and sharing stories over ale or through his letters to friends.

Within months, however, this life of idle frustration was replaced with hopeless desperation as many of Nathan's men deserted him after seeing the carnage of war. Men on the march resorted to eating dog meat to survive, and Nathan nobly "promised the men if they tarry another month they should have my wages for that time."[25]

During a rare granting of leave, Nathan spent that Christmas with his family in Coventry, even taking a ride to Salmon Brook to visit his Strong relations. By January he was back with a new appointment by Congress—captain of the Nineteenth Regiment of Foot, under the command of Charles Webb. The war was changing day to day, and Washington's defense strategy was shifting from New England to New York, which the regulars were keen to seize.

Gaining insights into British plans for this seizure was critical. At the end of 1775, Congress had established a Committee of Secret Correspondence whose original members included the likes of Benjamin Franklin. Other Founding Fathers like Adams and Jefferson were among those who not only would control the flow of intelligence but determine how to punish those who spied on them. On August 21, 1776, less than two months after the Declaration of Independence, the first Espionage Act stated that "all persons not members of, nor owing allegiance to, any of the United States of America, who shall be lurking as spies shall suffer death."[26] Such was the important role espionage played in the founding of our country. The battles were not always won or lost through cannon fire, but with a pen or a set of ears.

That August, the Continental Army was exhausted, starved, and drained of energy thanks to the extreme heat and heavy storms. Washington braced for the imminent attack on New York under General Howe, and Nathan, who had become very ill, and his fellow men made their way toward Brooklyn. "Our situation is now bad," Washington wrote, in what could be the biggest understatement of his career.

During the bleakest days of that summer, Washington rallied his troops with his unshakable composure and courageous battle cry. "Remember that liberty, property, life, and honor, are all at stake, that upon your courage and conduct rest the hopes of your bleeding and insulted country; that your wives, children, and parents, expect safety from you only. We have every reason to believe that heaven will crown success so just a cause."[27]

Nathan, who had not seen his courtship with Alicia to the alter before joining the militia, had no wife or children, but was buoyed by the letters he received from his many female admirers and friends. His sister Elizabeth Rose did her part for the cause by sewing garments for her brother. She asked via letter where to send it. He would retrieve it himself, he said, on his next trip to Coventry. Nathan had to be circumspect in his letters home and to his friends at this time, because unbeknownst to them, he had been selected as a ranger in the new elite intelligence-hunting unit, led by Thomas Knowlton.

Knowlton was one of the war's stalwart figures. Massachusetts bred, from an old family like Nathan's, Thomas enlisted as a soldier in the French and Indian War at the tender age of fifteen. Knowlton earned the admiration of Washington for his fierce bravery as he picked off Redcoats with startling ferocity in Bunker Hill skirmishes. Reporting directly to Washington, Knowlton was commissioned a lieutenant colonel to form Knowlton's Rangers, the army's first elite unit, akin to the Green Berets.[28]

Knowlton sought a new ranger who could infiltrate General Howe's orbit, glean information, and report back in time to save New York from falling under British control. Knowlton knew Hale and had also recruited two Hale brothers for the unit, which would number 150 of the best in the army. Hale felt conflicted about taking the job. For one thing, he had thus far seen little to no combat. He was hungry for action, and eager to do his part. "It would grieve every good man to consider what unnatural monsters we have as it were in our bowels," he wrote. But, on the other hand, although he may have been loath to admit it, espionage was not the occupation of a gentleman, and he may have felt spying was beneath him.

In Alexander Rose's book *Washington's Spies*, which inspired the AMC series *TURN*, he writes of the derision with which spying was regarded by Nathan and his peers at the time. Rose explains that there were three distinct categories of espionage. There was military scouting done by officers, almost always in uniform, which was considered aboveboard, and in fact honorable as this type of "intelligencing" had been done since the days of Homer. The second type, diplomatic reconnaissance in high society circles like palaces, was equally respectable. The third type, however, was for the lowborn and the lowly in morals. Any espionage done for payment involving an agent sneaking behind enemy lines to gain, and then abuse someone's trust, was for "blackguards," as Rose writes.[29]

It was with this in mind that Nathan came to his decision, with country, not money, as his motivation. "I will undertake it, sir," a weary Nathan told Knowlton, after he had conveyed Washington's appeal for the mission. Although Nathan was just twenty-one, and pale and tired after a bout with what at the time was believed to be influenza, he commanded the attention of the room of selected rangers, just as he had the previous year in New London when he volunteered to join the army. Nathan's illness was so grave, he thought he would soon die, which may account for the vigor of his conviction to go to war. According to the historian Henry Howe, everyone in the room pleaded with him to not do it as it was surely a suicide mission, but Nathan was resolute. In fact, the first man Knowlton tapped for the job, James Sprague, turned him down, saying, "I am willing to go and fight, but as for going among them and being taken and hung up like a dog, I will not do it."

"I think I owe to my country the accomplishment of an object so important, and so much desired by the commander of her armies—and I know of no other mode of obtaining the information, than by assuming a disguise and passing in the enemy's camp," Nathan explained. His biographer, M. William Phelps, firmly believes that Hale was very ill at this point, and perhaps this terminal illness influenced his decision.[30]

That Washington himself had once been a spy may have ameliorated any doubts Nathan had, and he was also eager to impress his hero. Washington fell, of course, into the "officer and gentleman" category of espionage. In 1753, during the French and Indian War, a young George, then an officer in the British Army, was asked to scout the wilderness for signs of French forts on British territory. He was given a letter to give to the commander at Fort LeBoeuf, but while the Frenchman was reading it, Washington snooped around, taking notes and making sketches of what the French were up to.[31]

"I am fully sensible of the consequences of discovery and capture in such a situation," Nathan wrote to his friend William Hull, "but for a year I have been attached to the army and have not rendered any material service. If the exigencies of my country demand a peculiar service its claims to perform that service are imperious."

New York was perfect for spying as Tories and American patriots cohabited, albeit grudgingly, and shared conversation and physical space. Markets, taverns, churches, and every institution was rife with soldiers and civilians on both sides of the war. Information was everywhere, if only you knew who to talk to, and knew how to listen. The city was mostly pro-Patriot, while Long Island was Tory country. It was also only one square mile, which made intel gathering easier.

The plan was for Nathan to glean information about the British invasion plans by going through Connecticut, crossing the Long

Island Sound, and entering the other British stronghold in Brooklyn. Enoch Hale reported that his brother left the American camp around September 14, with his letter of identification from Washington instructing anyone on his journey to assist him with transportation. Some historians believe that Washington and Nathan shared a New York candlelit meal together before Nathan departed on his mission, but this cannot be confirmed absent documentation. However, Nathan and Washington did meet in September of 1776, with Washington advising Nathan on his cover—that of a schoolmaster fleeing New York on his way home to Connecticut to find new employment. This cover was wholly believable as New Yorkers were leaving their city en masse with a British invasion looming. There was a palpable sense of panic permeating the city that September as people frantically packed, not knowing in some cases where to go, or how they would get there. General Nathanael Greene had advised Washington to burn Manhattan to destroy British supplies and keep the British from gaining a stronghold, but Congress forbade it. Historians differ on what Washington's position was.

Nathan and his old chum Stephen Hempstead, his partner on the mission, left the city en route to the Bronx on September 15. They would eventually arrive in Norwalk, Connecticut where they could cross into Long Island Sound. (He was also supported by his friend from Connecticut and the Nineteenth Regiment Captain Charles Pond.) Nathan boarded the fast four-gun sloop *Schuyler*. As soon as he boarded, he took on the persona of a schoolmaster, which included changing clothes and taking off the silver buckles on his shoes. Nathan and Hempstead arrived in Long Island in the early morning hours of September 16.[32]

As this patriot walked toward his destiny in the moonlit mist, another patriot was meeting his. Knowlton, the namesake of Nathan's unit, whose bravado had inspired Washington and others, was shot in the head in battle at Harlem Plains near Hollow Way. "Continue to do your duty in the action for you can do me no good," Knowlton told a comrade who tried to get him off the field. Disobeying Knowlton, the soldier dragged him into a wagon where he was seen by Washington an hour before he passed away. Some of the last words he heard came from his friend Washington who whispered to the fallen hero a deathbed ode to gallantry and honor.[33]

As these two friends said their heartfelt goodbyes, so too did Nathan and Hempstead. When Nathan arrived on shore, it was time to make his salute and thank Hempstead for accompanying him. Nathan handed Hempstead a watch as a parting gift as he stepped off the boat.

Now the real mission started, although the purpose of which was now moot, as the British had already completed their invasion of New York while Hale had been traveling. His plan, however, was to pass through Long Island capturing notes, sketches, and observations about British movements and any useful information from Howe's fortifications. On September 21, Nathan would rendezvous with Captain Pond again near Huntington for safe passage back to wherever Washington needed him. Nathan would keep his Yale diploma in his pocket to prove that he was just a sweet Dutch schoolteacher looking for a decent job.

This is what led Nathan on that night in September 1776 into that tavern with Robert Rogers. Although in the course of the two men's friendly conversation Rogers convinced Nathan that he was a fellow patriot, he was, in fact, a British spy for hire and ready to serve up Nathan to the enemy. As the two men talk, Rogers realizes Nathan is the perfect catch and will bring him a handsome price. Rogers had just escaped rebel custody and had started a spy ring of his own in His Majesty's service called Rogers' Rangers. Born in New Hampshire, Rogers had spent five years in England and was a dedicated soldier in the British Army, earning a reputation for bravery, and simultaneously, for deceit and reptilian tactics.

By the time his path crossed with Nathan Hale's, he was on a mission to convince uneasy Americans to join his side, usually through bullying and his usual ruthless modus operandi. He had heard of rebel officers in and around Huntington that September, and when he got word that someone had landed there and was talking to locals, he knew he was onto something. With a predator's gaze, he tracked Nathan and suspected he was a spy too. Rogers only needed the final trap, and when he saw Nathan enter the tavern, he knew exactly how to lay it.[34]

Rogers did an able job of convincing Nathan that they were comrades. Nathan was no doubt impressed that Rogers had fought alongside Washington in the French and Indian War. A Tory storekeeper named Consider Tiffany eavesdropped on their conversation that evening. "This intrigue not being suspected by the Captain made him believe that he had found a good friend, and one that could be trusted with the secrecy of the business he was engaged in." It is also likely the flow of alcohol inhibited Nathan's discretion and loosened his jaws. Soon, Hale had confided his mission and plans to the duplicitous Rogers.

While the two men enjoyed their tête–à–tête, Manhattan was taken by the British—and then by flames—on the evening of September 20. One of the greatest fires in American history swept through the city that evening and into the early hours of the morning, ravishing buildings and homes. Historians differ on the cause of the fire. Many still believe the Manhattan fire of 1776 was started by rebels in retaliation for the British capture of the city. The more likely scenario is the flames started from a simple cooking mishap inside the Fighting Cocks Tavern. Whatever the cause, the fire had effectively destroyed British high command in the colonies. "Providence, or some good honest fellow, has done more for us than we were disposed to do for ourselves," Washington later reflected.

General Howe had set up shop at 51st Street and First Avenue, at what was then the mansion of James Beekman, while Rogers planned to reel Nathan in. While they were dining, Rogers invited Nathan to breakfast with him the next morning at his quarters. Nathan, still believing Rogers was a new friend and fellow patriot behind enemy lines, accepted the invitation with alacrity. For years, it was believed that Samuel Hale, Nathan's Loyalist cousin, saw him in the tavern that fateful day and turned him in, but the veracity of the Consider Tiffany account, and Hale family denials, have cast this version in a highly dubious light.

Nathan arose the next morning, perhaps still in the fog of the heavy spirits he had enjoyed the evening before, combined with his already poor health. The first thing he would have noticed that morning was the blanket of smoke smothering the air, even as far as Long Island. A part of him would be relieved that he escaped the fire as many rebels were thrown into it by British troops who blamed them for starting it. Another part of Nathan was indeed relieved that his mission was over, and he could return to his men and the fight before them. But before he made his way back, he was to enjoy breakfast with his new friend Rogers. Maybe Rogers could explain what he knew about the fire, as details were then unknown. One can only imagine the thoughts and questions racing through Nathan's mind that day.

Nathan arrived at quarters where he was greeted by Rogers, who had been watching Nathan through the night to make sure he did not get away. Rogers, Nathan, and a few of the men at quarters shared a meal and continued their conversation from the night before. Talk of missions, rebellion, hatred of the ghastly British. Then, troops began to surround the house. The trap was set. The game was up.

When Nathan came out of the house, having been confronted by Rogers "by orders from the commander," he was poked with muskets and ambushed by sneering grins. As a prisoner of war, he was shackled, tied, and denied a trial, since he was a soldier behind enemy lines in civilian clothes. These were the rules of war, and Nathan had broken them.

As the waves thrashed about the HMS *Halifax*, carrying Nathan to enemy headquarters in Manhattan, his mind must have been equally turbulent. Anger, humiliation for his errors in judgment, and fear of what was to come swirled through his young brain. His destination was General Howe at Beekman mansion where he would join hundreds of other war detainees.

Howe's sadist in chief was William Cunningham who, having been a prisoner of the Americans, was out for revenge. Indeed, his favorite form of torture was a long and vile run of starvation in which rebels were placed in the basements of churches by the thousands. Cunningham's drunkenness only amplified his cruelty.

According to the recollections of American Captain William Hull, Nathan firmly and confidently stood before Howe, and realizing the truth was unavoidable, stated his name, rank, and the purpose of his mission as a spy. A British soldier noted that "the frankness, the manly bearing, and the disinterested patriotism of the handsome young prisoner, sensibly touched a tender chord of General Howe's nature."

As impressed as Howe may have been, he denied Hale his final requests—a Bible, and a chaplain—and was jailed inside the greenhouse on the Beekman estate, with two guards outside the door. Cunningham was overseeing the operation as he had a special detestation for spies, whom he considered to be the lowest of the low.

"He was calm, and bore himself with gentle dignity, in the consciousness of rectitude and high intentions," recollected British Captain John Montresor, another eyewitness. Montresor, an engineer for Howe, used Nathan's drawings and sketches for British intelligence, but took an instant liking to the prisoner. Historians would later note that Montresor's humane treatment of Nathan in his final moments provided the only redeeming quality to horrible episode in young America's history. Montresor allowed Nathan to use his quill and his ink to compose his final letters: one to his brother Enoch and another to his commander Knowlton, not knowing of Knowlton's death a short time before. Cunningham nastily took the letters from Nathan. Some historians believe he tore them up with a devilish laugh.

It was now the morning of September 22, the first day of autumn. The official end of summer, and in many ways, the end of American innocence. For all the talk of gallantry and patriot hearts beating, there was now a human face, soon to be a hanging corpse, to remind the world that the true act of rebellion is to face death for a cause.

The boy from Coventry had come full circle. His birth had been celebrated in the middle of a field and his end would come in farmland, probably an apple orchard, not far from Montresor's tent. Montresor and a few others accompanied Nathan on his final march to the tree where he would be hanged, having been denied another request: to be shot. When Nathan was asked what his confession or statement would be, he uttered perhaps the most famous apocryphal phrase in American history. American schoolchildren are taught that a young Nathan Hale said, "I only regret that I have but one life to lose for my country," which Nathan never said. These words, while true to the spirit of his sacrifice, have been falsely attributed to him through the legends and mythology that have surrounded his life and death. There are conflicting reports from various newspapers and eyewitnesses of what he actually said, but all agree he died with fervent patriotism.

"Swing the rebel off," Cunningham ordered, at which point a rope was fastened around his neck, tightly squeezing the ill-omened birthmark. Tunis Bogart, a Loyalist farmer, was present that day. Despite being on different sides, Bogart was haunted by Cunningham's conduct and years later, in 1784, noted that he had still not been able to "efface the scene of horror. Cunningham was so brutal and hung him up as a butcher would a calf."[35] Meanwhile, the women in the small crowd were weeping loudly enough for Cunningham to threaten them with hanging if they did not control their distress.

Nathan's body stayed on the tree for three days, likely mocked and spat on. In David McCullough's *1776*, he writes that "a slave finally took the body down and buried Nathan in an unmarked grave without a Christian burial."[36] Montresor received permission to cross enemy lines to personally convey news of Nathan's death to Alexander Hamilton, who surely passed it along to Washington. Washington's reaction has been lost to history, as there are no letters or accounts to explain it. Nathan's remains have also been lost to time. The body of one of our most revered heroes lays in an unknown tomb, somewhere far below the busy streets of Manhattan.

It took weeks of anguish for Enoch to confirm what he had suspected when he did not receive a letter from his brother. Now "Father Hale," Enoch had followed the Strong and Hale tradition of entering the clergy after graduating from Yale. Waiting for a parish assignment, he was occupied that autumn of 1776 with building a new home on the Hale homestead and acting as the head of the family with so many of his brothers away at war and his father of an advanced age. Rumors began circulating around Coventry that Nathan may have been apprehended and killed by the British, but because there were other Nathans and Hales, and military communications are not what we expect today, hearing of a loved one's death sometimes took weeks if not months of tedious investigation.

Enoch leaned heavily on his Strong family during this time, especially his uncles Joseph and Elnathan Strong, his mother's other brothers. While we do not know what if any communications he had with his Uncle Benajah about the matter, we do know that Enoch considered his Uncle Joseph Strong, a war chaplain, a second father. The two men prayed together, discussed scripture and homilies, and inspired each other in their faith. On the last day of September, Enoch rode to Joseph's farm, twenty miles outside Coventry. Joseph was likely to have news as he was often on the front lines ministering to the downtrodden soldiers.

Joseph secured Enoch's travel to New York to speak with a friend from Yale who would have definitive sources on Nathan's whereabouts. Sadly, on October 16, Enoch finally concluded that Nathan had, in fact, been hanged. "N York Accounts from my brother are indeed melancholy," he wrote in his journal that day. His brother had been "taken & hanged without ceremony." On October 19, Enoch summed up his mood as "gloomy dejected hope." By October 26, the valiant brother rode into Colonel Charles Webb's camp in White Plains, New York, to talk to men in Nathan's unit who corroborated the source from Yale. The fact that Enoch went to camp during the Battle of White Plains is testimony of his brotherly love and tenacity.

In June of 1777, the family losing hope of ever recovering Nathan's body, received the trunk of his belongings containing his uniform, diary, and a few other personal items. His father, Richard, was present on the trunk's arrival. When he opened the trunk, he was stirred by the emotions of seeing and smelling the last tokens of Nathan's life, and vowed to never talk about Nathan again, because his life as a spy was deemed embarrassing for the family at the time. These tokens of Nathan's life were given to his lady love Alice Adams and his brother Billey, and eventually made their way to what is now the Nathan Hale Homestead in Coventry.[37] America would take its revenge for Nathan and claim victory on October 19, 1781, when General Cornwallis surrendered at Yorktown. Across the sea, King George's state of mind, according to Andrew Roberts, was "saddened but not downhearted, and extraordinarily enough, he still believed Britain should continue with the war."

Roberts says that the king resisted the urge to fight fire with fire. He could have done several things, like liberate and empower Native Americans and the large population of the enslaved to take up arms against the colonists, but he did not. Why? In the first instance, there was no guarantee that the Native Americans or freed Black people would have much motivation to remain loyal to the Crown either. The latter because he was "a civilized, good-natured, Christian and enlightened monarch . . . a good Patriot King to all his subjects. It was partly because George was not a tyrant, therefore, that he lost the war against the so-called tyranny."

After a glorious and history-making career as a statesman and military leader, George Washington was the most famous and beloved figure in the young nation. Many assumed he would take on a king-like or emperor status in the new country he helped found, but the only kingdom he wished to rule was within the boundaries of Mount Vernon, to which he returned after the war, taking up another pastime both he and King George loved: farming. Both men relished their "Farmer George" monikers.

On December 23, 1783, George Washington resigned his commission as commander in chief of the Continental Army, and in 1797 when Washington readily gave up the presidency, King George praised him as "the greatest character of the age."[38] Before his death at Mount Vernon in 1799, George Washington returned the favor, calling King George "our great and good friend," and assuring him that while they were "enemies in war," they would remain "friends in peace." These two men with so much in common recognized the greatness—and goodness—in each other, although they were never to meet.[39]

Others too dealt with the fallout of the war with incredible generosity of spirit. Richard Hale, the patriarch of the Hale family, died in 1802 with a grieving heart, but without rancor. He would see four of his sons die between 1776 and 1785, but even Nathan's execution and the circumstances around it did not dim his devoted Christianity. "A child is gone," he wrote. "We are all through the divine goodness well." Cousin Samuel Hale, who had been accused in the local papers of turning Nathan in, fled to England, vociferously denying any involvement for the rest of his life. Enoch Hale would die in 1837, never forgetting his brother Nathan. In fact, he named his first son after him, and there are Hale family descendants scattered throughout the country, who plan to convene at the Nathan Hale Homestead in 2026 to honor the country's 250th anniversary. Asher Wright, Nathan's loyal friend, would mourn him for the rest of his life, and by most accounts, would never recover from the loss of his friend. Wright would never marry or have children and lived until the age of ninety with mental illness. He is buried in Nathan Hale Cemetery, where town historian John Holmy looks after his grave.

It seems Robert Rogers, Hale's Judas, received his just desserts. General Howe sacked him after his Rangers unit fell to an embarrassingly low head count due to desertion. His wife, Elizabeth, left him, and he never saw their son again. By 1781, ravished by alcohol and crippled by debts, he was captured by the Americans. He went back to London with the defeated British Army, and spent his remaining decade broken physically and mentally, coughing up blood and prone to hallucinations.[40]

Benjamin Tallmadge went on to live the kind of life that would no doubt have also awaited his friend Nathan Hale. He came back to Connecticut, became a Federalist congressman, and, despite becoming a wealthy landowner, was a zealous warrior against slavery, arguing, presciently, it would be a blight on our country's reputation. Perhaps thinking of Nathan, and their shared Christian tenet of "love thy neighbor as thyself," Tallmadge cofounded the Litchfield, Connecticut, Auxiliary Society for Ameliorating the Condition of the Jews, and established schools for Native American and Asian missionaries.[41]

The whereabouts of Nathan Hale's body remains a mystery, but his hometown of Coventry keeps an eternal vigil for their native son. At the Nathan Hale Homestead, visitors can tour his family's farmhouse and see the forty-five-foot obelisk erected in his honor in 1837 at the Nathan Hale Cemetery, overlooking Coventry Lake. In 1985, the Nathan Hale chapter of the Sons of the American Revolution, which still exists today, convinced the State of Connecticut to make Nathan Hale its state hero in the US Capitol. Cities, schools, buildings, and military bases bear the name Nathan Hale, which has become synonymous with American patriotism.

His final words about only having one life to give for his country, while dubious, have inspired generations for service to country. Perhaps his last thoughts were on a more spiritual note. In Nathan's Bible, on which he meditated frequently, there was found an underlined passage of scripture, one of his favorite verses from the Gospel of John. It brings solace to those who think of his sacrifice, and the rewards given to those who hold the line for eternity:

In my father's house are many mansions
If it were not so, I would have told you
I go to prepare a place for you

And if I go and prepare a place for you, I will come again and
receive you unto myself
That where I am, there ye may be also.

His biographer M. William Phelps says that Nathan would have gone on to be a leading statesman in Philadelphia and would have held his own among the greatest early presidents. In the shadow of Nathan's mammoth obelisk lies the simple grave of his uncle Benajah Strong. It is modest and nondescript, like the simple New Englander he was. The epitaph reads:

"An angel's arm can't snatch me from this tomb
Nor can a host of angels keep me here."
Benajah Strong, Esq, who died Nov 25th, 1809,
lies here, food for worms, Aged 69 years.[42]

It is a stark contrast to the burial and tomb at Windsor Castle that awaits his sixth great-grandson, King William V.

4

YANKEE DOODLE DUCHESS

While King George III may have made peace with George Washington before his death in 1799, he continued to fight political battles with his fellow countrymen and women. Some of these came from the highest echelons of British society, like Prince William's aunt Georgiana, Duchess of Devonshire, the dazzling supporter of the Whig party and the king's most vexing opponent during and after the American War of Independence.

Georgiana—like Diana, Princess of Wales, in the twentieth century—was too glamourous for her own good. She spent her life at the center of all things cultural, historical, and political in the late eighteenth century, when towering personalities with powdered hair reigned supreme. Charisma was her byword, and it got her into plenty of mischief. "She exchanged kisses for votes, something she always denied in her troubled marriage, but a charge that has stuck for over two centuries," writes her great-great-great nephew, the ninth Earl Spencer, in his book about his famous family, recalling that this scandal was the first thing he remembered hearing about Aunt Georgiana as a child.[1]

Her allure and success with men—and women—is something she accepted without any feigned modesty. "I know I was handsome, and I have always been fashionable," she said on her deathbed.[2] This self-assessment was rooted in truth as the sumptuous Gainsborough portrait of Georgiana (pronounced George-*jayna*) confirms. "When she appeared, every eye was turned towards her; when absent, she was the subject of universal conversation," recalled one of her many admirers.[3]

Born on June 7, 1757, to the Earl and Countess Spencer, she grew up in splendor surrounded by lush countryside tended by servants, five residences, and the vast Spencer arsenal of decadent artwork and jewels. The greatest jewel in the Spencer arsenal was Althorp, the family seat, and her Spencer blood was a source of pride and inspiration to her, as her own legacy would be for future generations. Among her ancestors were those Spencers who were neighbors, friends, and comrades of the Washington family in the decades before the English Civil War. Today, portraits of the Spencer luminaries stare down visitors in the main hall, known as the saloon at Althorp, as if to say, "welcome to the palace of champions."

Ever ambitious for their children—their son and heir but also their two daughters—Georgiana's parents brought her up to be the consort of a great man. She was given a classical education for an upper-class girl of her time, which included singing, drawing, and multiple languages, but Georgiana's greatest asset was her ability to charm, which she wielded with alacrity. Georgiana adored being adored, and, according to her biographer Amanda Foreman, an addiction to love and excess was her life's passion and tragedy. Her mother summed up Georgiana succinctly as a child when she said, "She is one of the most showy girls I ever saw." She likely said this with a combination of amusement and exasperation.[4]

By the time she was sixteen, her family was positioning Georgiana for marriage to the most eligible bachelor of the day: William, Duke of Devonshire, heir of the Cavendish clan, whom she met while on a family trip to Spa, Belgium. The Cavendish's grander fortune and fame, coupled with William's experience as a much older man, must have been intoxicating for the young Georgiana.

The Cavendish dynasty was built by men named William. Sir William Cavendish had been a henchman for Henry VIII. His son,

William, purchased the earldom from James I, ultimately securing a dukedom in 1688 when he helped William of Orange seize the throne from James II, establishing a centuries-long alliance between the subsequent Dukes of Devonshire and the Whig political party.[5]

During the summer that Georgiana met the duke in 1773, King George III had been on the throne since 1760. His was a throne tarnished by what George perceived as fifth column, namely the Whigs, the party that positioned itself as supporting the common man and resisting overreaches of the monarchy. Most of the Whig supporters would be described as "limousine liberals" today—the aristocracy and educated elites who hosted salons and jumped on every underdog bandwagon they could find. One of George's first actions was to cleanse his cabinet of Whig troublemakers, including William's father, fourth Duke of Devonshire, who would lose his position as lord chamberlain and as a member of the Privy Council.

Thus, William Cavendish held a political as well as personal animus toward the king and took on the leadership of the Whig party with great relish on his father's death.

Although intelligent, William was deadly dull compared to the luminous young Georgiana. His only sources of enthusiasm were his dogs and evenings at home reading Shakespeare. He was also known as a lackluster dancer during a time when dancing was the mark of a well-bred gentleman. (This was a transatlantic distinction—George Washington, for instance, was renowned as a spirited dancer well into his advanced years). Despite his shortcomings, Georgiana fell in love with him that summer—or at least fell in love with the position he could offer. They married in 1774, after which she was known as Her Grace the Duchess of Devonshire. Although still a teenager, she instantly became one of the most-watched women in the country at a time when newspapers were ravenous for details on the high and mighty. Georgiana provided perfect prey and copy. She would use this new exposure by entertaining on a grand scale, becoming a fashion plate, and promoting the Cavendish brand. In short, she would become the influencer of all influencers.

Home base for the new power couple was Chatsworth, the Cavendish family home since 1549. Today, it is widely regarded as the favorite country house for tourists as it reminds one of being in a Jane Austen novel. Stately and grand, its façade is meant to impress visitors while its endless green lawns soften its imperious magnitude. In Georgiana's time, she opened Chatsworth for "Public Days" when everyday folk could see how the other side lived, while she commanded elaborate functions at the dining table that could seat one hundred.

During the social season, which ran from October through June, the Duke and Duchess called Devonshire House in London home. There they could interact with members of Parliament in town for business. Among what was known as the *ton*, London's chicest set, Georgiana was the definitive "it girl," inspiring awe and her fair share of resentment.

"She gives me the idea of being larger than life," remarked one catty grandee. Georgiana also aimed to be taller than life as her signature look was a three-foot hair tower, which required a small army of hairdressers, and careful negotiation of ceilings. Soon women in the *ton* were stacking their hair as high as possible to keep up with the "most envied woman of the day," according to the press, always on her heels for the latest pearl of gossip.

A perk of the new duchesses's status was her easy access to the royal courts on the continent. Georgiana became fast friends with Marie Antoinette, with whom she shared a love of decadence. The two ladies of luxury maintained their friendship for decades, some say even venturing into an intimate affair.[6] Outside of entertaining and dazzling world leaders, Georgiana's primary responsibility was producing an heir, something that nearly drove her to the brink of insanity. In fact, unbeknownst to Georgiana at the time, her new husband already had a child, a girl, with his mistress, Charlotte. After suffering miscarriages and chafing at the suffocating press attention, Georgiana turned to escapism in the form of gambling and drinking. She also may have suffered an existential crisis in the throes of eighteenth-century extravagance, flitting from one party to the next, wondering what it all means, and trying to arrive at a sense of purpose.

It was at a Devonshire House salon that she met Edmund Burke, one of the elder statesmen of her set, whose ideas of liberty and support for the rebels in America made an impression on the young and increasingly disillusioned duchess. Another beleaguered guest in London was one Lady Diana Spencer, Georgiana's cousin, the namesake of the future Diana, Princess of Wales, who was struggling with her own marital discord. Lady Diana's grandmother, Sarah, Duchess of Marlborough, tried to organize Diana's marriage to Frederick, Prince of Wales, but to no avail. Like the twentieth-century Diana, the original Lady Diana died tragically young.

The seeds of rebellion were beginning to quicken in Georgiana, and she soon realized she had a chance to be not just a frivolity, but an agent for change. As she struggled with more miscarriages and the subsequent shame of not producing an heir, she developed two pivotal relationships that would change her life and the course of history.

In 1777 Charles Fox, a fellow Whig, came to stay at Chatsworth, and became friendly with the duke and duchess. Charles and Georgiana had many virtues and vices in common. Fox was a hopeless gambler and drinker, but shared Georgiana's vivacity and warm-heartedness. *Dull* is a word that could never be used to describe either one of them. In fact, they both vibrated with color and dazzle. Like Georgiana, Charles expressed himself through rakish dress, including brightly colored shoes and by powdering his hair red and blue. Charles Fox was on a fast track to be leader of the Whigs while still a young man, and inspired not just his political colleagues, but the young rebel inside Georgiana.[7]

Georgiana read the libertine Jean-Jacques Rousseau and was stimulated by *The History of the Revolutions in Sweden* by Rene-Aubert Vertot, which may have been recommended to her by Charles. Her observations about the book bear striking similarities to the cause for freedom across the Atlantic at the time. Vertot wrote:

> Especially at seeing a generous and open-hearted hero fighting for the liberty of his country and to revenge the memory of an injured friend against lawless cruelty and oppressive tyranny.[8]

Charles himself was a recent convert to this new ethos of freedom. He had served as a junior minister under the Tory government of Lord North, the king's prime minister pushing the American rebels into submission. When George fired Charles for his perceived disloyalty, Charles took up the Whig flag and started studying under Edmund Burke. The ideas of constitutional rights were passed from Burke to Charles, and then to a very receptive Georgiana.

Despite rumors, Georgiana's relationship with Charles was indeed platonic and based on intellectual interests. Georgiana had been playing with adulterous fire with Mary Graham, a renowned beauty Gainsborough had painted several times, the ultimate achievement in vanity during the late 1770s. Whether the two women were lovers is unknown, but what is indisputable is the affection bordering on obsession that Georgiana felt for Mary. It is as if Georgiana was on a discovery of freedom—freedom from her marriage, freedom with her sensuality (which was always a palpable part of her character), and freedom from what was expected of her. Thanks to Fox and the Whig salons in which she moved, Georgiana had also discovered that once freedom is discovered within, it must be shared and unlocked in others—even with those in other countries.

The year 1778 was Georgiana's year of enlightenment, encouraged by Fox's interest in her not as a beautiful woman, but as a political advocate. She was likely under Charles's ministration when she anonymously published *The Sylph*, a thinly veiled novel about a country girl who marries into chic society and gets stuck with a brute of a husband. Her heroine, Julia, is saved by the "The Sylph," her advisor and lover, whom she finally marries. The novel was a success, but its exposure of the inner workings of Georgiana's circle soon revealed her to be the author.

If the book was indeed autobiographical, it also revealed troubling secrets of her marriage. The antagonist is a Sir William who is carelessly philandering, abusive, and cold while Julia suffers failed pregnancies. Georgiana must have been brave to write this book, even threatening her own safety, knowing the duke would discover the book's authorship. Even though *The Sylph* was criticized, even by female intellectuals, for its frank sexuality, it was Georgiana's personal declaration of independence and courage.

While Georgiana made a daring move on the chessboard of her marriage, the French entered the increasingly bloody chess game between the colonists and King George, and all Britain prepared for a possible French invasion. Georgiana, bolstered by her newfound energy, organized a female auxiliary corps. She may have supported the American cause, but she wasn't about to let their French allies, centuries-old foes of England, to march on Chatsworth unopposed. "Her Grace the Duchess of Devonshire appears every day at the beauteous Amazons of Coxheath, who are all dressed *en militaire*, serve and charms every beholder with their beauty and affability," exclaimed the *Morning Post*.

Despite her obvious anger at the duke's adultery, at which she took aim in *The Sylph*, Georgiana, to her great credit, welcomed the idea of raising his child Charlotte as her own when the child's mother, the duke's longtime mistress, also named Charlotte, died in 1778 or 1779. Her de facto role as a mother did not deter Georgiana's interest in politics or supporting the Whigs. By 1780, Georgiana sent a clear social statement by skipping Queen Charlotte's birthday celebration. This was her way of joining the Whig disapproval of monarchic aggression in the colonies and around the world.[9]

Georgiana's influence reached new heights in April when she joined Fox at a major rally for his reelection as foreign secretary. Standing under a banner that read FREEDOM AND INDEPENDENCE and waving enthusiastically,

Georgiana, by this time a high priestess of fashion, wore the colors of the Continental Army, blue and buff, to signal the Whig support for their American compatriots. Fox and Georgiana became such stars that hat makers designed fans with their images on them that flew out of the shops. Georgiana-mania was in full swing.[10]

Georgiana's new friend in this fight was none other than the king's son George, Prince of Wales, known as "Prinny" and recently turned eighteen. He would later become prince regent and eventually King George IV, but at the moment he was chafing under the restraints of his father, with whom he had been at odds for years. Like his grandfather Frederick, Prince of Wales, who was constantly feuding with *his* father King George II, so too did these Hanoverian men have a lifelong acrimonious relationship that not only blighted the family but had pernicious effects on world politics.

The rebel Prince of Wales first met Georgiana and Charles Fox at Devonshire House, and soon fell under their spell, looking to them both for advice on everything cultural and familial. The king deeply resented Fox's influence over his son and blamed him for the prince's foray into cheeky behavior, typical for a teenage boy, but scandalous to the sometimes stodgy king.

The rumor mill was stimulated by the closeness of the prince and Georgiana, but Georgiana always maintained a strictly sisterly affection for the prince. His feelings for her, not surprisingly, given her attractiveness to everyone, may have been more amorous.

On January 18, 1781, the prince made his official society debut. The entertainment for the evening featured nasty jokes the prince dished up about his father, which delighted the Whig guests. When the guests were not laughing and drinking, they were dancing or watching the prince dance with Georgiana. "The Court beauties looked with an eye of envy on her Grace of Devonshire as the only woman honoured with the hand of the heir apparent, during Thursday night's ball at St. James," reported the *Morning Herald*.[11]

Later that year, after the Battle of Yorktown, Georgiana went about party planning with her usual dramatic flair in honor of the American victory. A series of celebratory balls, most of which went until the small hours of the morning, were held at Devonshire House where roses hung from the ceilings, and furniture and paintings were removed to make way for the packed crowds she welcomed. Never one to miss a party or a chance to spit in his father's eye, the Prince of Wales attended. He took in an opera earlier that evening but asked them to shorten the last act so could arrive on time at his beloved Georgiana's fete.[12]

The Devonshires' continued their closeness with the prince through 1783, when Georgiana finally gave birth to her first child. Unfortunately for the duke, it was a girl, and not the heir he had hoped for, but on the bright side, the Prince of Wales agreed to be baby Georgiana's godfather. The baby would be known as "Little G" to distinguish her from her namesake mother and would eventually grow up and lead an equally grandiose lifestyle.

"She has a present coming from the Queen of France," Georgiana wrote to Lady Elizabeth Foster, her lover, but "I don't know what it is yet." Elizabeth, known as Bess, had been Georgiana's great distraction, outside for politics, for years. She would later learn that Bess was simultaneously enjoying the Duke's bed, creating one of the most notorious ménage à trois in London society.

Her biographer, Amanda Foreman, makes it clear that while Georgiana enjoyed a physical as well as emotional affair with Bess, there is no evidence to suggest that she and Fox, or indeed the Prince of Wales were lovers, despite hearsay to the contrary continuing to make the rounds. Foreman notes that as an aristocrat, Georgiana understood how to skirt the rules without breaking them. Before she produced a son and heir for her husband, Georgiana could not and would not risk pregnancy through another man.

But this did not stop the press from making a spectacle of Georgiana, particularly as she defied convention yet again, and canvassed for the Whig party in 1784. Walking through the streets of London in her blue and buff and with foxtails in her hair to support Fox as leader of the party, she was doing the unthinkable for a woman of her rank—engaging in retail politics. Hosting salons in the confines of her houses was one thing, but walking among shopkeepers (and worse) was another matter.

"During her canvass, the Duchess made no scruple of visiting some of the humblest of electors, dazzling and enchanting them by the fascination of her manner," observed Horace Walpole. Not everyone was enchanted. She was subjected to verbal abuse, sexual references, and even physical threats in the most misogynistic manner.[13] The *Morning Post* mirrored the sexism in the streets that spring of 1784 during Fox's Westminster campaign. "We hear the Duchess of Devonshire grants *favours* to those who promise their votes and interest to Mr. Fox." The paper would go on to accuse Georgiana of being Fox's vixen in bed as well as in the political arena. A cartoon titled "The Two Patriotic Duchesses on their Canvass" depicts Georgiana making love to a butcher while handing him money.[14]

Georgiana had the last laugh when Fox was elected and the Whigs paraded to Devonshire House in victory before circling the Prince of Wales's residence, Carlton House, three times in an homage to his support. Fox was lifted in a chair by triumphant Whigs, wearing their buff and blue, foxtails, and singing special Whig fight songs, rather like a high school homecoming parade. The Prince of Wales and Georgiana were seen hanging from ladders leaning into Devonshire House while waving laurels excitedly. The prince's revelry was heightened by seeing his father's carriage pass by Carlton House on his way to Parliament. Petty and looking to score cheap points, the prince held a raucous celebration in his garden the king was sure to notice and hear.[15]

The year 1784 had established Georgiana "as head of opposition public," according to Fanny Burney, but the damage done by the hostile press to her reputation had lasting effects. Her mother, Lady Spencer, was appalled that the Whigs allowed her daughter to be used and traduced the way she was. She and other aristocratic women never canvassed in public again. It would be another hundred years—the dawn of the women's suffrage movement—before women again took to the streets the way Georgiana did.

The duke was resentful of Georgiana's ascendancy as a political powerhouse, and continued his affair with Bess, ignoring Georgiana's pleas for help paying her gambling debts, her constant Achilles heel. As her marriage trundled on through the 1780s, she met another political rising star, another Charles. This was Charles Grey, seven years her junior, the son of a general with what Lord Byron called "the patrician thoroughbred look." Georgiana soon took this new Charles under her wing. She introduced him to her elegant circles and the two eventually embarked on a passionate affair, which did not seem to bother Bess as she was still carrying on with the duke even as her physical relationship with Georgiana cooled. Bess would eventually bear two children by the duke.[16]

In fact, Bess had essentially elevated herself from secret mistress to second wife. She sailed through the family homes as the lady of the manor. The duke had managed to contrive a domestic situation in which both women maintained an almost equal status in the household, which must have been humiliating for Georgiana. Strangely, as she assumed more and more political power, the power dynamic in her personal life positioned her as a pawn, not a queen. Her powerlessness was made ever more dire by the fact that after nearly a decade of marriage Georgiana had failed to produce a boy.

It is easy to see why she fell hard for Charles Grey and maintained her close friendship with the Prince of Wales, whose own love life was equally dramatic and public, causing even more woe to his war-weary father. By 1788, King George III's mental and physical health were at a breaking point. "I wish to God I may die," he told his family. By this time, the Prince of Wales, who had been ignobly careless of his family in the past, was often at court to console his mother and sisters as his father declined. In private the women were grievously worried and confused, but in public they functioned as if nothing were amiss. On one occasion the royal family attended a concert, where the women sat demurely as the king writhed in his seat and blurted out disturbing gibberish.

In November, the king lunged at Prinny at a family dinner, thrashing him against a wall. The queen was in a justifiably fractious state and no longer felt safe in her husband's presence. Her personal effects were moved into a different bedroom, but the king followed her into it where he found his doctor and a cadre of attendants and relatives huddled together. The king cornered the physician in a rage but was miraculously lured back to his own room by one of the braver souls.[17]

Prinny was keeping Georgiana informed of the domestic violence at the palace. In fact, it is because of Georgiana that we have a firsthand account of the king's illness and the regency crisis that ensued. Her letters, according to biographer Amanda Foreman, remain the most quoted source documents of this time, invaluable for historians. "My letters will be a regular newspaper," Georgiana said presciently. "The truth is, I believe, that the King is quite disordered in his mind."[18]

In all crises, the resourceful find opportunities, and in this case the Whigs found theirs. If the king could not fulfill his duties, the Prince of Wales was by right able to assume the role of regent, allowing him to ask for the government's resignation and appoint his own cabinet. The Whigs were salivating at this stroke of good luck. The chance of having one of their own on the throne had come earlier than they had dreamed. For the Prince of Wales, having Charles Fox as prime minister would give him more latitude and resources, which the king's cabinet had reduced due to his wild overspending. Both of Georgiana's Charles's—Fox and Grey—jockeyed with others and each other for the role of chief negotiator for the prince. Their opponent in this fight was William Pitt, the king's advocate and prime minister, who wanted the prince to accept a limited regency with certain conditions. The prince, and by extension the Whigs, of course, wanted the full power of the monarch. While it appeared the prince had the winning cards, he did not have public support. His dissolute extravagance had become legendary, and Pitt took advantage of the growing concern that the prince was no more sensible to rule than his father.

The other complication in the crisis was the unknown. The king's illness was a mystery, making a diagnosis or prognosis impossible. One day he could be stark raving mad, and the next he could be lucid and stable, creating havoc inside the Devonshire House proceedings, as no clear leader or strategy emerged. "Great disturbances in the arrangements," Georgiana deadpanned in her diary.[19] Fox and the prince were, ultimately, outfoxed by Pitt who persuaded Parliament to pass, by a vote of 268–204, a series of restrictions on the prince's regency. The most humiliating of these was the proviso that Queen Charlotte remain head of the household, neutralizing her son's authority.

The outmaneuvering and eventual checkmate by Pitt was a disaster for the Whigs, the prince, and Georgiana, as it brought into sharp relief how disadvantaged they were against the establishment forces. Their Tory opponents to cast them as crass opportunists and power grabbers, and most alarmingly, as hypocrites. The chaos and finger-pointing were at fevered pitch inside the Whig central command, and in the streets, where the common people, the Whig's central constituency, defaced the walls of Devonshire House with insults against Fox and the prince. "Really London is now the most odious place I ever was in," wrote Georgiana's sister-in-law, Lavinia. "Party rage is so high and people all so outrageous and absurd that there is even less comfort in society now than there ever was." The actions of the Whigs backfired horribly and produced an epic surge in monarchic support.[20] The blue and buff, once colors of liberty and chic, were now replaced by blue and red—the colors of the king. The grand balls once hosted by Georgiana were objects of derision.

Things went from bad to worse in 1789 when the king's mystery ailments began to subside, nullifying (at least temporarily) the regency debate. When the king opened Parliament that March, he was honored with fireworks and deafening cheers of goodwill. While the festivities exploded around them, Georgiana and her Whigs stayed home to pout and lick their wounds. But Georgiana did summon up the courage to appear at the queen's drawing room later that month to celebrate, feignedly, the king's recovery. Georgiana was a gracious guest but drew the line at wearing GOD SAVE THE KING in her cap like the other ladies.

Later that year, her American compatriots would enact their own Constitution after beleaguered deliberations in Philadelphia. The king and his allies may have been on a high in England, but across the pond the Whig ideals of liberty were put into tangible motion—a small, but important bright spot in a ghastly year for Georgiana. Although she tried to encourage helpful discussions and postmortem reflections at Whig dinner parties that winter and spring, the party was deflated by defeat, and so was the usually ebullient Georgiana, who now had to contend with the smug faces of the "Tory ladies," as she called the wives of her political enemies.

But she also had problems of the domestic variety. Her gambling debts were still monumental, and there was still no son for the duke. The family, including Bess, headed for France to escape their ostracizing society; Georgiana hoped to relax enough to conceive an heir. While in Paris, Georgiana came face to face with yet another political rebellion—the French Revolution. Thomas Jefferson was the American ambassador in Paris at the time and recorded that near Versailles "the mob was violent, they insulted and even attacked all the clergy and nobility." Georgiana checked in with her old friend Marie Antoinette, whom she said was reduced to tears when she and the French King Louis XVI were shouted down by rioters when they appeared on their balcony.[21]

While in Parisian society, Georgiana struck up a friendship with none other than the Marquis de Lafayette, who had earned hero status in America while serving as one of George Washington's top generals. Georgiana and Lafayette exchanged spirited letters and engaged in forthright debates on politics. Their frankness with each other is evidence of their mutual admiration.

The heated situation in France would encourage most British aristocrats to return to England, but Georgiana was not keen to travel. She had finally conceived another child—the son that would be the Cavendish heir. On May 21, 1790, Georgiana gave birth in France to the Marquess of Hartington, who would be known by his nickname "Hart." After years as a political arbiter and hostess, Georgiana had hit the apex of her achievements as a duchess: She had produced a boy. The news quickly spread across the English Channel, and church bells sounded with joy near Chatsworth. The next Duke of Devonshire had made his debut.

After the birth, the family made its way back to England, but the French Revolution, at least in discussion, followed them back home. Everyone in their Whig world was talking about Edmund Burke's *Reflections on the Revolution in France*, but Burke's ideas on republicanism created even more fault lines within the Whig ranks. Burke was appalled by the violence of French Revolution, while the Whigs, with Fox at the helm, were in sympathy with the popular uprising that created it. This debate precipitated the dissolution of the Fox-Burke friendship, and Georgiana became a bystander to what she saw as a misunderstanding. Fox never advocated for a republic in France or England, but a constitutional monarchy as England had adopted in 1688. While Fox and the Whigs saw the merits of the French Revolution, they tried to save the king and queen from riotous mobs by writing to their friend Lafayette. Their efforts were in vain; the French monarchs lost their heads to the guillotine in 1793. On hearing news of their deaths, King George and Queen Charlotte wore black in mournful solidarity.[22]

Georgiana had seen firsthand the glories and ghastliness of politics and the revolutions she supported. She had learned that politics is bigger—and sometimes uglier—than idealist talk inside a gilded London salon. "I cannot express to you the horror I feel," she wrote. "The impression of the Queen's death is constantly before my eyes." The Duchess of Devonshire would also see the ugliness of social exile when she discovered she was pregnant again—this time with the child of Charles Grey. Despite his own flagrant adultery over the years, the duke was enraged and assumed the moral high ground, despite the fact that not only had Georgiana tolerated Bess, but she had also become her closest friend and had taken the duke's illegitimate children under her wing as her own. Bess tried to intercede on Georgiana's behalf, but the duke, with his family's full support, demanded Georgiana go to the Continent to have the child and see that it was adopted. If Georgiana did not submit to this plan, the duke would see to it she never saw their children again. Grey was of no solace and was "very cruel" to Georgiana when she explained her limited options. "He has one consolation that I have given him up to my children only," she said.

In early 1791, Georgiana gave birth to a girl named Eliza Courtney. The child was immediately taken from her and nursed by another woman before the baby was sent back to Grey's parents in England. Amanda Foreman writes that Eliza turned out to be the most beautiful of all of Georgiana's children but never knew the identity of her parents. She married General Robert Ellice in 1814, but Georgiana never lived long enough to see Eliza—born into such a sad situation—achieve happiness in her own marriage.[23] After Eliza's birth, Georgiana remained in exile and had not seen her other children for twelve months when she wrote to her daughter, Little G, that "this year has been the most painful of my life."

But by 1793, Georgiana was back in England, having ameliorated the duke's anger. She had made a promise to her mother that November that she would never engage in politics again. It was politics, and the charismatic men involved, that had gotten her into trouble, but trouble was something that Georgiana could not resist. Before long, Devonshire House and her dinner parties resumed, but this time with a much smaller group. This did not include the Prince of Wales, who had had a falling out with the Devonshires, later to be repaired. Despite the water under their marital bridge, the duke and duchess remained in accord in their support for the Whigs, still led by Fox.

As for Charles Grey, he did not inform Georgiana of his engagement to Mary Ponsonby, and let her read about it in the press, which naturally brought her great distress. "I had one kind letter from him," she said. "I think our correspondence is likely to end there."

"Grey's marriage increased Georgiana's sense of isolation," writes Amanda Foreman. "She had devoted her life to the Whig party; its ideology had become a religion for her, its leaders she had obeyed and venerated. Without these props she had no means of expressing her own suppressed political ambition."[24]

Georgiana watched from the sidelines as the Duchess of Gordon was now the leading political hostess, and Prinny continued to divide society with his bad boy behavior. Like the duke, he was unfaithful to his wife Caroline of Brunswick, and also followed the duke's example by treating his mistress Lady Jersey like a second wife. This scandal caused universal condemnation of the prince and Lady Jersey, who became the most hated woman in Britain.

The Whigs, however, achieved a public victory in 1796 by sending Charles Fox back to Westminster, and celebrated their win at Devonshire House. Although Georgiana was there to welcome the revelers, she became a virtual recluse over the next year due to an eye infection that rendered her nearly blind and necessitated a series of agonizing medical procedures. When she returned to public life, her political entertaining was on a smaller scale. The Whigs were a reduced entity by the late 1790s, and Charles Fox had retired by this time. She turned her ever curious mind to a broader, more aesthetic set of interests like gardening and poetry writing, but her passion for beautiful things never abated as her debts, mostly from her inveterate gambling and spending, haunted her always.

"My eye goes on well," she wrote of her partial eyesight loss. "I can and examine all the flowers and prospects to store my mind with images if I lose my sight. I have learnt to love my age, and not be ashamed of it and my illness perhaps was a benefit."[25] Now forty, Georgiana made peace with her erstwhile lover Charles Grey, inviting him and his wife to dine at Devonshire House. Just as she not only tolerated but befriended her husband's mistress Bess, so, too, did she come to form a friendship with Mary Grey, who had no knowledge of her affair with Grey, or their child.

Georgiana had also mended fences with the Prince of Wales, and now that she was a confident woman in her forties, had newfound strength in her opinions on world affairs as Napoleon dominated the continent and the headlines at the time. "We draw out the only virtues they have," she wrote of the French people. "Their miseries and the frivolity of their character would tell against them."[26] As a new century dawned, Georgiana reflected on the rise and fall of the great men of her time, including her hero, Charles Fox. Having overcome illness and personal betrayals, she had gained so much personal empowerment that had she been a man, she reckoned, could have led as his equal. "I think myself a very deep politician. To unite my talents, my hopes, my fortune . . . to make common cause, and fall or rule with him."[27]

It is with this early feminist mindset that she turned her attention to her daughter who was making her debut in society. Georgiana was closest in affections with Little G, and had high hopes for her, which perhaps explains the extravagance of her debutante balls, including a supper for one thousand guests. It was customary for the leading debs to make their court appearance in the presence of Queen Charlotte, who was noticeably civil to Little G, despite her history with Georgiana, and the fact that just a few years earlier Whig ladies had been banned from the palace. As Georgiana saw her children grow, her own popularity soon resurrected, and she was greeted in the streets like the superstar she once was.[28]

By 1806, she struggled with kidney stones, and that March she was tormented with feverish fits that lasted for hours. The undisputed queen of fashion and glamour of her day lay in bed in hysterics, bald and blistered. What was thought to be a disorder of the kidney, was, in fact, an abscessed liver. News of her illness spread. A distraught crowd gathered outside Devonshire House, while her closest family and friends stood vigil at her bedside while they tried in vain to keep her comfortable. Finally, and some would say mercifully, Her Grace the Duchess of Devonshire died in the small hours of March 30.[29] The Prince of Wales summed up the sentiments of his countrymen when he observed that "the best-natured and the best-bred woman in England is gone."[30]

Bess would eventually marry the duke and become the next duchess, which is what Georgiana wanted. Indeed, tellingly, Georgiana entrusted her papers and letters to Bess, not her children or mother. The duke died in 1811; Bess outlived him by over a decade. The three continue their ménage à trois into eternity as they are all laid to rest together in the Cavendish family vault in Derby.

By this time, King George III was entering his final decade in virtual isolation after a relapse of his mysterious illness and madness. By 1810, as he prepared to mark fifty years on the throne, he came down with severe symptoms of stress and agitation probably brought on by the impending death of his youngest child, Princess Amelia. He had been free of these attacks since 1804, but within weeks of the relapse the king was forced into a straitjacket every day to prevent harm to himself and others. By February of the next year, the king was considered incompetent, and his son was sworn in as prince regent with the proviso that Queen Charlotte, in consultation with her husband's doctors, have the final say in the king's health. The king was now based exclusively in an apartment at Windsor Castle where he would stay for the rest of his life, often carrying on "conversations" with Lord North, who had been dead for years. "I must have a new suit of clothes and I will have them in black in memory of King George III," he said in a moment of madness, according to his biographer. He had other "conversations" with the dead Princess Amelia during which he would give her a blow-by-blow account of her funeral. When he was not talking to ghosts, he would laugh and babble frighteningly. Historians and physicians are still confounded by the exact nature of the king's bouts of psychosis and differ on his exact diagnosis.

By 1818, he was deaf, blind, and immobile. Queen Charlotte would die that year, and the care of her husband was passed onto her son Frederick, Duke of York, who did not visit him, creating what Andrew Roberts aptly describes as a "King Lear Redux," the children of the king acting with callous disregard and betrayal.[31]

So it was a mercy, in a way, that King George died on January 29, 1820, at age eighty-one, then the oldest monarch until Queen Elizabeth II. He was mourned from the lowliest of shopkeepers to the poshest of Eton students who wore black coats for his funeral, which remain the school uniform today. Strangely, his biographer refers to him as "The Patriot King," a sobriquet that "his father had urged him to be, and what all his life he had considered himself to be."[32]

Later he would have an admirer in King Charles III, who observed, "The tragedy is that the American colonists never received a tour from him . . . the leaders of the colonies might have understood him better. Perhaps Americans will soon come to see the true George III without bias."[33]

Prinny would become King George IV but betrayed his Whig friends by failing to appoint them to his cabinet. He did stay faithful, however, to his mistress Maria Fitzherbert, by giving her place of honor at his dinner parties. He died ten years later in 1830, mostly because of his overly indulgent lifestyle. Georgiana's great love Charles Grey would become prime minister that year. "I have been in the midst of action," Georgiana observed of her life, often musing her objective would be to one day write a "secret history of the times."[34]

Devonshire House in London, which had been the locus of American support during the Revolution and a center of British political debate for decades, would be demolished in 1924. But today, Georgiana's legacy is stronger than ever. During the ensuing two centuries her descendants have produced the most influential people in the world, ranging from Winston Churchill to Diana, Princess of Wales, and, in her own way, Georgiana would bring together the two countries she loved—England and America—better than any of her salons ever could.

5

PHILADELPHIA FREEDOM

Benajah Strong's son Joseph sat by candlelight in Connecticut Hall at Yale in 1788, the school of choice for the men in his family and class. As engrossed as he was in his book, an unusual but frequent flickering in his peripheral vision tested his powers of concentration. Could it be the ghost of Nathan Hale, his cousin, who had lived in the same room decades before? Joseph thought that requesting Nathan's dormitory would provide a connection to his heritage, instead it was a connection to the supernatural. He would often feel stirrings of Nathan's presence. A sudden chill. A fast-moving shadow. Joseph thought for a moment and then went back to his reading. He could not be distracted by superstitions. He was a man of scholarship, and such things should have been beneath him, but the spirit of Nathan, be it real or imagined, would follow Joseph out of Connecticut Hall, and throughout his brief but distinguished life.[1]

Only six years old when Nathan was executed, Joseph's life would follow a similar pattern: work hard and die young. After coming of age in Coventry during the American Revolution, Joseph had seen the sacrifice of the men in his community—his father, cousins, and neighbors—many of whom had given the ultimate price. He had grown up hearing about them, savoring stories about their lives and even their deaths, and trying to live up to their legends. By the time he graduated from Yale in 1788, at the age of eighteen, he had decided his calling was medicine, breaking with the family tradition of pursuing the military or clergy. The origins of his interest in medicine are unknown. Perhaps being the eldest of a large brood of children engendered caretaking sympathies, and his intake of war stories from friends and relations could have inspired his future as a military physician.

At that time, formal study at a medical school was not required, and men could practice medicine—even conduct major surgeries—without advanced degrees. Apprenticing under learned men was the credential he needed, and he wasted no time associating with the best. He began in Hartford under Dr. Lemuel Hopkins, working in his apothecary. It was common practice for doctors to run shops where herbs and drugs would be sold to help patients self-diagnose and eliminate their diseases—before these diseases and their cures were better understood. Hopkins was a physician and poet, distinctions that appealed to the budding Renaissance man in young Joseph. It was likely through Hopkins that he was introduced to the Hartford Wits, a tight circle of writers who satirized the changing world around them with rapier humor and intellect—the college humor magazine nerds of their day.[2]

By 1790, Joseph was recommended by Dr. Ebenezer Beardsley, one of the most imminent physicians in New Haven, to Founding Father Dr. Benjamin Rush. "Permit me to introduce to your favourable notice & attention the bearer Mr. Joseph Strong who has had a liberal education & has lately completed a course of medical studies under the direction of one of our most able physicians," reads the letter Beardsley wrote to Rush maintained by the Library Company of Philadelphia. "Any civilities you may please to show him will confer a fresh obligation on me & should any of your friends come this way I shall be happy acknowledging the obligation."[3]

This letter set Joseph on his path from Connecticut farm boy to the riveting metropolis of Philadelphia. The City of Brotherly Love in the late eighteenth century was one of the major cities of the Western world, with only London, Dublin, and Edinburgh boasting larger populations. Then the capital of the newly formed United States, it still retained a marked diversity with Quakers, pacifists, and patriots all creating a "fertile soil for enlightenment thinking, radical political theory, and mass mobilization [that] was closely tied to the British networks of commerce, culture, and religion that stretched across the Atlantic," explains the historian Aaron Sullivan. This city would have seemed like a world away from the comfortable, unified community of Coventry, and the lectures that Joseph attended by Dr. Rush must have been true revelations to Joseph's young mind.[4]

The only physician to sign the Declaration of Independence, Benjamin Rush is to American surgeons what Alexander the Great is to Greek warriors. At his death, his closest friend, John Adams, summed him up as "a man of science, letters, taste, sense, philosophy, patriotism, religion, morality, merit, usefulness, taken all together, Rush has not left his equal in America, nor that I know in the world."[5]

Born on January 4, 1746, in a Quaker family farmhouse on the Delaware River, he was five when he lost his father, a common theme among the country's founders. When he was fifteen, he enrolled at Princeton where he indulged in "idle, playful, and mischievous" conduct but earned his degree in two years and found an apprenticeship with Dr. John Redman, Philadelphia's leading doctor. Rush also audited the first anatomy course in America in which Dr. William Shippen would dissect the corpses of enslaved persons and paupers—bodies that had been stolen from their burial place by grave robbers. During one lab session, Rush and his fellow students were attacked by an angry mob that had smashed through the windows, demanding Shippen and his students stop mutilating the innocent dead.[6]

There were riots in the lab and more riots in the streets for liberty, as colonial American discontent grew during the early 1760s. In 1766, Rush left for Scotland to attend the University of Edinburgh's medical school, then the best in the world. While across the pond, he developed a lifelong friendship with Benjamin Franklin, then stationed in London as Pennsylvania's agent. Franklin looked out for the young Rush, offering to introduce him to other good contacts, a courtesy that Rush would one day pass along to the young Joseph Strong. The historian Harlow Giles Unger recounts Rush's trip to London in which he visited the Houses of Parliament. Rush sat "like a mischievous schoolboy, on the throne of the House of Lords, then going to the House of Commons and thinking to himself, 'this is the place where the infernal scheme for enslaving America was first broached.'"[7]

Rush returned to Philadelphia, and without funds to open a shop or practice, began what Unger calls "street medicine," ambling the filthy roads of the city, looking for lice-infested poor people who needed medical assistance. The city's center gleamed with fresh gardens and regal architecture, but its slums reeked with abject poverty. This was a time when chamber pots were poured out of windows, leaving raw sewage in the streets. Families would often fill a tub once and use the same bathwater. Lice and bedbugs were rife. The poor walked around with open bacterial and fungus sores, passing their infections like air. These were Benjamin Rush's patients, whom he courted by declaiming: *Doctor calling! Anyone need a doctor?*

"Within seconds they responded, like ants marching from their hills to feast on prey," Unger writes. Although Rush exposed himself to infection and filth, he would look back on his treatment of the destitute with great pride and recalled "the innumerable blessings of my life to my services to God's poor children." Unger says, "He believed Man himself determined the lot of the advantaged and disadvantaged and that the former had an obligation to improve the lot of the latter."[8]

Rush advocated for the education of women, prison reform, and joined the Pennsylvania Society for Promoting the Abolition of Slavery and the Relief of Free Negroes Unlawfully Held in Bondage. "The first step to be taken to put a stop to slavery in this country is to leave off importing slaves. Let such of our countrymen as engage in the slave trade be shunned as the greatest enemies of our country," he explained. Rush also was an early advocate for temperance, blaming alcohol for many of the social ills and poverty he encountered, and he presciently called out tobacco use as "uncleanly. Many diseases are produced by it, some of which become fatal."[9]

By 1774, after having acquired degrees, made friends in London and Paris, and absorbed knowledge from the streets, Rush was able to establish his own practice in Philadelphia. His practice was built on a new and innovative way of treating disease, mainly smallpox, through the practice of bloodletting. Rush's small and painless puncture—rather than the traditional deep and ghastly cut—gained the attention of his fellow Philadelphians, looking to rid themselves of infections. Bloodletting seems ridiculous to us now, but from ancient times to the early nineteenth century, it was established practice for purging the body of disease and bringing balance to the "humors."[10]

Every Tuesday, Independence Hall would fill with Philadelphia's poorest who would be injected with Rush's pox-infected serum as part of a campaign he started called Society for Inoculating the Poor Gratis. Within weeks, the rate of smallpox declined markedly.

Rush's reputation as an innovative healer made him ideal for the lecture circuit, and students flocked to hear him speak, paying $15 for the privilege, according to Unger. One of those students was Joseph Strong. "I visited Dr. Rush to know the fee he received from his pupils," Joseph recalled in his letters about his visit to Rush. "He told me $100 per annum with the privilege of hearing his lectures and attending the practice of the Philadelphia Hospital. This is a uniform establishment for tuition by the year. He makes an abatement when the pupil contracts for 3 years; for this term he receives $100 Pennsylvania currency." Joseph, like Rush's other pupils, would take inspiration from Rush's mission to use medicine to not only heal wounds, but heal social evils.[11]

As 1775 and 1776 unfolded and revolution gripped his adopted city, Rush became part of the inner circle of Founding Fathers, thanks to his eminence as a doctor and man of conscience. He did not let his aversion to tobacco keep him from establishing a friendship with tobacco farmer

George Washington, whom he celebrated at a party on the Schuylkill River shortly after his appointment as the commander in chief of the Continental Army. The onetime "street doctor" was now a leading statesman by 1776, and at twenty-nine, one of the youngest of the Founding Fathers. He and John Adams would forge an especially tight bond due to their mutual antipathy for slavery.

As fighting with the Crown progressed, Rush was on the front lines of battle, overseeing health and hygiene policies for the troops. He insisted on regular bathing, handwashing, haircutting and shaving, and the avoidance of setting up camp near damp environments, like marshes. At Trenton, Rush treated British troops as well as his own, which won him the respect of an enemy colonel. Rush's passionate, consistent criticism of the failure of military camps and hospitals to meet his recommended health standards led to a temporary falling out with Washington, who was under enormous pressure to balance military expediency and doctor's orders. But the commander in chief, eventually recognizing Rush's well-intended motives, reconciled with his friend by the end of the war.[12]

Still, by 1787, Rush's constant complaints about public health standards had discontented enough of his fellow patriots that he was denied a place at the Constitutional Convention. At this point, however, Rush had found a cause as noble as the Constitution—helping freed slaves in Philadelphia. He encouraged the founding of the African Episcopal Church of St. Thomas—the first to be established in the United States in 1792 by free Blacks in the newly independent Episcopal Church (formerly the Church of England). At their opening night dinner he toasted: "May African churches everywhere soon succeed African bondage."

Rush wrote to his wife, Julia, recounting a "day to be remembered with pleasure as long as I live. In order that my other friends, the criminals in the jails . . . might sympathize a little in the joy of the day, I sent them a large wheelbarrow full of melons."[13]

While Rush was building churches, his protégé Joseph Strong was building a career as a military surgeon's mate—or assistant. His army commission was signed by Washington on March 19, 1793—though the paper itself has disappeared from the Strong family archives, according to later research. Joseph served in the Legion of General Anthony Wayne in the Ohio campaign against the Native Americans until 1796. The roster of the Officers of the Legion of the United States commanded by General Wayne lists four surgeons and eighteen surgeon's mates, including Joseph, who was placed in charge of hospitals at posts in what was then wilderness territory.[14]

General "Mad" Anthony Wayne—the Historical Society of Pennsylvania delicately suggests "the nickname may have been awarded for his short temper and use of off-color language"—was a dynamic officer who had fought British and Hessians during the Revolution, leading a heroic charge at the Battle of Stony Point in New York.[15] After a brief retirement that involved a stint farming in Georgia and representing that state in Congress, Wayne was back in uniform, assembling troops at Pittsburgh in the summer of 1792. By November, they were sent down the Ohio River by boat where they established a training camp Wayne named Legion Ville, near what is now Rochester, Pennsylvania. It is here that recruits were trained intensively in Native American warfare. Several forts were created up and down the river, mostly named for the country's founders. "The Army is sickly at present, though the ruling epidemic is abating. The common disorder has been a Typhus fever," Joseph related in a letter in manuscripts held today at Yale. "It has proven mortal in a few instances. You can readily form an idea of my opportunities for improvement both in politeness and professional knowledge."[16]

By 1794, Joseph was stationed at Fort Washington, the site of present-day Cincinnati. He wrote of the "immense wilderness" around him and his "little society apart from the Army . . . many painful occurrences constantly accompany the progress of the War, I was appointed in charge of the General Hospital on the movement of the Army from this place on their intended campaign. It consists of about 100 patients of various complaints requiring the aid of medical surgery. It has been a slavish task to me but attended with satisfactory improvement. I have but few sick now in the hospital and enjoy myself very well."[17]

On March 16, 1794, he wrote to Ezra Stiles, president of Yale, describing the landscape of what would become the American Midwest. "The prairies of the country are extremely beautiful and covered with fine grass and flowers and variegated with small bunches of trees which appear at a distance like islands in the sea." He also described encountering the remnants of the earlier inhabitants of the region, now thought to be part of the early American culture known as the "Mound Builders." "The mounds of the earth and the circular fortifications observed in this country are full proof of the immense labor and industry of some former nation. What nation that was none can tell."[18]

It was at Fort Greenville, near today's Ohio-Indiana border, that Wayne signed a treaty with the Native Americans in August 1795. "Four tribes of hostile Indians have lately arrived at Green Ville to supplicate peace with General Wayne," Joseph wrote of the negotiations. "They declare that all the other tribes—the Shawanese excepted—will soon be with them to unite in their wishes . . . I feel much happiness in the occasion."[19]

A year after the peace agreement, Joseph went to Philadelphia, not back to Connecticut, as some of his family may have hoped. He had resigned his commission in the army but was determined to fight another war—the battle against yellow fever, which was ravaging Philadelphia in a second outbreak in 1797 and 1798. For this fight, he would rejoin his teacher, Benjamin Rush.

The first yellow fever outbreak in the summer of 1792 had rendered Philadelphia and New York virtual graveyards as citizens fled to the country. The poor were left behind to live or die, depending on their luck. The fever was remarkably similar to COVID-19: it began with headache, chill, stomachache, but then became decidedly fatal, usually resulting in death within days. The patient would expire with the fever's signature:

a morbid yellowish pallor. Decades later, at the turn of the twentieth century, an army doctor named Major Walter Reed would discover that yellow fever was caused by mosquitoes. But at the end of the eighteenth century, Rush was convinced it was caused by squalid urban conditions, pollution, and odors, made all the more pungent by the summer heat. He believed patients became infected by breathing in noxious air.[20]

By August, deaths rose to twenty a day—only to spike to forty-two and then forty-eight a week. Rush was one of a handful of the "noble group" to stay behind to treat the infected, using his bloodletting methods on some one hundred patients a day. Rush, according to his biographer, was "among the few doctors left in Philadelphia who dared to venture into filthy slums and neighborhoods where the living hurled the dead into the streets to rot with the garbage and the contents of their chamber pots."[21]

Death came calling to the Rush household as it claimed the life of his sister, who had been a loyal nurse for him. Rush fainted at the bedside of a patient and nearly succumbed to the fever himself. Finally on November 1, 1793, the *Federal Gazette* declared the pandemic over, and four days later, church bells rang out, bonfires were lit, and guns fired in celebratory joy. "We may ever remember the Thirtieth of November," John Adams wrote in one of his many letters of affection to Abigail. "It was the day which I entered the city in 1793. The principal families have returned, the president is here; several members of Congress are arrived."[22]

As the aftermath of the pandemic set in, finger-pointing commenced in Rush's direction as bleed-and-purge methods were largely seen as more harm than good by the public. Undaunted, Rush continued in his campaign for cleaner living conditions, especially for the poor. He pleaded with officials and citizens to clean and remove stagnating water from streets and privies, thereby inadvertently reducing the breeding sites for mosquitoes. Rush, activating his clean streets campaign, effectively stopped the disease, without knowing the exact cause.

With the worst behind him, Rush continued his studies into yellow fever and the practice of bloodletting, but by 1798, yellow fever had broken out again in Philadelphia. By this point, Joseph had also established himself firmly inside the Philadelphia medical establishment and with Rush and others formed the Academy of Medicine whose purpose was to better understand and alleviate the effects of the menacing disease.

Joseph's grandson Lockwood Barr wrote later that Joseph and Rush "found a common ground of interest in their study of yellow fever, in bloodletting as a remedy." A key area of interest to Rush was an invention by Joseph—a new, stronger type of tourniquet used to control bleeding during operations, and after bloodletting. By 1801, Joseph, after having spent four months in Washington, DC, secured a patent for his invention, which was used in the army and navy. The patent was signed by John Adams on January 29 and attested by Charles Lee, his attorney general. It reads: "Whereas, Joseph Strong, a citizen of the state of Pennsylvania, in the United States, hath alleged, that he has invented a new and useful improvement, called the Axle Tourniquet; which improvement has not been known or used before his application: has made oath, that he does verily believe that he is the true inventor, or discoverer, of the said improvement."[23]

Joseph had the inventor's entrepreneurial instinct and turned to his colleagues in the medical community back in New England for their help getting the tourniquet into the mass market.

"I am willing to sell them at 4 doll [dollars] complete & to allow any commission they may think proper to receive," Joseph wrote to a colleague. "I have expressly mentioned in my specifications that the size of the tourniquet may be varied to answer the purposes of compression from the highest operation in surgery to the act of phlebotomy. I shall have small ones manufactured for bleeders in a short time, which may be sold for 1.50 doll (dollars) & answer for compressing the arm or leg in the extirpation of tumors which may require a tourniquet . . . Let it be plainly mentioned to the public that such an instrument is for sale & the medical men requested to examine it for their own convictions."[24] Decades later, Lewis and Clark would carry a Strong tourniquet—purchased in

Philadelphia for $3.50 (about $95 in 2025)—when they set off on their expedition in 1804.[25]

Lockwood Barr recounts that while his fellow Americans were happy to try a new product, the former mother country was not. "England had done all within its power to prevent the establishment of manufacturing in the colonies. Machinery could not be exported from Great Britain; processes were held secret and skilled craftsmen in all lines of industry were prevented from migrating. The United States put an embargo on imports and exports. That embargo brought ruin upon the Philadelphia businessman."[26]

In response, the leaders of the Federalist movement in the early American Republic intended to organize for a boom in American industry. American-made silkworms, sailcloth, woolens, carpets, dyes, chemicals, and drugs were promoted for the preservation of the new and feeble American economy. Philadelphia, as the country's pulse point, was at the heart of this push, and so was Joseph Strong. In November of 1808, he attended a dinner for the freshly formed Philadelphia Society for the Encouragement of Domestic Manufacture of which his grandson Barr referred to him as the "leading spirit."[27]

In 1812, Congress, at the behest of President James Madison, declared war on Great Britain, with New York and the New England states refusing to join the war effort as trade with Britain was too profitable. Sadly, that year Dr. Joseph Strong's life came to a sad and ironic end. He died of yellow fever, leaving behind his wife Rebecca, and their children. He was only forty-two.[28]

Now in his sixties, this latest war provided another opportunity for Benjamin Rush to serve his country as the demand for doctors increased. By January of 1813, his crusade turned to medical education. He called a two-year medical school education woefully inadequate and "a danger to life." Today, American medical schools are what they are, thanks to the standards set by Benjamin Rush, while Rush University in Chicago, named in his honor, is one of the most eminent.[29] On April 19, 1813, after having been bedridden with possible pneumonia, Rush called an acolyte and asked him to extract ten ounces of blood, perhaps using the bleeder's tourniquet that his protégé had invented. When the doctor on call was told to extract more, "only three viscous ounces oozed out," according to his biographer. Rush died that afternoon.[30]

Even in death, Rush was a healer. He was a gentle guiding light in the lives of his two friends—John Adams and Thomas Jefferson, who made a rapprochement after years of bitter feuding and public insults, thanks to Rush's encouragement. They exchanged letters on all the subjects Rush loved—science, country, politics, faith, and family. "Another of our friends of seventy-six is gone, my dear sir," Jefferson wrote in one of those letters, after hearing of Rush's death. "A better man than Rush could not have left us; more benevolent, more learned, of finer genius, or more honest. We must go, and that ere long. I believe we are under half a dozen at present; I mean the signers of the Declaration. I am the only one south of the Potomac."[31] Jefferson and Adams would die on the same day—July 4, 1826.

Joseph and Rush lived and died in the City of Brotherly Love, one a national hero and statesman, and the other an obscure but loving man whose goodness never matured into the greatness more time would have likely given him. After Joseph's death, his wife Rebeca remarried and moved to Ohio with her family, settling into the new American prairie that Joseph had so admired.[32] It was here in American's heartland that William's family sowed the seeds of its ultimate fortune.

6

THE DEAN OF
MADISON SQUARE

It is the summer of 1876 in New York. As the sweltering heat descends on 10 Washington Square, so too does terminal illness visit this address's master, Cornelius Vanderbilt, known as the Commodore, a man so wealthy and powerful, it seemed he could conquer everything. But not mortality.

Despite having amassed one of the greatest fortunes of all time, Vanderbilt lay stricken on his bed just like a pauper stricken in a Bowery alleyway. He was suffering from a variety of ailments; in such pain he often begged for death. Downstairs in the parlor loomed the image he wanted the world to see: a bust of himself, conveying the bold, brave, and resolute man whose dynasty has become synonymous with American success—or greed, depending on one's point of view. A larger version of this bust stands tall and proud at Grand Central Terminal today, eyeing droves of travelers to and from the city he helped to make.

The great and good of New York passed by this parlor bust during the last months of the Commodore's life and made their way to his sickbed, commanded by his wife Frank, decades younger, whom he had married only a year after his first wife Sophia had made him a widower. Vanderbilt's second union was sealed only after an iron-tight prenuptial agreement had been signed. His children remained skeptical of the depth of Frank's affections and did not attend the wedding. As the Commodore wished death would take him away from his agony, he stroked Frank's hand hoping she would join him in eternity soon. The Commodore had adopted his wife's spiritual and religious affiliations, purchasing and giving the former Mercer Street Presbyterian Church to Rev. Charles Deems who set up the nondenominational and chillingly named Church of the Strangers in its space. Deems was a frequent visitor to the Vanderbilts that summer, offering the couple solace as they contemplated the hard reality of "till death do us part." Vanderbilt had already made plans for their burial together in the Vanderbilt cemetery on Staten Island where the family, including descendant Gloria Vanderbilt who died in 2019, now rest in peace.[1]

He may have hewed to his wife's and Rev. Deems's idiosyncratic faith, but the extent of his Christian attitude toward his flesh and blood was another matter. Some of his children, like his wayward son Cornie, were denied entry to their father's home that summer. Thanks to this melodrama, and the spiritualists and mediums who joined Rev. Deems in preparing Vanderbilt for his journey onward, the scene at his deathbed took on a theatrical quality.

The other Frank, who was likely at his bedside, was of a much more down-to-earth sort. His name was Frank Work, and he was Vanderbilt's stockbroker, fellow horse lover, and Madison Square neighbor. Frank had a portrait of Vanderbilt in his own parlor, signaling his admiration for the man who had made Frank Work one of the richest men in the city.[2] Leonard Jerome, who had also made his fortune thanks to the Commodore, was also likely passing through to say his goodbyes. The daughters of these two financiers, Fanny Work and Jennie Jerome, would play pivotal roles in linking the American Republic with the British Crown in the person of William, Prince of Wales.

The Commodore had one foot in the hereafter in 1876 and one foot firmly in the here and now as he gathered his business associates, like Frank and Leonard, for postmortem financial planning. He had spent a lifetime building wealth, and though he could not take it with him, he whispered "keep the money together" when he was strong enough to utter something coherent in his final days. These may have been his last words, and surely his last thoughts, when Cornelius Vanderbilt finally died in January 1877, at the age of eighty-two.[3] In *Vanderbilt: The Rise and Fall of an American Dynasty*, co-written with Katherine Howe, Anderson Cooper, Gloria Vanderbilt's son, would describe his family's patriarch as a "master manipulator, disseminator, and inventor of his own legend."[4]

The same could be said of Frank Work, who may not have the fame of the Commodore, but whose bloodline will one day produce a king. This is a legacy not even Vanderbilt's fortune could buy, and a story almost too good to be true.

The town of Chillicothe, Ohio, is today a blue-collar Rust Belt oasis, less than an hour outside of Columbus, which supplanted it as the state capital in 1816. Today, its population is about twenty-two thousand, and the city's claim to fame is the annual Feast of the Flowering Moon festival, which draws some eighty-five thousand spectators annually to celebrate the area's Native American heritage. In some ways, the area hasn't changed much since Franklin Work, known as Frank, William's great-great-great-grandfather, was born there in 1819. His story from small-town misfit to Gilded Age tycoon is a credit to the Midwestern values he gleaned from Chillicothe, but he would have been unlikely to admit it. He was eager to forget his hometown as soon as he left it.

Frank's father, John Wark, was an Englishman from Plymouth whose father had served in the Royal Navy. John and his wife, the former Sarah Boude from Maryland, would have five children, but Frank was the only one born in Chillicothe, in the city's Dogsburg section, according to the local historian Patricia Medert. John came to town to work as a civil engineer on the Scioto River Bridge but died in 1823 when Frank was just four. Young Frank would always remember the stories his father told him about his adventures sailing on the Mississippi to Baton Rouge, and one day Frank would have his own river odyssey on a steamboat as he made his way out of Chillicothe.

Left broke after the death of John, Sarah opened her home at South and Mulberry Streets as a boardinghouse while rearing the children. Her most difficult child was little Frank, who was often tangling with the local marshal when he was not trying his own poor mother's patience with his shenanigans. "He loved horses and was not content to ride at a normal pace, but raced up and down the streets, terrorizing those in his path," Medert explains. But his most infamous misadventure involved skinny dipping in the river, and not bothering to put his clothes on, mount his horse and ride back home "like Lady Godiva." With the town marshal breathlessly running behind him, Frank sat proud on his nag, unflappable as he ducked the fruit and stones pelted by scandalized neighbors.[5]

Even as a child Frank had a manly stoicism that would serve him well in the years to come. He did not seem to care what people thought, and in fact, seemed to delight in irritating his peers and elders. While in Ohio, he did manage to make at least one friend—Edwin Stanton, who would later become Abraham Lincoln's secretary of war and lead the manhunt for his assassin.

By the time he was fifteen, he had had enough of Chillicothe and his mother. Reports vary on the nature of their parting. Medert says Sarah beat Frank for his profanity, while it is also reported that the rattan whip of a schoolmaster made Frank cast off his hometown in a "complete medium of divorcement." Once Frank had left, he was never to return or speak to Sarah again. He made his way to New Orleans, Columbus, and finally to New York City in 1839 with a gold piece and thirty cents in silver in his pocket.[6]

He would hold on to that gold piece for the rest of his life as a symbol of his American ascent and ingenuity. His lifelong axiom, according to his children, was "show me a man or woman who does not get up in the morning, and I will show you a man or woman who will never amount to anything."[7] He started his rise with WJF Daily, a dry goods merchant, and discovered his natural affinity for business and retail. Within a short time, his lucky gold piece was yielding results and Frank, having changed his name from Wark, was a partner in the company of Daily and Work. As Frank was building his fortune, he saved his pennies. His source of amusement was hanging around stables, dreaming of the day he could buy horses of his own. Finally, he had saved enough to buy a broken-down horse struggling with early onset lameness. Not only did he get the horse back on his feet but trotted him down the streets of Manhattan as if the horse were a purebred champion. One day a distinguished older gent noticed Frank and his horse and followed them to the local tavern where he asked Frank for a drink. Frank sheepishly replied that if he was paying, he would be happy to join. Frank's new drinking buddy was none other than Cornelius Vanderbilt, who had been riding his champion, Maude S, that day. The two men took an instant liking to each other. Vanderbilt saw the potential in this fearless rider who could make a lame horse run like the wind.[8]

This friendship that young Frank forged and maintained with Vanderbilt is a testament to his resourcefulness and charisma. Frank would remain loyal to Vanderbilt for the rest of his life, often gazing admiringly at the portrait of the Commodore he had in his parlor. William Vanderbilt, the Commodore's son, would also figure in Frank's life as a friend. As the Commodore was ravenous for control of the ever-growing railroad industry, he placed Frank as his representative on the board of the Erie Railroad. Although he and Frank both lost money in their railroad ambitions, Frank earned Vanderbilt's trust as he went to battle with the courts and other tycoons in the so-called Battle for the Erie.

By 1873, there was a financial panic in the city, and Frank's dry goods business was going under. Not only did Vanderbilt loan Frank the money to save Daily and Work but he gave him some advice that would make Frank one of the wealthiest men in the country: Go to Wall Street. In due course, Frank sold his stake in the dry good business and got himself a seat on the New York Stock Exchange the following year. Together with William Strong, another Chillocothean and a descendant of the Strong family of Coventry, they formed the banking firm Work and Strong.[9]

The family that Frank married into came, perhaps surprisingly, from the town he'd sought to forget. He picked the belle of Chillicothe, Ellen Wood, who had also fled Ohio for New York as his bride in 1857. She was the daughter of one of the wealthiest men in the city, John Wood, whose house at West 5th Street, was one of the grandest in the area. "I recall the lithe and lissome form of the pretty faced Ellen Wood," recalled a local in the *Chillicothe Gazette* in 1894. "She was an energetic and captivating young lady. A society belle of more than ordinary conspicuousness and of unusually quick repartee." Ellen had a distinguished American pedigree—her grandfather was Dr. Joseph Strong of Philadelphia, and her great-grandfather was Benajah Strong, who had served during the Revolutionary War, from Coventry, Connecticut. For someone as proudly American as Frank Work, Ellen and her solid Yankee roots were highly appealing, and he courted her with his typical ferocity. He pulled out all the stops to win her, even sending her quotes from Lord Byron. Frank may have lost a railroad deal, but losing a catch like Ellen Wood was unthinkable.[10] Family historian Mary Burke Roche, before her death in 2008, still had the note with Frank's Byronic wooing of Ellen in her personal papers.

Frank provided a life of luxury for his bride and his horses. His stable opposite Carnegie Hall was worth a staggering $100,000 in the late nineteenth century. Built with Wyoming rock, it had oak and bronze doors, beveled glass windows, and was heated with steam. The stable's fanciest feature was its glass dome, which allowed his horses to sun themselves on their days off the streets of Manhattan. A tough and ruthless businessman, Frank melted with fondness for his trotters, especially his favorites—Pilot Boy and Dick Swiveller. "All that was needed to dispel the mantle of brusqueness and gruffness in which he cloaked himself was to talk horse with him," explained his obituary in the *Chillicothe Gazette*. "Horses were his ruling passion. They brought him health, entertainment, and the opportunity to display tenderness and affection which he possessed abundantly but which he apparently chose to conceal in his walks with men."[11]

In his book on the Gilded Age, *A Season of Splendor*, Greg King explains, "There was a nearly universal obsession with horses: gentlemen owned, bred, and raced horses, and enjoyed coaching and driving, diversions adopted from English models. Although an American Gilded Age gentleman tended to hunt and shoot less than his European counterparts, many enjoyed—or pretended to enjoy for the benefit of their guests—such endeavors at their country estates."[12]

When Dick Swiveller died at the age of thirty, Frank stayed at his side on his final night cuddled up with his old friend in his heated stable and was said to have been uncharacteristically tearful at his passing. Frank later provided for his horses in his will and made sure that all of them would be transferred to a Long Island farm upon his death for a life of pastoral luxury.[13]

While his contemporaries were buying the new automobile, Frank is known to have proudly never driven anything but a horse-drawn carriage, usually alone. "It's not a pleasure to have another man in the wagon," he said. "I just want myself and the horse. I keep a good trotter or two for the use of my friends when they call, but the horses I drive are for no one now or hereafter." His affinity for horses is on display at the Museum of the City of New York in the painting *Frank Work Driving a Fast Team of Trotters* by John McAuliffe. He drove well into his eighties and was arrested for reckless driving in Central Park by two mounted policemen. Frank, still as feisty as ever, threatened to spend six figures to have the charges dismissed, and the police officers fired. He was successful on the first point, when a judge threw out the speeding violation, although it's unknown whatever happened to the cops, who no doubt got an earful of the old man's indignation.[14]

Frank would ultimately earn the moniker "The Dean of Madison Square" for his stubbornness, which his peers saw as his best virtue. He stayed in his East 26th Street house long after "fashion had moved out—and skyscrapers had moved in," as one observed at the time. In 1876, Delmonico's, the New York hotspot, relocated across the street from the Dean, who spent many an evening indulging in decadent evenings of masked balls, multi-course dinners, and smoking with his fat-cat friends.[15]

In addition to his four-legged children, Frank had three human ones with Ellen. They had a son, George, and daughters Lucy and Frances, known as Fanny, who inherited her father's rebellious spirit. Like a thoroughbred mare, Fanny was beautiful, obstinate, with a mind of her own. She was a creature that could not be tamed, much to the consternation of her father whose version of love—when it came to his horses and his daughters—was through the prism of control.

Frank's constant irritation with his daughters could be summarized by two frequent fatherly complaints: their lack of appreciation of money and America, Frank's favorite things, apart from horses. He insisted that they marry Americans, something he would later try to persuade his grandsons to do too.

"It's time the international marrying came to a stop," Frank said with his usual direct manner. "Our American girls are ruining our country by it. As fast as our honorable, hard-working men can earn their money, their daughters take it and toss it across the ocean."[16]

Lucy Frank-proofed her marriage when she wed Peter Cooper Hewitt, the son of New York mayor Abram Hewitt, and grandson of industrialist Peter Cooper. Like Frank, Peter was hardworking and resourceful, becoming an engineer who produced the first mercury-vapor lamp in 1901. Unlike Frank, he was not a good husband, and fathered a child with his mistress, whom he later married. While Lucy's tenure as Mrs. Peter Cooper Hewitt was brief, she did manage to have her portrait painted by Giovanni Boldini. This sumptuous painting, decadent in pastels, now is in the permanent collection of the Rhode Island School of Design Museum.[17]

Fanny famously ignored her father's marriage diktat, and in doing so, took the Work legacy far beyond Chillicothe and New York, and into the world.

7

CASH FOR CLASS

Here are the names, don't you know, on the authority of their great leader, you understand, and therefore genuine, you see . . . read the *New York Times* on February 16, 1892. Ward McAllister, the right hand of society queen Caroline Astor, needed to make it absolutely clear who was still "in," and Mrs. Astor's social list was the apex of New York power and money. Money, for Mrs. Astor, "represents energy and character; it is acquired by brains and untiring effort; it is kept intact only by the same means."[1]

While the men like Cornelius Vanderbilt and Frank Work made the money, the women, like Mrs. Astor, decided how it would be used, and how it could be parlayed into money's ultimate currency—power. Social position was a ruthless sport during the Gilded Age. Battle lines were set in parlors, and Caroline Astor, known as Lina, was the field marshal who made all the rules. In militaristic fashion, she rose through the ranks and established her primacy with an iron fist beneath an elegant silk opera glove.

Caroline Schermerhorn Astor, forever known by her far more imperious moniker "Mrs. Astor," was born in 1830 to a Knickerbocker family whose patriarch was a multimillionaire. According to Anderson Cooper in his other family book *Astor: The Rise and Fall of an American Fortune*, Lina's marriage to William Backhouse Astor Jr., while making for a glamourous Gilded Age coupling, had deteriorated by the 1870s, and she had turned to a cadre of gay men for companionship while her husband entertained himself with other ladies (sometimes prostitutes), racing, and yachting. One of Mrs. Astor's companions was Ward McAllister. McAllister served as not only a companion, but an advisor, and, of course, dutiful sycophant. "Mystic Rose" was what he wistfully called her. She ate it up almost as blissfully as being called "Mrs. Astor," a name she had molded into an almost royal title.

The two fast friends had come of age during the Civil War and saw the tumults of history from both sides—Lina as a New Yorker and young Ward as a child from Savannah, Georgia. As they absorbed the devastation of Reconstruction, according to Anderson Cooper and Katherine Howe, they both pondered the same questions. What is American society? "Someone had to set the standard," Cooper writes. "Someone had to decide what constituted American taste. After the Civil War, a sense of American cultural inferiority persisted, even as the newly reunited United States emerged as an international player." Lina Astor decided that she would be the arbiter, and Ward McAllister would be her primary propogandist. He had earned the right to be in her circle after metamorphosizing into a dandy thanks to long stays in Europe. New York would be their oyster.[2]

Like a scientist working on his first patent, Ward devised a system for categorizing New York society. The "Nobs" would include the old Dutch settlers of Mrs. Astor's ilk, while the "Swells," such as the Vanderbilts and the Frank Works, would be the thrivers and newcomers. To be a respectable "Nob," one needed to be at least three generations removed from your immigrant ancestor, or the original moneymaker. To be a proper "Swell," a bank account holding a million dollars—around thirty million in today's money—was the ticket price for admission, or "respectable poverty," as Ward called it.[3]

While the landed aristocracy in their country houses set the rules for Georgiana, Duchess of Devonshire, and her descendants in Britain's ruling class, Mrs. Astor would define the new American elite in the new

Gilded Age—a term coined by Mark Twain to mark the years from the 1870s to late 1890s.

This era's advent was best represented by the Patriarch Ball in 1872, one of Mrs. Astor's inventions under the ministrations of Ward. Patriarchs—those deemed deeply entrenched in the Nob camp—would be given invitations to pass out to people in the Swell camp who could use some social boosting. Elaborate balls would bring both camps together in an opulent nineteenth-century approximation of *West Side Story*.

Besides the Patriarch Ball, Ward and Mrs. Astor created "the Four Hundred," the Phi Beta Kappa of Manhattan's elite, revolutionary in its mingling of the old and new families. "There are about 400 people in fashionable New York society," Ward explained. "If you go outside the number you strike people who either are not at ease in a ballroom, or else make other people not at ease."[4]

Mrs. Astor remained at the top of this new social caste system, setting the standards for the modern New York hostess. According to Mrs. Astor, a society figure's biggest failure was the seeking and flaunting of publicity. This is where Ward McAllister fell short, and fell out with Mrs. Astor, who Cooper writes, could be "pitiless in her expectations of adherence to an ideal."

Ward published a book in 1890—*Society as I Have Found It*—without Mrs. Astor's blessing, and much to her shock and horror, broke the cardinal rule by releasing the list of The Four Hundred to the newspapers two years later. Ward died shortly thereafter, and Mrs. Astor maintained her pitiless intransigence by not attending his funeral.[5]

One of the names on the list of four hundred in 1892 was one Mrs. Frances Burke Roche, the former Frances Work, Frank's daughter. She would adhere to Mrs. Astor's expectations by marrying high but fail miserably at keeping herself out of the papers. Her life, like her father's, was always good copy.

Born in New York on October 28, 1857, Frances had the kind of upbringing her father didn't—one of privilege and luxury. Portraits of Frances show a young woman of arresting beauty and poise, starring into the viewer's direction, daring him to question her right to be young, beautiful, and rich. In the painting, she wears a golden ornament in her hair with a tiara quality. Over the years, she developed a keen eye for art and fashion, and thanks to her father's wealth, could indulge her passion for luxury with clothes, jewels, and furs.

When she traveled, she would catalogue the baubles she was taking in case any of it went missing. "Pearls, little pearls and drops, ruby bracelet, ruby earrings, ruby crown, bracelet three pearls, sapphire and pearl bracelet, big diamond ring, sapphire and diamond ring, sapphire two diamonds, small ruby single diamond ring, antique necklace, watch chain, sapphire barrette and earrings," she wrote of her inventory. Her great-great-granddaughter Diana, Princess of Wales, would later wear jewelry and tiaras with a similar effect as the most photographed woman in the world.[6]

Fanny, from when she was young, was an assiduous curator of all things beautiful and artistic whether man-made or from the natural world. Her collection of exotic birds included a Japanese nightingale, whom she nursed with whisky, and a Brazilian bird she named Lincoln. Horses, dogs, flowers, paintings, and music would all be lasting companions and bring her solace and joy throughout her life. "It is necessary for me to ride every day," she explained of her frequent jaunts through Central Park, usually with her dog Daphne at her side. On her bay mare, Glenna, she would attract (and adore) the attention she received. "Me in chinchilla with yellow roses and fur turban. Daphne in yellow. Down avenue at good clip, everyone looking." Yellow and black became her signature color combination, which adorned everything, including the rugs in her carriage. "I am supposed to have the best taste; and why not have?"[7]

Like her father and future husbands, she became a formidable horsewoman, huntress, and carriage driver, at a time when the sport was an elegant, yet unconventional avocation for a lady. Fanny always had one foot firmly in society, and one foot ready to kick up its backside. "Try and get some spirit into your blood," she would say when a friend or relation needed her inspiration.

Her passion was often used to help and support the underdogs in her life, and to fight injustice. "Will not be patient with a person who gives me endless arrogance," she said. A case in point is recounted in her diary from 1909 when she describes racial prejudice at her riding academy, where the people of her class would exercise and train their horses. "I have been requested to say that ladies object to the colored man being in the ring . . . I will take my horses away rather than be dictated to . . . I cooly decide that the episode will not for one moment be tolerated." Two days later she removed her horses to another location.[8]

Fanny was educated at home, unlike her brother George, who was sent to St. Paul's, where she would one day send her sons. She had a French governess and learned to speak the language with ease. Her diaries show a fine mind behind the glamourous façade as she quotes from the great writers of classic literature. One of her favorite lines, which may explain her penchant for vanity, comes from William Shakespeare's *Henry V*. "If it be a sin to covet honour I am the most offending soul alive."[9]

Fanny's neck was said to be the best in the city, and she loved showing it off. Later in life after seeing the women of London wearing dresses sans the traditional high ruffle collars, she conspired with Gilded Age "funmaker" Mamie Fish, also known as Mrs. Stuyvesant Fish, to bring the daring sartorial look to New York. She said it was "absurd for the general public to be deprived of the sight of a pretty neck just because an obsolete convention decreed that only nice women could appear in evening dress in the shelter of their own and their friends' houses." She and Mamie made a pact: The following Sunday evening at Sherry's they would go hatless (dear, oh, dear!) and would wear the new "Dutch" necklines that exposed the throat. A press report recounts the scandal Fanny and Mamie caused, and the new trend they started. The waiters at Sherry's "averted shocked eyes from the shameful expanse of bare throats . . . . If they had come in naked they could hardly have caused more of a sensation."

Louis Sherry, the owner of New York's chic establishment, tried desperately to maintain his poise amidst the commotion of chatter and jaws hitting the floor. He walked Fanny and Mamie to their table, giving them basic civilities. These were, after all, two of New York's leading hostesses. Nobody else would have gotten away with this spectacle, but Mr. Sherry's disapproval was evident.

The report ended by calling "the victory of the décolleté necks" an unqualified success. Fanny got what she wanted—she turned heads, defied her class—and the next Sunday, other women turned up wearing the same neckline. There was an appeal to Fanny's innate defiance, and this was the leitmotif of her life.[10]

She carried herself as if the world were her oyster, and she was its most luminous pearl. "If born of a most beautiful, thoroughbred mother and a father who had exceptional beauty, health, ability, magnetism, and force, that there should have been at least some trace of my parents. But it would be a poor creature indeed who, with such a pedigree, did not at least attempt to be something and not let herself with the crowd be spent."[11]

Her debut as a desirable young heiress came as the "Million Dollar Princess" wave swept across the Atlantic. Over three hundred British aristocrats married American women between 1870 and 1914. Some of these marriages were for love, but many were hard and cold "cash for class" transactions. As robber barons created wealth and expanded the American elite, the aristocracy across the pond was foundering because of economic and agricultural decline. The income from vast estates like Chatsworth and Althorp struggled to support staff, family members, huge households, and property expenses.

The new advances in steamships made transatlantic travel between New York and London a virtual dating app. Young Americans with rich fathers were "swiping right" to meet titled heirs, and vice versa. The

Chicago Tribune cynically noted that "it was taken for granted that the possession of a coronet is the highest possible standard of female happiness as well as ambition. There is some doubt, however, whether such is the case."[12]

This transatlantic trend was the trap Frank Work had always warned Fanny—and indeed all of her peers—against falling into.

"I am an American to my backbone," he said. "Therefore, I have only contempt for the helpless, hopeless, lifeless men that cross the ocean to carry off the very flower of our womanhood. I'd like to give our girls some good advice to tell them to stay at home and realize that American men make the best husbands even if they have not any foolery like 'sir' or 'milord' attached to their honest, substantial names."[13]

But just as young Frank had given his mother grief back in Chillicothe, so too did Fanny express the familial Work propensity for disobedience. The rebel apple did not fall far from the tree the day she clapped eyes on James Boothby Burke Roche of the Fermoy family.

Jim, as he was known, was the second son of the Irishman Edmund Burke Roche, first Lord Fermoy, and was born at his mother's house Twyford Abbey, Acton in Middlesex in 1851. His father was named for Edmund Burke, a first cousin twice removed, and the revolutionary writer who had inspired Georgiana, Duchess of Devonshire, and the American Founding Fathers. When Edmund Roche was elected to Parliament in 1837, he represented County Cork, and formed an alliance with Daniel O'Connell, a hero of Irish republicanism. He would later serve as Lord Lieutenant of the county and city of Cork, and would become the first Baron Fermoy, after which he added "Burke" to the family name of Roche in honor of Burke's writings. Although the new baron and his wife had political power and status, they had little cold hard cash, and the family struggled to keep up with their aristocratic surroundings, a fate that would haunt Jim for the rest of his life.

They occupied two family homes in Ireland—Trabolgan, their summer house on the coast, and Kilshannig in the winter. The estates and their contents would eventually be sold off to pay off debts and stay afloat, but, like Fanny, Jim grew up riding, hunting, and reveling in the country pursuits of the landed gentry.[14]

The prestige of titles in Britain is measured by their antiquity, and the Fermoy title had only arrived a few years after Jim's birth, when Queen Victoria created it. Further eroding his aristocratic credentials was Jim's misfortune to be the second son, after his brother Fitzy, who was destined to inherit the title.

After getting his degree at Trinity College, Cambridge, young Jim embarked on his first trip to America on a hunting expedition with other English lads in 1878. The exploration of Yellowstone National Park was a common rite of passage for men of his class, and young Jim was ready to conquer it. On August 19, 1879, he was reported killed by Indians in Yellowstone River, but this report was proved wrong, and Jim set out on his next adventure.

He made his way to New York by 1879 for a hunting expedition of the more civilized wife-hunting variety. The big game in Manhattan was young American flesh, with daddy's money to go along with it. As Jane Austen famously wrote in *Pride and Prejudice*, "It is a truth universally acknowledged, that a single man in possession of a good fortune, must be in want of a wife."

The Fermoy family may not have been the richest, nor the holders of grand and old titles, but Jim was a catch for any American girl. He "created quite a stir in New York and London society in the fall of 1879," wrote the *New York Times* in 1897. "The most exclusive circles took him up. He was at the time an honorary member of the Knickerbocker and Union Clubs." With great stature, a sweeping mustache, and a British bearing, not to mention his adventurous past, he must have been devilishly attractive, and soon he and Fanny Work fell in love, or at least lust.[15]

In 1877, her mother, Ellen, had died, leaving Frank in charge of his daughter's future. He was adamantly opposed to the relationship with Fanny's "noble ruffian," but Fanny was determined to have her way.

Frank's increasing irascibility could be explained by the fact that he was a widower without his Chillicothe rose at his side when he needed her the most.

On September 22, 1880, nearly one hundred years to the day Fanny's ancestor Nathan Hale was hanged by the British for defending America, Frances became Mrs. Frances Burke Roche, a member of the British establishment. Fanny was patriotic enough, however, to exchange wedding vows on American soil at Christ Church, New York on Fifth Avenue, the same church where Ellen Work's funeral was held just three years earlier. *The Sun* noted that the wedding was "strictly private with only near relatives and very intimate friends having been informed that the event was to take place." We don't know if Frank gave the bride away that day in 1880, but if he did, we can only imagine the behind-the-scenes fights leading up to it due to his animus to anything "not American," as the *New York Tribune* would later put it.[16] Fanny left her father and city behind and sailed for London for her new life as an expatriate, although she did maintain friendships with her fellow Americans, like Clara Frewen, the daughter of Leonard Jerome, who married Jim's friend Moreton Frewen, a British entrepreneur. The couples spent time together at Castle Frewen in Wyoming, reliving Jim's adventures as a bachelor in the American West.[17]

Back in London, Fanny brought a good deal of cache into the marriage but was still an American and seen as inferior by her new British peers. While someone like Frank Work could crack into the upper echelons of New York society, Fanny's new family was embedded in a much older system, highly averse to change. In the year of her marriage, 580 peers were in the House of Lords—nearly all of these seats were hereditary. The ruling class both in the House of Commons and the House of Lords dominated the political and social fabric of Britain. The legal system, military, and even the church were run by the same men, from the same schools, from the same backgrounds. Outsiders, especially Americans, were not warmly welcomed. By 1914, sixty of the peers and forty of their sons of peers had married Americans. Their money was appreciated; their new American ways were not.[18]

The women in the Gilded Age, those with money and position, occupied their time running large estates, entertaining, and breeding. Fanny performed her marital duty and produced children immediately, but shared Georgiana's frustration by not birthing babies of the right gender. Her first daughter, Eileen, was born in 1882, but died soon after. Cynthia came in 1884, and finally by 1885, Fanny had given birth to two boy twins, Maurice and Francis. Maurice would ultimately inherit his father's title and become fourth Baron Fermoy, as he was the eldest by a minute.

While Fanny performed her duty and produced children, Jim proved to be feckless, and an inveterate gambler. Frank had been bankrolling the couple from the beginning, sending some $7,000–$12,000 a year, to avoid creditors from seizing furniture and belongings from the Burke Roche residence.[19]

By December 1886, the fairy tale was over and the couple had separated. Fanny faced the unthinkable social stigma of divorce, but even more glumly, she faced the truth no daughter ever wants to admit: *Daddy was right*. Swallowing her pride with a little champagne, Fanny packed her bags and her daughter, and went back to New York to live with Frank, who was himself exultant to be rid of the son-in-law he had pegged as rotten from the beginning.

The twin boys stayed behind in London with their father, but the following March, Jim showed up at Frank's Madison Square residence with the twins, whom he shockingly left at the house's entrance. The following day, Jim, desperately in debt, made a cold and hard transaction—he effectively sold his sons to Frank Work. The two men made a deal that allowed the boys to be raised by Fanny in New York in exchange for Jim never being a part of their life. Jim took his check and departed.[20]

In 1891, Fanny obtained a divorce decree from Jim in a Superior Court in Wilmington, Delaware, and custody of the children, who became naturalized Americans. Meanwhile, Jim lived at 60 St. James Street in London and enjoyed a dandy's life as a member of the Bucks and Hurlingham Clubs.

By 1896, he followed his father's political example and won a seat in Parliament, representing the East Division of County Kerry, but not without a character debate. Divorce, especially in his circle and among public servants, was a sacrilege, and despite Fanny's Delaware writ, Jim maintained he was still a married man, a source of pearl-clutching gossip on both sides of the pond. When the aristocracy's who's who of the titled—*Burke's Peerage*—listed him as divorced, he sued for damages and won. He maintained the divorce was not recognized outside of the United States for the rest of his life.[21]

The War of the Burke Roches spilled over into the raising of the children. A standoff between Fanny, Jim, and their fifteen-year-old daughter Cynthia in May of 1899 is documented for all to peruse with delectation in the *New York Times*, whose headlines added further embarrassment to the family drama. HE OBTAINS AN ORDER FOR THE PRODUCTION OF HIS DAUGHTER . . . THE FATHER CHARGES THAT HIS EX-WIFE DEPRIVES THE CHILD OF HER LIBERTY.

This episode started when Jim was staying at the Albemarle Hotel in New York and wanted to see Cynthia while he was in town. When he sent a lawyer to 18 East 26th Street to request Cynthia be delivered to the hotel, Fanny told the lawyer Cynthia was away at boarding school—which, according to Jim, was a blatant lie. So he went to the Supreme Court of New York and secured a writ of habeas corpus to have his daughter appear in court, arguing she was being "imprisoned" by her mother. The paper ended the story with "this last move will not surprise New York society. The controversy has been a *cause celebre* for some years." But for Fanny, this was just the beginning.

8

THE MOTHER OF THE SPECIAL RELATIONSHIP

In the late 1890s, as the Burke Roche transatlantic alliance was going sideways, Lady Randolph Churchill, formerly Jennie Jerome of New York, was basking in vindication. She stood victoriously in front of her mirror, being fitted for a gown by Charles Frederick Worth, the leading dressmaker at the time. She had commissioned the frock in the perfect shade of blue to complement the medal she would receive, the Insignia of the Order of the Crown of India, which the Prince of Wales had persuaded Queen Victoria to give her. *How far I have come*, she must have thought.

When she married Lord Randolph Churchill in 1874, she, like Frances Work, became one of the first Americans to bag an aristocrat, but also confront the snobbery and envy that came as the price of admission. As an American, she was looked down on by Englishwomen. As an American from a wealthy background, she was tolerated by their debt-ridden noble families. But her son would one day save the very nation they held so dear.

Although her father, Leonard Jerome, whom we previously met at Vanderbilt's bedside, was a titan in New York with a Madison Avenue mansion boasting its own theatre and three-story stable, the Spencer-Churchill family of Blenheim Palace, who had carried the Duke of

Marlborough title since 1702, viewed Jennie, her mother Clara, and father as social climbing upstarts. And, frankly, they were.

Leonard, born in 1818, grew up near Syracuse, New York, and was working in the village store by his early teens. Young Leonard earned a place at Princeton but had to drop out for lack of funds and enrolled in the far less prestigious Union College. By 1844, he and his brother Lawrence were practicing law in their Uncle Hiram's firm in Rochester where they fell in love with the fetching and wealthy Hall sisters. Catherine would be the bride of Lawrence, while Leonard won the hand of Clara.

Thanks to Clara's family's loan of $30,000, Leonard branched into the newspaper business by starting the *Daily American*, the go-to journal for supporters of big government and federal projects like canals and railroads. The paper was successful enough that he and Clara could move to Brooklyn, where their daughter Jeannette was born in 1854. Some say Leonard was fond of the name Jennie, the lasting nickname of the child, because of his amorous attachment to an opera singer of the same name. Leonard's interest in opera, and opera singers, would be a lifelong amusement.

With his new proximity to New York, Leonard reinvented himself again by turning to Wall Street, selling short stocks with the ambition of joining the small club of millionaires in the city. In the mid-1850s there were only nineteen, and Leonard Jerome was determined to be number twenty in a business he described as "a jungle where men tear and claw." Like his grandson, Winston Churchill, Leonard was a lion of a man, who stared down any challenge as if it were easy prey.[1]

Clara Jerome's ambition was to rise socially, but she and her husband were not good enough for Mrs. Astor's Four Hundred, so had to "fake it until they made it" by showing off Clara's dazzling jewelry collection and their mansion at Madison Square and 23rd Street.

They threw an opening ball—the Gilded Age version of a housewarming party—with champagne fountains and crimson tapestry lining the walls. Leonard's dinners became legendary for their party favors. At one such gathering at chic hotspot Delmonico's, the lady guests were gifted with bejeweled gold bracelets.

Elisabeth Kehoe, in her biography of the Jerome women, explains that Leonard lavished Clara with worldly gifts to ameliorate the pain of his extramarital dalliances. Kehoe writes that Clara was of the belief that a woman should never confront her husband or else he will retreat "where he is not scolded." While his infidelities may have caused cracks in the marriage, they were steadfastly united in their ambition and love of high society.[2]

In 1866, he built a racetrack with a grandstand for eight thousand spectators, a luxurious clubhouse, and additional space for other outdoor upper-class excursions like polo and shooting. True to form, Leonard named the area Jerome Park, and it would eventually become the American Jockey Club whose opening that September the *New York Tribune* called "the social event of all time . . . a new era in the horse racing world." Mrs. Astor be damned. Leonard Jerome was now "the Father of the American Turf," and a Wall Street mogul, although his fortune would experience constant upheavals.[3]

Now that he and Clara had showed the "Nobs" what they were made of, they wanted to show the world what their three beautiful daughters could offer. Jennie and her sisters, Clarita and Leonie, were all accomplished linguists, writers, and pianists thanks to a cultural education and European travel afforded them by their parents.

In 1867, after having been rebuffed by Mrs. Astor and excluded from Ward McAllister's social list, Clara moved the family to Paris where she was intent on marrying her girls off to European royalty. It was in Paris that Jennie polished her French and adopted her lifelong patina of sophistication. By 1873, she was a dark-haired beauty, an exotic foil for her fair and blue-eyed sister Clarita. The death of Louis Napoleon that January had dispelled the magic and splendor of the Paris they had come to adore, and the women found new socially upward hunting fields in England where Jennie made her debut.[4]

The social scene in London was led by the Prince of Wales: Albert Edward, known as "Bertie," the oldest son and heir of Queen Victoria. As his predecessor, Prinny, had lorded over the Devonshire House set, so Bertie ruled supreme over the Marlborough House clique, the movers and shakers of chic Victorian London. It was into this milieu that Jennie found herself launched that summer of 1873 when she met Lord Randolph Churchill, the Duke of Marlborough's second son and a close friend of the Prince of Wales.

The Dukedom of Marlborough was created in 1702 by Queen Anne for John Churchill in appreciation for his career as an undefeated military leader. With the dukedom came Blenheim Palace, the seat of the family to this day. Another American lady who would later marry into the family, Consuelo Vanderbilt, described Blenheim as an "expensive absurdity" with its 775 rooms and 1,450,000 square feet. The exorbitant scale of the house and gardens reflects the family's primacy in Britain's cultural and political history.

The current occupant of Blenheim, James, Duke of Marlborough, is casually known as Jamie Spencer-Churchill. His family has styled itself Spencer-Churchill since the fifth duke obtained a Royal Licence to add the name Churchill to their patronym to honor the merging of the two families in 1733 when Charles Spencer, through a complicated twist of deaths and marriages, became the third duke. The Spencer family of Althorp and the Spencer-Churchills of Blenheim had both risen to the top of the British hierarchy and would rise even higher in the years to come.

The meeting of Randolph Spencer-Churchill and Jennie Jerome could not have been better written by the most imaginative romance novelist. Jennie, bare-shouldered in the sun and corseted, stood on the deck of the *Ariadne*, perhaps holding a parasol, looking like a Renoir painting. The boat party that day was in honor of the future Tsar Nicholas II of Russia and his wife. As the Royal Marine band played, Jennie was asked to waltz by one of many admiring men on deck that day. This is when Randolph instantly decided she would be his wife.[5]

By the time they had their third meeting, he had proposed, much to the consternation of both families. Randolph wrote to his father asking for an increase in his allowance to ask Leonard for Jennie's hand. Inside the letter, he enclosed a photograph of his beloved, believing her magical beauty would sweeten the deal.

Randolph, like James Burke Roche, was expected to take his place in British society and seek a seat in Parliament. Randolph argued that Jennie would not only be an outstanding asset but would motivate him to settle down and take life more seriously.

"She is as nice, as lovable, as amiable and charming in every way as she is beautiful, and that by education and bringing up she is in every way qualified to fill any position," Randolph implored.[6]

Randolph's father, the Duke of Marlborough, took his time replying while he made inquiries about Jennie's provenance. The reports were varied, to put it kindly. The duke wrote to Randolph that Leonard was "a sporting, and I should think, vulgar kind of man."[7]

For their part, Jennie's parents were equally resistant to the match. Randolph Churchill was, like James Boothby Burke Roche, a second son. Therefore, he was not in line to inherit Blenheim, or any fortune of consequence. Mrs. Jerome was still champing at the bit to advance socially, and she believed her daughter was cut out to be a duchess or princess, not merely Lady Randolph Churchill.

The couple did have one high-profile champion in Albert, Prince of Wales, who had been an early witness to the sparks that flew between them. Bertie would remain a lifelong friend, driven, perhaps in part, by his admiration for American women. He described them as "livelier, better educated and less hampered by etiquette . . . they are not as squeamish and they are able to take care of themselves." His grandson, a later Prince of Wales and briefly King Edward VIII, inherited this fondness for transatlantic liaisons with historic consequences.[8]

Jennie, for her own part, was forthright in what she perceived as prejudices against American women, which agitated against her, despite the prince's endorsement. "As a rule, people looked upon her (an American) as disagreeable, or even dangerous, to be viewed with suspicion, if not avoided altogether. Her dollars were her only recommendation."[9]

The couple dug in their heels and persuaded their families with the strength of their commitment to each other. Unlike the Burke Roche marriage, this was no transaction. Randolph knew Leonard Jerome could not and would not bestow millions on the couple, and Jennie knew that they would never inherit Blenheim and the titles of duke and duchess. In other words, they were in it for love. Their eyes and hearts were wide open.

"This was a love match if ever there was one, with very little money on either side. In fact, they could only live in the very smallest way possible to people in London Society," their son would later reflect. "If the marriage became famous afterwards it was because my father, an unknown sprig of the aristocracy, became famous, and also because my mother, as all her photographs attest, was by general consent one of the beauties of her time."

They married at the British embassy in Paris in April of 1874 with the Duke and Duchess of Marlborough conspicuously absent. The duke, however, sent a letter to be read on the day of the wedding in which he wrote that while he had wished his son had deliberated more on his choice of bride, he believed "as time goes on, your two natures will prove to have been brought not accidentally together." The Prince of Wales sent his best wishes in the form of a locket of pearls and turquoise.[10]

After their honeymoon, the couple stayed at Blenheim, which left the new bride cold with its stodginess and strict protocols. In her memoir, Jennie describes her every move being watched by the duchess, Randolph's mother, and his sisters during mind-numbingly boring teas and meals. "Even breakfast was made ceremonious," Jennie recalled. For someone as chic and cultured as Jennie, the Spencer-Churchill women, while thinking themselves her superiors, were to her mind frumpy and grumpy. Dinner, she describes as "solemn full dress" affairs after which guests repaired to a decadently-appointed room for reading or games.

"Many a glance would be cast at the clock . . . No one dared suggest bed until the sacred hour of eleven had struck." Jennie then describes the mandatory ritual of kissing the duke and duchess at the end of the night before carrying candles upstairs to bed. Jennie was a free spirit who chafed under regimented procedures from which no deviation was tolerated.[11]

Despite their own home in London, Randolph and Jennie were obliged to spend many nights at Blenheim, which is where one of the happiest moments for Jennie—and the world—occurred in the early morning hours of November 30, 1874, when she gave birth to one Winston Leonard Spencer-Churchill. The baby was named for his "vulgar" American grandfather Leonard Jerome and would later joke about the curious timing of his arrival—less than nine months after his parent's wedding that spring. For the record, historians maintain that Winston was a "premature" baby.

Jennie was a young woman in her early twenties, and like most women of her class, relied on staff to look after her child while she became a professional social butterfly, twirling around London in her Worth gowns. Winston would later remember her "brilliant impression. She shone for me like the Evening Star. I loved her dearly—but at a distance."

She was living in frequent separation from Randolph after Winston's birth, because he had contracted what most historians believe was syphilis, a highly contagious but common sexually transmitted disease. This separation gave Jennie the excuse (or opportunity) to take lovers of her own. She was at the height of her legendary beauty, and she enjoyed sharing it immensely.

"I have the clearest recollection of seeing her for the first time," recalled an aristocratic banker in poetic terms, who saw her in Dublin. "A dark, lithe figure, standing somewhat apart and appearing to be of another texture to those around her, radiant, translucent, intense. A diamond star in her hair, her favorite ornament—its lustre dimmed by the flashing glory of her eyes. More of the panther than of the woman in her look, but with a cultivated intelligence unknown to the jungle."[12]

Jennie and Randolph, despite their glittering social lives, found a cause to support in the downtrodden people of Ireland, perhaps the most pressing political and humanitarian issue of their time. Randolph's father was named lord lieutenant of Ireland by Queen Victoria in 1876, and the couple assisted with the Famine Fund, which helped ease the burden of the potato crop failure in 1877.

This cause brought Randolph Churchill and James Burke Roche together in admirable alliance. Both as members of Parliament advocated for the Irish during a time when few British leaders deigned to visit Ireland at all and acted with shocking disregard of the starvation going on so close to their own backyards. Jennie and Randolph visited nearly every county on the island, and Randolph, against his father's wishes, agitated for independence for Ireland from Britain.

Jennie's second son, Jack, was born in 1880 with his paternity a matter of historical debate. The father, according to most scholars, was the child's official godfather, Colonel John Strange Jocelyn, who had been living in Dublin, where Jack was likely conceived.

Jennie continued to leave the rearing of her children to nannies and governesses while she campaigned for her husband and consolidated their influence as a power couple. In addition to their work in Ireland, Randolph was appointed Secretary of State of India in 1885. Randolph and his contemporaries knew that despite his natal talents and noble birth, his rise would not have been possible without the beautiful American at his side.

"Randolph's growing prominence in the political world was attracting considerable attention in the social world," Jennie said. "We were bombarded with invitations of every kind. The fashionable world, which had held aloof, now began to smile on us once more."

By 1886, he was one of the most popular statesmen in England at the age of only thirty-seven. He was not popular, however, with Queen Victoria, who noted in her diary that Randolph was "mad and odd and also has bad health." Perhaps Her Majesty knew the tawdry nature of

Randolph's illness. Despite the queen's reservations, Randolph was a star, mainly because Jennie made him one. While Randolph thrived in Parliament and in debate with opponents, Jennie thrived on bringing people together. She was every bit the saloniste that Georgiana had been at Devonshire House a century before. "Our house became the rendezvous of all shades of politicians," Jennie remembered, while her biographer Elisabeth Kehoe goes one step further by describing Jennie as one of the most influential women in London. Far from being an upstart, Jennie was now a power player.

Perhaps inspired by President Lincoln's "team of rivals" approach, Jennie thrived on what Kehoe calls "dinner parties of deadly enemies," which a guest described as "a hazardous experiment, but proved a complete success. The talk flowed on smoothly." Her son Winston would employ his American mother's strategy to vanquish the Nazis in the 1940s, as we shall discover later.

Nobody was more pleased by Jennie's success than her father, Leonard, who continued to bankroll the couple from across the Atlantic. "You have no idea how universally Jennie is talked about and how proud Americans are of her," he wrote. When Jennie, as the secretary of state's wife, accepted the Insignia of the Order of the Crown of India in her blue Worth dress in November of 1885, she was accepting a badge of victory for herself and for all the Americans that had been regarded as inferiors in her new country. She had simply proven them wrong—this belief gave her medal a little more sparkle on her chest and a little more beam in her eye that day.

She carried this sense of belief with her when she and Randolph dined with Queen Victoria at Windsor Castle. The couple's firsthand knowledge of Ireland gave them rare insights into the most discussed political issue of the day. But their time at the top was not to last.

By 1886, Randolph was chancellor of the exchequer, which required tedious attention to numbers and details, a skill he did not possess. He was better suited to oratory and ideas. His ongoing battle with syphilis wore down his ability to concentrate, while his physical and mental challenges caused friction at home and at work. He was at the end of his tether when he finally resigned.

While only in his thirties, he was considered a busted flush, and Jennie, who thrived on political intrigues, was utterly disappointed for her husband—and herself. Jennie would be equally galled when Randolph's request for an ambassadorship to Paris, something much more his style, was denied.

She cheered herself with lovers and social pursuits. In 1890, she joined "The Souls," a club for the bold and beautiful of London. Although the organization's official mission was to gather for the reading and appreciation of poetry, it soon got out that there was more than reading going on behind closed doors. Despite her moniker in the press as "Lady Jane Snatcher," due to her penchant for passionate liaisons with a variety of men, Jennie maintained her friendship with the Prince of Wales and his wife, Princess Alexandra. Jennie's biographer Elisabeth Kehoe records that like the Duchess of Devonshire and the previous Prince of Wales, the two had formed a mutual admiration society that stood the test of time and social vicissitudes. Jennie "was one of the very few who could enjoy a relatively unsychophantic relationship with him. He granted her rare favor of using Buckingham Palace's private garden entrance and relied on her to organize parties for him. She understood how to please him and manage him; in return he lavished gifts and affection upon her." Kehoe proposes that Randolph's guilt at having contracted syphilis and his intimate friendships with men himself might explain his openness to Jennie's extramarital friendships.[13]

Leonard Jerome, her stalwart father whose American grit and charm she had inherited and passed down to her teenage son, Winston, had died by 1891, and she leaned more readily into the arms of men, older and younger, who could comfort her. Kehoe also writes that Jennie's sons knew of her friendships with other men, and that Jennie used her lovers to advance Winston's career when she could. One of Jennie's boyfriends,

Charles Kinsky, had married another woman by 1894, signaling what she described as a "fin de siècle" (end of the century) affair. It was also the end of Jennie's married life as the Spencer-Churchill family came to terms with the inevitable: Randolph was dying. As his syphilis raged, his moods became irascible, and Jennie, as his caretaker, was as much the victim of the disease as her husband.

In January of 1895, at the age of forty-five, Lord Randolph Churchill passed away after being in a coma, two weeks after Kinsky's marriage to a countess. Jennie was now forty, virtually ancient for a woman in those days. Never on good terms with Randolph's mother, and her own father dead, Jennie's financial situation seemed desperate.[14]

As she sat in Westminster Abbey that winter's day for Randolph's funeral, looking every inch the glamorous widow, her thoughts must have been miles away, thinking of the life she could have had with Randolph, or with one of her many admirers. *Who will want me now? I'm as dead as Randolph.* But, then her back stiffened, her chin lifted. She remembered something she would never forget. *I am a Jerome. I am a New Yorker. I must do what we do best—keep buggering on.*

9

"NOT WITH THE CROWD TO BE SPENT"

Frank Work, now a retired banker, sat in the vestibule of his New York mansion on East 26th Street, looking into the distance. It was a beautiful summer day in 1906, and his home offered a perfect vista of Madison Square Park, lush and green, but his view was encumbered by a most unpleasant pest—a *New York Times* reporter at his doorstep. In fact, there were many muckraking insects he wanted to swat down that day. Rather than acknowledge their presence, he sat stone-faced, a wool hat studiously obscuring his eyes. Finally, after being harangued for hours, he snapped.

"Present my compliments to the newspapers and tell them I don't know any more about my daughter's marriage than they do," he said, according to the *Times* article on July 16. "Damn it, I don't know anything about it."[1]

The last few years had been hard on Frank Work—even his vast wealth and horses could not heal the suffering. In 1900, his son George had died in Switzerland from health problems caused by alcohol abuse. Like his father and his sister Fanny, George had been an excellent equestrian, known as the "best jockey in the country," and "champion steeplechaser." But drinking caught up with him, and he died a young and tragic death with his sisters at his bedside.[2]

Now Fanny had done it again. The first time she had married a man despite Frank's express objections. This time she married a man without his knowledge, a Hungarian riding instructor by the name of Aurel Batonyi. The *Times* explained that Aurel's parents, based in Budapest, had made the wedding announcement, an "unusual" break in tradition.[3] Other press reports at the time of his marriage to Fanny said that his Hungarian parents spent most of their time in Monte Carlo, and that his mother had one of Europe's most impressive collections of emeralds.

Aurel had arrived in New York in 1889 with a dubious curriculum vitae and provenance. Like Fanny, Aurel had been married before, but to whom and for how long was unknown. Some speculated that Aurel Batonyi was not even his name. He claimed to have studied at a prestigious German university, but this is also subject to doubt.

What is clear is that Aurel was one of the most gifted horsemen in the city. Before his arrival in Manhattan, he had raked up hundreds of ribbons in thoroughbred riding competitions in Europe. He started his New York career at the Central Park Riding School on Seventh Avenue, but after discovering his ability as a "whip," or carriage driver, he branched into driving carriages for the high and mighty. "Few in New York can manipulate the lines over a four in hand as expertly as he can," one observer noted. He started his own carriage firm called Good Times, which would shuttle the upper crust around the Waldorf Astoria and to Newport, the new summer stomping ground for the elite. Press articles say that Good Times "was not a success and lost several thousand dollars."

But it did provide access to affluent women who swooned over the Hungarian whip with the irresistible charm. It was not long before Aurel fell into Fanny's orbit, or maybe it was she who was the primary mover.[4]

Fanny had become an accomplished carriage driver in her own right, which surely impressed Aurel. In 1902, she was the first woman to drive a four-in-hand in Central Park. A 1903 article in the *New York Times* documents "the spectacle" she and her fellow members of the Ladies Four in Hand Club made when they paraded their carriages in "very becoming—not mannish, but sensible" attire. "Mrs. Burke Roche has been driving all winter," the paper explained. "Her favorite speedway is Fifth Avenue where she is a familiar figure." She was also a dominant figure in Newport where she raked up all the prizes at horse shows with her black mare, Iris.[5]

By this point in her life, Fanny was perhaps the most socially successful divorced woman of New York. Under the headline, AN INTERESTING SOCIETY WOMAN, the *Philadelphia Inquirer* waxes poetic about the divorcée, then in her late thirties. "Though she is known all over the world as a great beauty and undoubted belle, she has scarcely lived long enough to attain the degree of fame which she now bears." The article goes on to rhapsodize about her demeanor, intelligence, and elegance, which allowed her to deftly navigate the scandal of her divorce from Jim, and the custody battles in the papers. The writer explains that Mrs. Astor was a friend and had been angling for Fanny to marry into her family—the highest social badge of approval.

Her parties were "fearless in the matter of invitations and never hesitated to include stiff dowager and stuffed shirts in a dinner company composed of artists, actors, cartoonists, horse trainers, etc," one observer noted.[6] She courted headlines driving carriages, hosting parties, and showing off her other four-legged friends: her beloved bull terriers, especially her favorite sidekicks, Daphne and Nellie, never far from her elegant skirts, in their custom-made sweaters in black and yellow, Fanny's favorite color combination. Fanny's motto of "not with the crowd to be spent" was a way of life for her, and something she repeated in her letters to her sons.[7]

Despite the social whirlwind and the strength of her personality, Fanny was middle-aged for the time, and likely lonely. Fanny and Aurel were often seen in Aurel's carriage around Newport and New York, and tongues began to wag. She had not learned from her father or from Mrs. Astor to stay out of the papers and out of the beds of foreigners. Her romance with a Hungarian stud, several years her junior, was the latest chapter in an ongoing saga that made a Russian novel look boring.

Less than a year before Cynthia's wedding, Fanny cemented her courtship with Aurel and became his bride on August 4, 1905, unbeknownst to her father, and possibly her children. Cynthia opposed the marriage and had received her mother's promise that she would not go through with it. But stubborn as ever, Fanny did it her way. Like her first wedding to Jim Burke Roche, Fanny's second was even more low profile. When Frank Work finally heard the news of Fanny's second marriage, she was persona non grata to him. Sadly, Frank would again be proven right in his objections to the mésalliance.[8]

Fanny and Aurel moved into Two Mile Farm, her stock farm near Newport, and were estranged from the Work family and her society friends. In December of 1906, her diary shows the early cracks and regrets of her marriage. "No relations: no wires: no presents: no communications of any kind. Deadly depression. Aurel very angry. Telling me to go back to my family."[9]

The couple placated their anxieties by sailing to Europe, Daphne in tow, where Fanny indulged her passion for fashion at the best Parisian dressmakers. Barred from her father's homes, Fanny stayed active in Newport social life with Mrs. Astor and Mrs. Fish, but it was made clear to her that her husband was not welcome. In her diary from one Newport summer: "Aurel very critical of many things. In some things quite right. I am not practical . . . I am a person of extreme moods. I feel so intensely . . ." A few days later she writes, "Terribly depressed. Just as unnerved and useless as I used to be. Out of conceit with myself. Depressing talk with Aurel. Fear the end will come . . . . Slept badly."[10]

That same summer Fanny had received a letter from Frank explaining that his financial support for her and her children was in jeopardy if she continued in the marriage. Maurice had received a similar missive from his grandfather.

ABOVE: King George III, the last king of America, never met George Washington, a former British military officer, but the two men had much in common: love of farming; happy, faithful marriages; and strong moral uprightness. The King was hugely impressed that Washington relinquished power at the end of his service to return to Mount Vernon, calling him "the greatest man in the world." LEFT: The first Lady Diana Spencer, the namesake of the future Diana, Princess of Wales, was mooted as a bride for the Prince of Wales at the time, ultimately becoming the Duchess of Beford. She, like the later Diana, would die young at the age of twenty-five.

This portrait of Washington was painted in 1772 by Charles Willson Peale, and shows Washington in uniform as a colonel of the Virginia Regiment. The original hangs in Lee Chapel at Washington and Lee University in Lexington, Virginia. It is the earliest known depiction of Washington.

ABOVE LEFT AND RIGHT: William's ancestress Georgiana, Duchess of Devonshire was born a Spencer and set the world ablaze with her glamour and penchant for scandal. She became one of the most visible Whig supporters, and as a result, was aligned with the Americans in their fight for independence.

The author by the statue of Nathan Hale, one of many monuments to the hero, and William's American relative, in Hale's hometown of Coventry, Connecticut.

Also in Coventry: the author at the gravesite of Benajah Strong, William's direct American ancestor who joined the Lexington Alarm to warn of an imminent British attack. Coventry was a hotbed of anti-monarchist sentiment, and Benajah Strong was in the thick of it. Strong was the uncle of American spy and martyr for the cause, Nathan Hale.

The Burke Roche twins, Maurice and Francis. Born in the United Kingdom but raised and educated in New York after their parents' divorce, the boys would grow up to be handsome and highly sought after bachelors in the highest echelons of society. They would attend St. Paul's, Harvard, and serve in the American military during World War I. Maurice, the eldest, would inherit the title, and become the fourth Lord Fermoy. He is the maternal great-grandfather of William, Prince of Wales and provides an American patriot bloodline for the future king that will set him apart from all other British monarchs. *Courtesy of the Fermoy Family Archive.*

ABOVE LEFT: Diana's maternal grandparents, Maurice, Lord Fermoy and Ruth, Lady Fermoy. The couple would become close friends of King George VI and Queen Elizabeth. They would name their daughter, Frances, after Maurice's mother Frances Burke Roche. She would name her daughter Diana Frances Spencer. All of the Frances's were beautiful and scandalous. *Courtesy of the Fermoy Family Archive.* ABOVE RIGHT AND BOTTOM IMAGES: Frances Burke Roche, known as Fanny, was a Manhattan heiress who created headlines in New York and Newport. She was passionate about everything: horses, clothes, music, and getting her way. Her beauty and scandalous life made her the perfect fodder for the growing society pages in the new American media. Her great-granddaughter, Diana, Princess of Wales, would lead a similar life, across the pond, decades later. *Courtesy of the Fermoy Family Archive.*

ABOVET: Maurice Burke Roche. RIGHT: The Burke Roche twins as older men, never losing their charm. Francis, the younger, missed inheriting the title by minutes, and would never marry. *Courtesy of the Fermoy Family Archives.*

Fanny with her dogs. She loved horses and birds too.

Frank Work was a force of nature who left Chillicothe, Ohio, as a young man and made a fortune in New York after befriending Cornelius Vanderbilt. He was adamant that his daughters, Fanny and Lucy, not marry foreigners. Fanny did twice, much to her father's consternation. When Frank died in 1911, he left millions that he said should remain on American shores, no matter what, and left strict instructions that his children and grandchildren should marry only Americans if they were to inherit his fortune. His wishes were outmaneuvered by clever lawyers.

ABOVE AND BELOW: Two Currier and Ives prints of Frank Work doing what he loved most—driving his carriage. His daughter Fanny would inherit his horsemanship, love of carriages, and stubborn streak.

Jim Burke Roche was a devilishly handsome young man from a titled, Irish family. He set out to find a rich American girl to marry and did. Her name was Fanny Work, and her father hated him from the start. Jim and Fanny would have a painful divorce that would have lasting emotional, and practical, effects on their children.

ABOVE LEFT AND RIGHT: Jennie Jerome, like Fanny Work, was born to a new money family in New York. Just a few years older than Fanny, Jennie was bright, lively, and one of the greatest beauties of her generation. She married into the British aristocracy and became Lady Randolph Churchill, and the mother of Sir Winston Churchill, who always credited his mother's American spirit for his success and winning personality.

ABOVE AND BELOW: King George VI was the first monarch to visit the United States in 1939 when lingering tensions between the two countries were beginning to abate. Franklin Roosevelt organized one of the most memorable events of his administration when he brought the king and queen to Washington, and then to his home in Hyde Park, New York. They got along famously over hot dogs and martinis. *Bottom image courtesy of the National Park Service.*

Sulgrave Manor, the ancestral home of George Washington, is just a short distance from Althorp, the family seat of the Spencers, the maternal family of William, Prince of Wales, and the burial place of Diana, Princess of Wales. The Washingtons and Spencers have a special relationship going back centuries, and former Lord Spencers have happily helped with Sulgrave Manor fundraising and restorations.

The seventh Earl Spencer, and Queen Mary at Sulgrave Manor, which has become the historical headquarters of the "special relationship" in the United Kingdom, teaching visitors about the family of George Washington. Earl Spencer was highly invested in turning Sulgrave Manor into the site it is today. *Courtesy of Sulgrave Manor.*

Winston Churchill receives his medal from the Society of the Cincinnati in Washington. He would later receive honorary American citizenship thanks to his love of the United States and American family through his mother. As members of the Spencer-Churchill family, he and William are related. *Courtesy of the Society of the Cincinnatti.*

TOP AND BOTH CENTER IMAGES: Elm Court on Bellevue Avenue in Newport was purchased by Frank Work in the late 1890s and has been occupied by his descendants ever since. Photos and portraits of Fanny, Frank, Maurice, and Francis throughout the house are reminders of the family's luminous cast of characters. The current owner is Guy Van Pelt, who raised his twin daughters here, with his wife, Mary.

BOTTOM RIGHT: The author in the dining room of Elm Court where a portrait of Fanny looms large.

LEFT: Diana with her mother, Frances Shand Kydd. Both women were named for their American grandmother and great-grandmother, Frances Burke Roche. *Getty Images*. CENTER AND BOTTOM LEFT AND RIGHT: Diana loved the United States, and the American people loved her. She was planning to spend most of her time in the country of her ancestors when she died in 1997. She made many visits to the White House, where she famously danced with presidents and John Travolta in the glamorous 1980s. *Getty Images*.

The current Lord Fermoy is the sixth Baron Fermoy, a former British miliary officer, photographed here in 1992. His cooperation was central to the research of this book. He is the father of two daughters, so the Fermoy title will pass to his brother the Honorable Hugh Roche. *Courtesy of the Fermoy Family Archives.*

As the health of King Charles III is in question, and the monarchy is rocked by scandals related to Andrew and Prince Harry, William has emerged as a steady and beloved presence. He is increasingly taking on more global responsibilities like meeting with President-elect Trump in France in 2024.

He and Catherine, Princess of Wales, are held in high affection, just like Diana was in the '80s and '90s. The couple's regal appeal and cozy family life mirror that of King George VI and Queen Elizabeth's. Americans await a William and Catherine state visit with great enthusiasm.

Fanny writes in her diary: "My situation is very sad and terrible. This beautiful day is ruined for me. I have no place and never have had in this rich happy community. I am not of it or in it. I feel like hiding somewhere out of sight."

From August 2: "There is so much fighting, intrigue. I cannot think it over anymore. I thought I did right. It was all so awful at home. My life so impossible and my self-respect so impaired by all the conditions [imposed by Frank Work] . . . Aurel is such a good man . . . I cannot understand all the opposition . . . It must come, I suppose, and I go back to prison [Frank Work's house]."

By August 13, Fanny was staring down the Dean of Madison Square in his sitting room for a "most stormy and disagreeable talk," as she wrote. "Ruin, desolation. My new state of health is strange, uncomfortable, and trying. I must try and adjust myself. If only my outlook were not so horrible and so humiliating. The going back, the appeal to a father so hard-hearted. The giving up all I had carefully built up . . . It is bitter."[11]

Fanny was in an invidious position. She had to give up the man she loved, or face financial instability for herself, and her children, not to mention further estrangement from her family. At a time when women, especially those of Fanny's background, did not work and earn an income, the reliance on their husband or father's money was vital for survival. Aurel's income was not nearly enough to keep them afloat. Yet the stigma of divorce, a second one, no less, was also a constant source of vexation for her.

Fanny was like Ellen Olenska, the heroine of Edith Wharton's Gilded Age classic, *The Age of Innocence*. Newland Archer, with whom Ellen is in love, gives her a harsh assessment of the terrain. He could have been speaking to Fanny Work: "New York society is a very small world compared with the one you've lived in. And it's ruled, in spite of appearances, by a few people with—well, rather old-fashioned ideas . . . Our ideas about marriage and divorce are particularly old-fashioned. Our legislation favors divorce—our social customs don't . . . . It's all stupid and narrow and unjust—but one can't make over society."[12]

By September, Aurel had left for good. "There are no words to describe my desolation, the wrench, the utter blackness, emptiness . . . The whole thing was madness on the existing financial basis," she wrote in her diary entry of the day.[13]

Aurel sued Frank Work, Frank Sturgis, and a host of other family members and associates for $1.5 million for deliberately trying to alienate his wife's affections. "I ask you again to let me have my wife back," he wrote to Frank, after Fanny fled back to Manhattan to live with her father.[14] This suit against her family was the final nail in the coffin of Fanny's fragile state of mind. "I am paralysed" she wrote in her diary on learning of his suit. "I am so unhappy. To have been duped by such a horrible villain. On reading this I can hardly believe I could be so blind, such a fool."[15]

PUBLIC GAZE CENTERED ON FAMILY AGAIN THROUGH SENSATIONAL BATTLE . . . read one headline from the breakup. BATONYI CLAIMS HIS WIFE IS HELD UNDER WHIP AND LASH . . . read another. Everyone from Newport to Chillicothe to Manhattan was devouring the details of the Batonyi separation and court proceedings in all their tawdry glory.

Fanny claimed seven correspondents, or extramarital lovers, in her divorce suit. In March of 1907, a private detective shadowed Aurel's apparent assignations in Central Park West and in a taxicab with a variety of women. Society page readers no doubt salivated reading the testimony of the cab driver and elevator operator brought into court to give their testimony of Aurel's comings and goings.[16] Not to be outdone, Aurel claimed his wife had her own stable of boyfriends, including an unnamed but well-known architect, and Frank Sturgis, the secretary of the Jockey Club and one of Frank Work's closest associates.

Aurel alleged that one of Fanny's rendezvous took place "in the dining room of Mrs. Batonyi's chateau on her farm near Newport." But perhaps the most salacious claim that Aurel leveled was that Fanny and the married Sturgis had an illegitimate child together, and that Sturgis, under the direction of Frank, had twisted Fanny's arm to leave Aurel, who further reported the couple was bribed with $24,000 to live in exile abroad. Aurel claimed Fanny was tempted with yet more money and jewels by Sturgis to dump her husband entirely.[17]

Fanny had gone from professional beauty to scarlet woman, with reporters following her every move, a situation her great-great-granddaughter Diana, Princess of Wales, would experience at the height of paparazzi culture. Her life and all its scandals came at a time when newspapers used socialites as celebrities. Long before movie stars, politicians, and musicians filled the column inches, people like Fanny were the news fodder. Her refrain was "no answer" when questioned about the divorce trials. One journalist trailed her on the street while Fanny wore a "big brown hat with white feather . . . worry was stamped on her face in deep lines and a casual acquaintance would scarcely have recognized her as the lively hostess at Newport two or three years ago."[18]

Aurel's horses and property were confiscated from the farm they shared together near Newport. "First these people took my wife away, now they take my horses and other property," he said, while threatening to expose the whole story in a book he planned to publish. "I am willing to compare my life with those who are behind this nasty work."[19]

As far as is known, the book was never published and the final years and whereabouts of Aurel Batonyi are unknown. Most observers agree that Fanny and Aurel loved each other to the end, but were the victims of their passionate natures, the powerful forces in Fanny's family militating against them, and Frank's constant threats to impoverish her and her children.

By 1910, Fanny finally won her divorce decree from Aurel, and his suits against her family were invalidated. "I WON," she wrote in her diary entry, explaining that her twin boys had called with their congratulations. During her marriage, she had not been on speaking terms with her father, sister, or daughter, but her sons, Maurice and Frank, had remained steadfastly by her side. She rewarded herself in Fanny fashion with a spending spree at her dressmaker and with a new victory ruby pin and pendant to celebrate her reversion to Frances Burke Roche, a name change she made sure was printed in the *Social Register*.[20] She also found acceptance again with her father and sister. The prodigal daughter had come home.

Fanny and Lucy were at Frank's bedside when the restless boy from Chillicothe who had become "the Dean of Madison Square" passed away at home in March of 1911. The kid who had arrived in New York with one gold coin and big American dreams was worth $14 million—nearly half a billion today. Fanny, Lucy, and their children would be provided for for life, and for generations to come.[21]

Meanwhile, Jennie Jerome was not letting widowhood slow her down. In 1897, as the new century was dawning, she donned another Worth gown for the fanciest of fancy dress balls at Devonshire House, Georgiana's former pro-American salon in London. The historian Charlotte Gray describes the fete for seven hundred guests where, naturally, Jennie was placed at the top table with the Prince of Wales at her side. "Gossip about such an audacious woman was inevitable, particularly because she remained close to the Prince of Wales while attracting the admiration of younger men."[22]

Now in her early forties, her children absent and her husband dead, Jennie, like Frances Burke Roche, was thrashing around for a new life of purpose. By 1899, she had done something truly scandalous—she went to work. She founded the *Anglo-Saxon Review*, for which she commissioned articles on a broad range of subjects, stimulating her eager mind. One of her projects was the publication of Georgiana's eighteenth-century letters. "A most delightful and enthralling period began, which absorbed me from morning till night in the most interesting of occupations."[23]

Men and the pursuit of their admiration would remain her other occupation. Around this time, she fell for a younger man—the age of her son, Winston. George Cornwallis-West was a dashing British Army officer from a distinguished background. According to George, Jennie "did not look a day more than thirty, and her charm and vivacity were on a par with her youthful appearance."

For her part, Jennie remained realistic about the relationship's prospects. "Of course, the glamour won't last forever, but why not take what you can." George's father was aghast at the age difference and Jennie's "insane infatuation for my son." The Prince of Wales joined the naysayers, and George was warned that he would lose his army commission, not to mention his father's money, if he went ahead with marriage. The only person who seemed to be approving, strangely enough, was Winston. On July 28, 1900, Lady Randolph Churchill became Mrs. George Cornwallis-West at St. Paul's Church in Knightsbridge, requiring police to hold back the hundreds of spectators. The bride was given away by the ninth Duke of Marlborough, while George's family was absent. "I bade farewell to Lady Randolph Churchill," she wrote wistfully in her memoir, *Reminiscences*. Despite the unconventionality of her new marriage, she did not lose support of her friend the Prince of Wales, who became King Edward VII shortly after she tied the knot. The glamorous American was at his coronation as his special guest in the king's box, according to Charlotte Gray. "Clever Jennie continued her role as confidante. The wider British public embraced their new king regardless of his appetite for twelve-course dinners, fast horses, and beautiful women." The Victorian era's stiff moralizing had come to a screeching halt, and the Edwardian era would be much more Jennie's speed.[24]

10
WINSTON TAKES MANHATTAN

In 1895, a young Winston Churchill first discovered his mother's country. He had been born at Blenheim and had been brought up on the Spencer-Churchill legends—men and women who had shaped England and served its monarchs. But he was eager to finally breathe in the Yankee air, the patriot spirit that would always be within him. Winston stayed at 763 Fifth Avenue and brushed shoulders with New York's elite including Cornelius Vanderbilt, who had helped Leonard Jerome and Frank Work build their fortunes. As a Sandhurst man, Winston was also eager to see West Point on the Hudson River. His host in New York was Bourke Cockran, a New York congressman and former boyfriend of Jennie's who would serve as a mentor, and would introduce him to the ideas of Edmund Burke, who had so fascinated his Spencer ancestress Georgiana and America's founders.[1]

Winston later recalled his early impressions of Jennie's countrymen as "a great, crude, strong young people . . . like a boisterous healthy boy among enervated but well-bred ladies and gentlemen. Their hospitality is a revelation to me and they make you feel at home and at ease in a way that I have never before experienced." [2]

After his Fifth Avenue whirl, Winston and a friend took a train down the East Coast to Florida. Winston's travels were part of Jennie's plan to make a great man out of him, picking up where her husband Randolph left off. She wanted him to read often, travel widely, and meet and interact with the best minds. Throughout the next decades, Jennie would use her social life and the amassed contacts to leave "no wire unpulled, no stone unturned, no cutlet uncooked," as Winston would put it.

Jennie's new husband, born just two weeks before Winston, was made to resign from the army as their marriage was deemed "too scandalous for the regiment to swallow," according to Charlotte Gray. The couple managed to maintain their grand lifestyle in London, although Jennie's exorbitant spending was a constant source of tension. They lived at Salisbury Hall, which included eight bedrooms, a garden for Jennie, and a pheasant shoot for George. While not as grand as Blenheim, Jennie saw its potential as a launching pad for Winston's career. So far this had mostly been in the army, with stints in India and the Sudan, about which he wrote successful books. After failing to win his first election, Winston went to South Africa as a correspondent covering the Boer War and gained greater fame when he was captured and escaped from a Boer prison.[3]

Riding this new wave of approbation, Winston made a second attempt at a seat in Parliament. Just a few months after his American mother's gossipy wedding, Winston Churchill, the soldier and writer, was elected, representing Oldham as a Conservative at the age of twenty-six. Backbench MPs were unpaid, but Winston would make a decent living as a lecturer and writer. Thanks to Jennie's encouragement, he had read everything from Plato to Milton and began early on what would become a dazzling literary career, publishing everything from short articles to his extensive memoirs and history books. Although his father had in many ways been a cruel bully, Winston hero worshiped him in death and read all of his parliamentary speeches. He would employ his and Jennie's colorful use of language for the rest of his own life and career.

The day of his first Parliament speech was a special one as his mother was there to see it, just as she had been for Lord Randolph's decades earlier. Ever the showman, like his American grandfather Leonard Jerome, young Winston placed his hand on his hip, another lifelong Churchill signature. Like his mother, he adored the attention and knew that he deserved it as he enthusiastically gobbled the nearly twenty newspaper articles that documented his debut. All of the observers pegged him a rising star. Randolph Churchill may have died in shame, but his son had fully vindicated the Spencer-Churchill name.

Not everybody, however, would be an admirer. "His brash overconfidence, which irritated some, was blamed on his mixed parentage." By 1903, the economist Beatrice Webb would sum Winston up as "egotistical, shallow-minded, and reactionary . . . more of the American speculator than the English aristocrat."[4]

This American brashness propelled Winston from backbencher to Cabinet member by 1908 by which point he had switched to the Liberal Party and become president of the Board of Trade by the age of thirty-three. He would become home secretary by 1910. Jennie, after the initial success and then failure of the *Anglo Saxon Review*, published her memoirs in 1907, following Winston's pleadings to tread lightly on the more colorful parts of her past and present. "You have a great chance of making a charming woman's book about the last thirty years and I do beg you . . . banish ruthlessly anything that will hurt other people's feelings. It is well worth while."[5]

Although *Reminiscences* was considered dull because of Winston's admonitions, it proved that there was still interest and fascination in Jennie, so much so that the novelist Henry James suggested she take her story on the road for a tour of her native country. But Jennie had problems at home. Her marriage to George was in constant strain due to her overspending and his affairs. Their divorce proceedings, like their wedding, garnered widespread press attention, and as soon as the ink was dried, George married his mistress. Jennie sent her rings back in the mail with the whimsical "I say Goodbye . . . a long, long goodbye."[6]

Just like Frances, Jennie reverted to her former name, Lady Randolph Churchill, in the *Social Register*. Despite her streak of independence in retaining a divorce during a time when it was huge albatross for a woman, Jennie did not approve of the burgeoning suffrage movement in London. "The female suffrage women are too odious. Every night they make a disturbance and shriek and rant. They damage their own cause hopelessly." Eventually, she would overcome her aversion to their methods and support their cause of women's right to vote.

When Jennie turned sixty, she found that the engraved invitations and glittering social life were becoming less and less accessible to her. "I shall never get used to not being the most beautiful woman in the room," she said. "It was intoxicating to sweep in and know that every man had turned his head." But as she did after Lord Randolph's death, and her scandalous divorce, she "buggered on" into her next decade as a matron. She would not be asked to the coronation of King George V, her friend's son and heir, who was a modest and simple man, unlike his glamorous father who had enjoyed the company of women like Jennie.[7]

If Jennie was no longer asked to major events, she would create them. She organized major Shakespearean balls as fundraisers for a national theater. The project, called Shakespeare's England, ran from May to October 1912. "As one talked with her and realized the enthusiasm with which she has approached her work and the complete grasp that she has of all the details, one begins to understand how very much Mr. Winston Churchill is the son of his mother," the reporter from the *Daily Express* wrote. "He may have inherited his political genius from his father, but he certainly owes to his American mother superb energy and thoroughness."[8]

The previous year Winston had assumed the position of First Lord of the Admiralty and had settled down to married life with the former Clementine Hozier, of whom Jennie was very fond. "Clemmie" would be at Winston's side for fifty-seven years, through many career upheavals, and war and peace.

On August 4, 1914, Britain declared war on Germany, and Jennie proved that her title as "the busiest woman in London" was not just idle chatter. As a proud expatriate, she chaired the executive committee of the American Women's War Relief Fund and toured American military hospitals. It is hard to imagine now, but at the time, the War of 1812 and even the Revolution were still close to living memory, and some animus still lingered among sections of the American populace toward the former colonial power. But in 1917, Americans stepped forward as friends to save Britain and Europe from a German takeover. This must have been a source of pride for her and Winston, always happy to claim his American credentials. It was around this time that Winston crossed paths with a young politician from his mother's home state of New York called Franklin Roosevelt, who was visiting his friend Viscount Astor. Roosevelt, ever affable and ready to make new friends, was snubbed by Churchill, something he never forgot. "I have always disliked Churchill since the time I went to England in 1918," FDR later explained to Joseph Kennedy. "He acted like a stinker at a dinner I attended, lording it over all of us."[9]

As a new decade beckoned, Jennie was embracing the flapper period with its new hemlines, zest for life, and peppy spirit. She had also fallen in love—again with a much younger man. This time her love was Montagu "Montie" Porch, this time three years younger than Winston. From a solid family in Glastonbury, with an Oxford degree, and a military background, Porch was suitable, and most importantly, adored Jennie. The couple wed in 1918 as the Great War was ending, and British-American relations were on the mend. "They say. What do they say? Let them say!" was Jennie's reported retort to scandalized reactions to her third trip down the aisle.

By 1921, Winston and his brother Jack, to their great credit, were supportive of their mother and her unconventional love matches. Winston was now Secretary of State for Colonies under David Lloyd George and could have opposed the marriage for fear of scandal brushing off on him. But Winston seemed to revel in his mother's devil-may-care way of living. Jennie shot back at a critic who was scandalized at the shorter hemlines in women's fashion. "There is no such thing as a moral dress

. . . It's people who are either moral or immoral." This was Jennie, and showed why Winston could not deny her anything, especially a great love story. But sadly, Jennie and Porch's story would be a short one.[10]

While her new husband was in West Africa, Jennie, never one to slow down her social life, fell and broke her leg while in the country. Gangrene set in, and her leg had to be amputated. Within a fortnight of the surgery, she suffered complications and slipped into a coma. When Winston heard the news, he dashed out of his house, never bothering to change out of his pajamas.

It was too late. The light and fire that was Jennie Jerome slowly went out on June 29, 1921. She was sixty-seven years old. Winston, in great Churchillian fashion, said of her, "The wine of life was in her veins. Sorrow and storms were conquered by her nature, and on the whole, it was a life of sunshine."

Winston kept the two hundred obituary clippings from around the world, one of which described Jennie thusly: "A brilliant and high-stepping figure who flung herself ardently into many occupations—literature, hunting, drama, politics, marriage . . . To the last, no illness, no social change, could dim her courage and kindliness."

She was buried at St. Martin's Church, Bladon, just outside Blenheim Palace grounds next to her first husband. This all-American girl from Brooklyn who became Lady Randolph Churchill was laid to rest in the cold ground of the Spencer-Churchill clan, whose members would intoxicate the twentieth century. Her wine of life would keep on flowing.[11]

11

DEAR BOY

Maurice and Francis Burke Roche had to meet for a very important drink. It was early November 1920 and their futures hung in the balance, so this was no casual gin and tonic—this was a time for a man-to-man huddle. Maurice was in New York that fall, while Francis was in Europe, against the vehement objections of Grandfather Work, whose presence still loomed large nearly a decade after his death. When Francis received Maurice's cable, he knew it was time for a brotherly summit back home. As twins, they shared a special bond, bordering on the telepathic. Maurice's letters to Frank, as his brother was called by the family, survive and were published by his daughter, Mary Burke Roche, in 2008. His missives to Frank always began with "Dear Boy," and usually ended with "Love, MR." They exchanged letters about their mutual passion for tennis, social gossip, and marriage prospects, although Frank would never marry.[1] There was a time when Frank, writing of severe "nerves," what today we would call anxiety, contemplated suicide, but the support of Maurice, his Aunt Lucy, and mother, Fanny, got him off the ledge. Theirs was a warm and affectionate brotherhood forged during times of personal and national crisis.

In 1916, their charmed lives were upended by the specter of World War I. They had become naturalized American citizens after Fanny brought them back to New York after the separation from their British father but always had a dual identity with one foot in the United States and one in Britain. While a mediocre student at Harvard, Maurice befriended Ted Roosevelt, the president's son whom he visited at the White House. The twins would later serve as ushers at Ted Jr.'s wedding. It was TR's "man in the arena" image that inspired the twins as young men coming of age. They both wanted to do their part in the military but did not know which side to join. It was ultimately decided their allegiance should be to the American armed forces. Maurice joined the army while Frank became a sailor, fully expecting to go to war soon.[2]

They spent Christmas 1916 with Fanny in New York, thinking it may be their last. In April of 1917, the US Congress officially declared war on Germany. Maurice was sent to Camp Dix after six months training in Plattsburgh, and Frank was assigned to the SS *Carolina* as an ensign. Although they were born in London, a photo of the twins in their respective military uniforms shows their unapologetic support for their mother's country. Maurice's diary entries from his army years chronicle the bravery of his generation, and his love for his brother in arms. "Dear Boy, . . . we were so crowded and the days were unending. I tell you it was depressing. I was glad to see the country of our birth, but unfortunately, we did not stay there long. Boy, I cannot realize that I am here. I look at the sky and think of the happy years I had at home . . . perhaps your letters may not reach me. Boy, do take care of yourself."[3]

The Lord Fermoy Memorial Clock, at St. Paul's School in New Hampshire, the twins' alma mater, was donated by Maurice in honor of the St. Paul's students who died during World War I, with the inscription AND TIME ITSELF SHALL NOT EFFACE THE GLORY OF THEIR SACRIFICE. Maurice and Frank remained loyal supporters of the school for the rest of their lives. Maurice also gave a portrait of George Washington, which today resides outside the rector's office.[4]

Although the war sobered their privileged existence, they embraced the Roaring Twenties with gusto. While Grandfather Frank Work may have been a Hemingwayesque character of rugged fortitude, the Burke Roche twins were right out of F. Scott Fitzgerald in their perfectly tailored suits with gardenias in the buttonholes. By 1920, they were in their mid-thirties, and were the quintessential American "preppies," making their rounds on the Fifth Avenue party circuit, on the lawns of Newport, and in the salons of Paris. When in New York, they lived with their mother Fanny on West 53rd Street and were the toast of society with all the requisites for it: graduates of St. Paul's, in the class of 1909 at Harvard, and memberships in the Knickerbocker, Racquet and Tennis, Tuxedo, and Southside Sportsmen's Clubs.

Photographs of the time show two men of striking dapperness with the aristocratic polish of "Chinese vases from the Ming period," according to the *New York Tribune*. Naturally, every young woman angled for their attention. As identical twins, they would delight in games of double trouble. "I know I'm talking to Francis because Maurice has gone abroad," one lady said during a flirtation. "The joke is on you," came the reply. "Francis has gone abroad. I am Maurice."[5]

Their bond had been sealed by their mother's scandalous divorces, the subsequent media embarrassment, and their grandfather's rank Anglophobia. After Frank's death, his heirs discovered in probate some fifteen codicils, or provisions, Frank had placed "for the protection and benefit of my said daughter (Fanny) and grandchildren and in the belief that they can find in the US enough to interest, instruct, and amuse them and all the varieties of climate at any time necessary or desirable for the purpose of health." This was Frank's way of saying "do it my way or forget about my money." The twins were meant to inherit some $3 million each so Frank's provisions, while ridiculous, demanded consideration.

Provision number one demanded that his grandchildren give up the name Burke Roche and take the name Work. Provision number two stated that they should have nothing to do with their father, James Burke Roche. Ever. Number three: that they never step foot back in the United Kingdom, and finally, that they settle down with nice American girls. Frank Work, after all, believed "international marriage should be made a hangable offense," after the ensuing fiascos of Fanny's unions with foreigners.

"I do hereby expressly will and provide that my daughter, Frances Ellen, and her children shall not during my lifetime, without my express consent, nor at any time after my death visit or reside in the Kingdom of Great Britain and Ireland, or the continents of Europe, Asia, and Africa," Frank stipulated, eliminating, he thought, any of his money going outside American shores ever again.[6]

Almost immediately after Frank's death, the twins ignored their grandfather's wishes and set sail for Europe, and, ironically, attended the coronation of King George V and Queen Mary on June 22, 1911, while Frank Work's body was still warm in his grave. "We've received legal advice and we have been informed that we are within our rights in going to England," one of the twins told a reporter who had caught up with them on their way to London. When asked about taking the name of Work, Maurice was even more defiant. "I am going to keep the name I've been carrying as long as I live," he said flatly.[7]

It appears the twins got away with breaching all the codicils of Frank's will with the exception of the one concerning marriage. In 1920, both men remained bachelors, and very eligible ones at that. In 1913, Maurice was reportedly engaged to a marquis's daughter in Rome and, according to society gossips, had a dalliance with Princess Vlora, the first wife of Frank Gould, a potential mésalliance Fanny was said to bitterly oppose.

How they were able to outmaneuver the codicils came into question in 1919 when the trustees of Frank's estate, including Frank Sturgis, whom Fanny's ex-husband had accused of being her lover, asked for an accounting of the will. It is said that Cynthia, through legal finagling, gave her brothers the millions they were due. In the end, Fanny, her sister Lucy, the twins, and their sister Cynthia, got the full benefit of Frank's largesse.

The ghost of Frank Work would have been well pleased with the women in his family at least. Fanny had divorced her foreign husbands. Lucy had married American, as had Fanny's daughter Cynthia. The men? In some ways, yes. In others, Frank would have been incandescent. By 1920, Maurice was working for Lackawanna Railroad. Despite the millions from Frank, he was said to be earning $60 a month. Flouting his grandfather's instructions, he not only visited London that summer but had a warm homecoming with his Uncle Edward, second Baron Fermoy, known as "Fitzy," and his father, Jim, living in Westminster, financially insolvent. Despite a pending bankruptcy, Jim was seen every morning walking across St. James's Park to Brooks, his fashionable club. He had somewhat compensated for his feckless life by serving as a respectable member of Parliament like the Burke Roche men before him and had daringly delivered a steamboat torpedo to a Russian port when the Russians were at war with the Japanese in 1904. In a foreshadowing of his descendants, Jim became a founding member of the Pilgrim Society, a mysteriously elite club with the objective of strengthening British-American relations. Joseph Choate, the American ambassador to the United Kingdom at the time, was an attendee at the society's first dinner.[8]

Because his brother Fitzy had no boys, Jim would become third Baron Fermoy, and Maurice, as the elder twin, fourth. Due to the complications of Maurice's American life, no doubt the future was a topic of conversation on that visit.

In September, Fitzy died, bringing Maurice one step closer to his fate much earlier than he had expected. In early November, Maurice visited Fanny and Aunt Lucy at Woodburn Hall, Lucy's home in New Windsor, New York. When he arrived back at West 53rd Street, he was accosted by a reporter with the *New York Herald*, something he and his family had come to accept as a frequent, yet irritating part of life. In the 1920s, newspapers, especially in New York and Newport, dedicated more and more column inches to the comings and goings of people like the twins, and with their perfect looks and wardrobes, they were camera and ink ready, just as their mother always was.

"Why do you ask me these questions?" Maurice wanted to know. "In view of your father's death," the reporter said. "My father's death," Maurice gasped. "When?"

James Boothby Burke Roche, third Baron Fermoy, and former member of Parliament for Kerry East, was dead at the age of sixty-nine, two months after he had joined the peerage, and just months after his last visit with his son. *The Times* later explained his cause of death was heart failure caused by pneumonia.

"I left him in London ten days ago," Maurice explained to the reporter, trying to make sense of the news. "He was in the best of health. I have heard nothing from London."[9]

Maurice was speechless as he stood on the New York pavement that day, his whole world shaken to the core. The only person who could understand was Frank. He went inside and immediately cabled him the news. Frank was living in Paris, not as a trust fund brat, but as a respectable banker. "I'm tired of wasting time at golf and the theaters and spending money," Frank told a journalist, following the news of his employment as a clerk in the letters of credit department at Guaranty Trust Company.[10]

"Dear Boy, I cannot begin to take in the fact that our father has died. I am also unable to know what to do. I am hoping that you will attend to the funeral arrangements and also get a good lawyer . . . I think it would be a good thing to have an inventory of the estate made and also I suppose I will have to pay a big sum to the crown if I accept the title . . . Take good care of yourself. Love, MR"[11]

The funeral for James Burke Roche, Baron Fermoy, was held at St. Martin-in-the-Fields with his son Frank and his old friend Moreton Frewen as principal mourners, while Maurice pondered the many questions this highly unusual situation presented.

Am I American? Am I British? Can I be both? How can I defy the wishes of the man who practically raised me and my brother? Will my grandfather's will be challenged if I move to London and take on the life of a baron?

The new Baron Fermoy would be stepping into a title with very few perks to go along with it, certainly no estate or land. Besides the title, the only thing Maurice was inheriting were his father's debts. His family—and the press—were waiting for his choice.

"I have decided to prove my claim and accept the title," Maurice explained in *The New York Herald* of February 1921. "It has taken me a long time to come to this decision, but I have decided to do it," further explaining to another newspaper that he still planned to visit the United States a few months a year. Maurice, never forgetting his American grandfather who raised him, visited Frank Work's grave to leave flowers on the tenth anniversary of his passing. Maybe this was his way of apologizing for contravening his wishes, but his life as an Englishman was set, and there was no turning back. Maurice's last act as an American citizen was indeed a very American one—he cast his vote in the presidential election of Warren Harding.[12]

12

BACHELOR KING
OF HEARTS

The Burke Roche twins were called the "best dressed of all" in their frock coats and top hats among New York society, but as the new Baron Fermoy stood in front of a group of friends at the Metropolitan Opera in February 1921, his new title lent even more glamour. Frank, now The Right Honourable, made equally good copy in the society pages. That they remained single rendered them irresistible.[1]

As Maurice chatted to his friends before making his new home across the pond, one of them waded into the geopolitical, with an uncanny prescience. "I congratulate you because half and half American and British blood men are needed now and will be needed more in the immediate future to take a sane middle road and to persuade others in helping our mutual British and American problems."

"That is one of the ideas that impelled me to prove my claim and assume British citizenship. I even tried to persuade Francis to take over the title," Maurice replied. "I am giving up my American citizenship with great regret." He added that his title would be "an Irish one, and I hope Ireland will be reconciled much as our southern states did after our Civil War."[2]

Despite his earnestness in addressing political and social issues to which he felt his title obligated him, Maurice and his brother mostly provided fodder for the society pages, not hard news. As the 1920s roared ahead, both men stayed single, turning up at the best parties in New York, Newport, and Paris—sometimes with their mother in tow. Fanny proved to be a tough critic of any future daughters-in-law. One poor girl Maurice brought to lunch was sized up thusly by the formidable Fanny: "A tall, very awkward, stooped girl . . . A very affected English voice, very rapid speech with no gradation or stressing, very indistinct. No manners. No distinction. Not one comment on my pictures, furniture, pretty things that showed she knew what she was looking at . . . I was so extremely bowled over by Maurice's want of discernment and discrimination that I finally made no more effort to speak to her."[3]

Fanny could be equally judgmental, and even cruel, toward her own family. Her granddaughter Mary Burke Roche recalls meeting her when she was three years old, and being told "Grandma Roche does not like fat little girls." It is no wonder then that Maurice married later in life, and his brother Frank never married at all.[4]

In Newport, Maurice stayed at Elm Court, the Work family home, at the time the summer residence of his sister Cynthia. When he came for a visit in 1923, hearts and tongues were aflutter. Maurice was not just a baron; he was a stag and in Newport it was open season. OH, BARON FERMOY—HOW COULD YOU DO IT? shouted the headline from the *Sunday Express*. "How the former Maurice Burke Roche's long bachelorhood could survive his summer at Newport with all the richest, most fashionable debutantes hovering about him?" the paper asked.

The young women, including the daughters of the richest and most influential men in the country, and their mothers had "upturned eyes and pouty lips" the paper explained, which "plainly expressed their hopes."[5]

The report went on to say that Maurice seemed to be more impressed with the girls of more modest backgrounds than the more obvious candidates. NEWPORT MATRONS GAZE FOR PROSPECTS ran the headline three years later when Maurice, alas, remained a lonely stag. "In artistic circles a woman nowadays can remain single with impunity, but in that assemblage of exalted souls known as New York Society such independence earns little but frowns. Society, in a way, is still mid-Victorian," the *Sunday News* explained, summing up the zeitgeist.[6]

One of the "normal" women Maurice fancied was Edith Travers, an American divorcee with two young boys. The two met on a train in 1915 from New York to San Francisco and, despite their social differences, became lifelong lovers and correspondents. Their love letters span four decades, encompassing marriages, children, wars, coronations, and idle chatter. These letters provided the basis for *Lilac Days*, a narrative account of their affair by journalists Gavan Naden and Maxine Riddington, published in 2005.

As a divorced woman, Edith understood she could never be Maurice's wife, and, despite their closeness, Edith was never introduced to Fanny, who would have been scandalized by Edith's past, notwithstanding her own scandalous relationships.

Fanny, now a white-haired grande dame, never lost her enjoyment of old-world glamour and jet-setted as much as her sons. She spent time with Maurice in England and Ireland, Frank in Paris, and Cynthia in Newport. In 1923, she sold her home on West 53rd Street, the place where she had held forth as one of the city's great hostesses, something that the following generations never forgot. Her new Manhattan pied-à-terre was a luxurious suite at one of the top hotels where she was greeted as "the peppiest matron who can recall when Fifth Avenue and Twenty-Third Street was an elegant residential section," as one observer put it.[7]

Her personality still reigned supreme and attracted lots of chic friends. One of her chums was Alice Longworth, the sharp-tongued daughter of Theodore Roosevelt, who famously quipped, "If you don't have something nice to say about someone, come sit next to me." In 1929, Fanny returned to New York, this time at 61 East 91st Street, the Manhattan home of Cynthia, for the debutante ball for her granddaughter, Eileen. Just as Fanny had commandeered Cynthia's debut in Newport at the beginning of the century, so too did she steal the show at Eileen's where a "veritable bower of flowers and Christmas greens" greeted guests, according to society columnist Nancy Randolph in her report in the *Daily News* that December.

"A personality so dominant as Fanny Burke Roche's gathers spotlight unto itself," she wrote. "No wonder she crowded into the spotlight last night and pushed Eileen out of today's story," she explained, although Eileen's photo was included alongside Fanny's. Not to be eclipsed, Fanny's image was the same size as her granddaughter's.[8]

That April of 1921, Maurice, the new Baron Fermoy, set sail for England on the RMS *Mauretania*. Although he was an Irish baron and had obvious interest in Ireland, settling there would have been dangerous as the fighting between Irish republicans and British Army and police was at a fevered pitch. London would be his destination, and once he arrived, he thought he would figure out what to do. With Frank's Work money, the need for instant employment would not be a pressing matter. While on ship, Maurice met Lord Queenborough, who encouraged him to enter politics at Westminster as his father and grandfather had. At this point, Frank was in Paris with Fanny, and Maurice's letters to the pair of them read like a fizzy London social diary as he took to the city like Earl Grey tea in a porcelain cup. He quickly joined the right clubs, stayed at chic hotels, met the right people, and wrote enthusiastically about his tennis competitions. "Dear Boy," he wrote to Frank, "Let us make this thirty-sixth year a good one. Am wonderfully rested. I suppose you're on the go the entire time in Paris."[9]

By January of 1922, Maurice had settled down with a house, at least, and became a candidate for a Conservative seat in Parliament, representing a rural constituency in Lincolnshire where he rented Hagnaby Priory, Spilsby, the first of many elegant country houses he would take during his days in England.

Now Maurice was a proper lord with a handsome house, staff, and a budding reputation with the local community. He threw himself into learning about agriculture, going to schools, and making friends with as many of the locals as possible who were impressed with his service in the Great War and his Anglo-American perspectives. Unfortunately, Maurice was defeated that November in his campaign for Parliament, but with his brother and mother at his side, he vowed to run again at the next election. The Conservatives, however, were victorious with a majority over Labour.

By the next election, which would prove successful for Maurice, he was living in Heacham, a coastal town near King's Lynn. He endeared himself to the community by appealing to the ladies, dancing with them at community parties, handing out prizes at local fairs, and being every woman's ideal son, brother, and, of course, husband. A reporter in the area chronicled his charm offensive under the headline BACHELOR KING OF HEARTS. But Maurice campaigned on weightier matters, too, arguing for a higher wage, benefits for veterans and their widows, and the rights of farmers.

On October 29, 1924, the Conservatives won a landslide victory, and Maurice was a new member of Parliament with a yearly salary of 400 pounds in 1924 currency. Fortunately, the American dollars of Frank Work allowed him to live comfortably and provide for his staff at the Shooting Lodge, his new seven-bedroom home, and travel frequently to Newport to stay close to his American roots. As he stood in the Assembly Room of the Town Hall, Maurice beamed as his new English neighbors shouted and cheered, *For He's a Jolly Good Fellow!* When Frank came for a visit, a photo of the two of them outside the House of Commons shows a mirror image of the same man. Now in their middle age, they had not lost their debonair good looks or their smart dressing; morning coats and top hats complete their dashing presentation.[10]

Over the next four years, Maurice transformed himself into the perfect country gentleman, who never lost his fondness for his mother's homeland when speaking to community gatherings, with a slight American accent that he never managed to fully expunge. On July 4, 1928, he reminded his audience of the significance of the date but incorrectly predicted that Britain would soon repay its World War I loans to the United States. In fact, the US Treasury still has an accounting of the trillions in loans from the war but has been noncommittal in collecting repayment.

Maurice also presciently talked about tariffs, nearly one hundred years before they would be the defining issue of President Trump's trade policy in 2025. "This summer I had the privilege of going to America," Maurice explained. "No country in the world had so high a tariff. The Americans are very clever people. Why should not Germany, France and other countries not give up their tariffs? Simply because it paid them and stimulated their industries. For that reason, many of the European countries are exporting huge quantities to England when really England had the coal mines to supply her own requirements. But, instead, the miners have little work."[11]

Maurice had his fair share of dissenters who, despite his generous personal contributions to a variety of community causes, accused him of living in the lap of luxury while his people starved. At town halls, he was heckled and shouted down by socialists. *Politics! Not Charity!* While Maurice did live well—playing tennis, shooting partridges with aristocrats and royalty, and summers in Newport, the people he served knew his heart was in the right place, and continued to reelect him. When the stock market crashed in 1929, Maurice looked out for his constituents through personal contributions and care. One child in the village remembers getting a green sweater from Lord Fermoy at Christmas. If Frank Work's money was being spent overseas, at least, he would not begrudge it being used to help disadvantaged British children.[12]

Maurice, at forty-six, finally made his way to the altar on September 17, 1931, but his bride nearly married Frank first. Ruth Gill, a classical pianist from Scotland, was in her early twenties when she met Frank in Paris while he was working for the bank and she was studying at the École normale supérieure under a top Frédéric Chopin interpreter. For whatever reason, Maurice ended up taking Frank's girl out to dinner when he visited his brother in Paris. "The dinner went well, but I shall always prefer Frank," Ruth wrote to her mother. "He is so kind."

According to her daughter, Mary Burke Roche, Ruth had striking similarities with Fanny. Both were cultured, with a special love for music and the French language, confident, and sometimes sharp-tongued. "She once told me that she assumed that men would find her attractive," Mary wrote of her mother. "She could express her annoyance very effectively in an icy, tacit way. Her own brand of humor was rather cruel, and she was inclined to make fun of people's weaknesses," she recalled. Also, like Fanny, Ruth had no time for overweight people and discarded a friend for getting too hefty.[13]

Not everybody across the pond was happy for the new couple.

"At the age of forty-six, Lord Fermoy is to wed Ruth Gill, a London pianist," sniffed one New York paper. "The chances he had to carry off the foremost debutantes of many past seasons, he embraces matrimony with an obscure London damsel. The younger folks about town are raising their eyebrows at the fuss, but the older set about the casinos of Newport and along Park Avenue is deeply shocked. Somehow it doesn't seem right after all these years for Maurice to become a benedick." We can assume the reporter is referring to Benedict Arnold, the infamous Revolutionary War traitor.[14]

Fanny was in favor of the marriage, and, characteristically, made her opinion known. "I pushed him unhesitatingly over the brink," she wrote. "It is the greatest success." Like her mother-in-law, Ruth compensated for her snobbishness with charm, charisma, and seduction, which she happily used to boost Maurice in his constituency. He became mayor of King's Lynn that year of 1931, and Ruth, as Lady Fermoy, was a true partner in his mayoralty.

The couple became a part of the royal family's circle of friends, and leased Park House, a royal residence since 1862, on the royal Sandringham estate. This would be their home for the duration of their married life, and where they raised their three children: Mary, Edmund, and Frances. Surrounded by a large park, Park House had seven bedrooms, and was divided into three sections, with one being designated for staff quarters. Maurice became a regular in the shooting parties of King

George V and had just been with him at Sandringham before he died on January 20, 1936. The same day his daughter, Frances, the mother of the future Princess of Wales, was born.[15]

Later that year Maurice, along with President Franklin Roosevelt, attended Harvard's 300th anniversary, joining alumni from all over the world for the historic homecoming. Maurice, like a young Winston Churchill, did not have a good first impression of the historic president. "He must be a radical of the first order," Maurice wrote to an American friend, but years later, Maurice would mourn Roosevelt at a special church service in London.[16]

As World War II intensified, Maurice was deemed too old, at fifty-four, for active miliary service, but got a job in France with the YMCA, organizing canteens for the British Expeditionary Force, selling every-thing from chocolates to shoelaces. "We had sixteen cars operating in my area, and I found the work very interesting. Young men in the Army and the Air Force who knew me kept dropping in to see me. I was struck by the splendid physique and fine spirit of our young men. All of them I talked to seemed determined that the job of ending the Hitler menace would be done."[17]

Maurice would hear "Hitler's menace" in the form of loud thuds from bombs while he was in Calais. Frank was in Paris during the war, and opened a Paris branch of the Lafayette Fund, which provided care pack-ages for French soldiers. In 1943, Maurice was in Washington, DC, as the personal adviser to Air Marshal Sir William Lawrie Welsh, because of his American background. While in the United States, he made time to revisit his old stomping grounds in New York and Newport, but the reunion was bittersweet. In 1942, Fanny had a stroke, which had left her unable to speak. Maurice, Frank, and their sister Cynthia had a happy reunion, however, at Elm Court, coming under the same roof that Frank and Fanny had estab-lished as the Newport family home in 1896.[18]

Maurice had stepped down from Parliament in 1935, but in 1942 when Somerset Maxwell, who had succeeded Maurice as MP for King's

Lynn, was killed fighting the Germans in North Africa, Maurice stood to represent his constituents once again and served until the war was over.

Fanny was still making headlines when she died at 1020 Fifth Avenue in January 1947 at the age of eighty-nine, outliving her sister Lucy by several years. She was laid to rest in New York with her father, the man she spent a lifetime defying. The old man likely got a chuckle to have the spirited Fanny under his domineering obelisk for eternity.[19]

That November, Ruth and Maurice would attend the wedding of Princess Elizabeth to Prince Philip, the future Queen Elizabeth II and the Duke of Edinburgh.

Maurice would die eight years later at the age of seventy in 1955, followed by Frank in 1958. Maurice would be one of the last people to see George VI, his tennis partner, before his death in February 1952. Ruth would form a close bond with her fellow Scotswoman, Queen Elizabeth the Queen Mother, and become her lady-in-waiting.

After his death, Lady Fermoy discovered a pile of letters from his American lover Edith Travers. Unaware of Maurice's death, Edith received the following from Ruth's secretary: "I am writing for Lady Fermoy to tell you that Lord Fermoy died rather suddenly in July . . . she is sorry that there had been some delay in answering your letter."

Devastated, Edith sailed to England, and took a train, then a taxi to Sandringham to pay her respects to her beloved Maurice. There she found his grave covered in lilacs, casting a shadow westward, toward America. Before her death in 1976, Edith would befriend Frank and Maurice's son Edmund, both of whom knew about the affair.

The grandson of the Anglophobe Frank Work, who was raised in New York and nearly made a home there, died the quintessential Englishman, a loyal subject of Queen Elizabeth II, whose coronation he had attended. His son Edmund succeeded him as the next Baron Fermoy. Six years after Maurice's death at Park House, his granddaughter, the Honourable Diana Frances Spencer, would be born there, carrying her grandmother Frances Work as her namesake.[20]

13

HOT DOGS AND MARTINIS

I n June of 1939, King George VI and his wife Queen Elizabeth embarked on one of the most consequential British invasions. Unlike their military subjects who had ransacked and burned the White House in 1812, these Londoners mounted a charm offensive—they would set America aflame with royal fever and reset Anglo-American relations forever with a history-making royal tour. The king and queen were relatively young at the time, about the same age as the current Prince and Princess of Wales today, and radiated the same youthful optimism during an uncertain era.

"I'm from Boston," one reporter covering the tour told the king. "You remember we'd trouble with another George once."

"Oh yes," the king replied with a smile. "I think I've heard about it. Something about tea, wasn't it?"[1]

This would be the king's (known by intimates as "Bertie") and Elizabeth's first time to the United States, and, more importantly, the first time a reigning monarch had deigned to cross the pond to see the land of the colonists who had cast off his ancestor and namesake King George III in 1776.[2]

Joe Kennedy, the father of the future president John F. Kennedy, was serving as ambassador to the United Kingdom at the time, and had been working behind the scenes to eventuate a state visit. Ever the operator, Kennedy had elbowed his way into royal circles. Over dinner, he and Elizabeth talked about the possibility of a visit. "You could charm them as you are charming me," he said. "I know only three Americans," the queen replied, "you, Fred Astaire, and J. P. Morgan, and I would like to know more."[3]

Elizabeth was a shrewd operator herself. In her conversation with Kennedy, she deliberately did not mention the American she really wanted—and needed—to meet: President Franklin Delano Roosevelt, whose reluctance to provide military and financial assistance to Britain as World War II began was a source of diplomatic strain. FDR, despite his democratic ideals, was a closet fan of the royals. "He was fascinated by kings and queens, half-amused, half-impressed, by the pomp and pageantry that enveloped royalty," explained his son, James Roosevelt.

The president would be easy prey for the royal couple, but getting into his orbit—and winning him over—would be a chess game requiring skill and patience.

Not only were Americans firm in their objection to getting involved in another war after the devastation of World War I just two decades before, but they still harbored suspicion—and indeed animus—toward the mother country. In 1937, seventy percent of Americans polled said it was a mistake to have supported Europe in the Great War, and nearly a third were involved with anti-war demonstrations. By 1935, the Neutrality Act, which prohibited giving arms to nations at war, passed through Congress with flying colors. Isolationism ruled the day, and FDR was keenly aware of the zeitgeist.[4]

But there were more deeply embedded cultural differences that fed the hostility. In 1902, then-president Theodore Roosevelt forbade his daughter, Alice, a chum of Fanny Burke Roche's, from attending the coronation of King Edward VII due to "raw and powerful antimonarchist" sentiments in America, according to the historian Will Swift.

He explains that some ethnic groups, particularly the growing Irish and Jewish communities in the United States, were offended by the monarchy and the aristocratic class structure that upholds it. In 1936, King Edward VIII had abdicated the throne to marry American Wallis Simpson, whose treatment in the British press and by the British public, still frustrated Americans three years later. Wallis, who was raised in Baltimore, was denied the Her Royal Highness style, and was living in virtual exile with the former king, much to her fellow Americans' dismay. She may have been a twice-divorced woman, but she was still one of their own. The majority of Americans, according to a 1937 Gallup poll, liked the idea of Wallis and her regal husband settling down in the States. How fun would it be to run into the duke and duchess at a Midwestern café or gas station, they naively thought. The duke and duchess, however, lived most of their lives in Paris in resplendent luxury, no longer royals, but far removed from the banalities of everyday life.[5]

British people, including the royal family, did not exactly have the highest regard for Americans either. Before he became monarch as a much younger man, King George V did his naval service in the area around Niagara Falls. "I half-walked across Niagara, took off my hat and walked back again. That was the nearest I ever got to the United States," he later recalled with sarcastic pride.[6]

Fast forward to the 1930s and the mutual antipathy between the two countries was still stewing. British Prime Minister Neville Chamberlain and Canadian Prime Minister William Lyon Mackenzie King were busy cooking up ideas to bring the royal couple to Canada. They thought that if they could get them over the border to the promised land, they would charm the pants off the Yanks, who despite their protestations of democracy for all, had, like President Roosevelt, secret adoration for royal splendor. For his part, Roosevelt needed the royal couple's glamour to convince Americans that joining the allies in World War II, which he had come to accept as unavoidable, was in the global interest.

Thus, a *bromance* was born. For the first time since George Washington traded letters and compliments with King George III, President Roosevelt initiated a pen pal relationship with King George VI.

"I need not assure you that it would give my wife and I the greatest pleasure to see you," FDR wrote the king. "And, frankly, I think it would be an excellent thing for Anglo-American relations if you could visit the United States."[7]

The president proposed a requisite stay at the White House, and then a more relaxed visit to Hyde Park, the Roosevelt family home near the Hudson River in New York. "It occurs to me that a Canadian trip would be crowded with formalities and that you might like three or four days of very simple country life at Hyde Park—with no formal entertainments and an opportunity to get a bit of rest and relaxation."[8]

Sensing the opportunity of his reign, and perhaps his lifetime, the king leapt at the offer.

To prepare for the American visit, Queen Elizabeth, painfully aware of comparisons to the chic and slender Wallis, went on a diet, and packed her best jewels and ensembles to razzle and dazzle the public. She and the king would travel with two valets and a page, five footmen, a private secretary, lords-in-waiting and ladies-in-waiting, servants, police officers, a physician, and other assistants. Elizabeth had two dressers, a hair stylist, and her own lord chamberlain. The royal machine was pulling no punches to impress.

In America, a flurry of preparation and excitement ensued from journalists hustling for details on the visit, to companies hankering for their products to be used and promoted to the inevitable ruthless elbowing for invites to events on the tour. The party that caused the most agony and ecstasy for Washington's social scene was the garden reception hosted by the British ambassador Sir Ronald Lindsay, who likened getting an invitation to getting past the pearly gates. "Some are taken and some are not," he said. Today, the ambassador's sprawling garden is still used for grand parties, and people still clamor for invitations, but nothing like the royal visit in 1939. The event "caused more heartburns, more adverse press comment, and more of a tempest in a teapot than any social event in this country," another diplomat explained. Sir Ronald and Lady Lindsay ruffled plenty of feathers by denying access to the minority leader of the Senate, and a significant number of US senators, but they were eventually included among the 1,350 chosen ones, who were given strict instructions on how to dress, curtsy, and address the king and queen. Lady Lindsay pointedly did not extend invitations to the Duke and Duchess of Windsor, or her relatives in Baltimore.

Eleanor Roosevelt was equally anxious about the tour as she prepared the White House, and her home in New York for the occasion, which amplified her deeply rooted sense of inadequacy. Long physically estranged from her husband due to his affairs, the First Lady still took her public role as the wife of a head of state seriously. Like Elizabeth, she felt mocked and ridiculed by the press for her less-than-perfect looks, a common burden for women in the harsh spotlight of global media.

The big day, June 8, 1939, came with a sweltering heat, that only those who live in Washington's swampland can appreciate. The royal couple pulled into Union Station that morning and walked onto a royal blue carpet flanked by marines. "Well, at last I greet you," Roosevelt said, offering what Ambassador Kennedy described as "perhaps the most important handclasp of modern times."

"It is, indeed, a pleasure for Her Majesty and myself to be here," the king replied as he braced himself for the ninety-four-degree day, a far cry away from misty London. The king and president, despite the weather, were dressed in heavy military uniform and suit and top hat, respectively.[9]

Nearly seven hundred thousand people lined the streets to see the king and queen's procession by the Capitol and down Pennsylvania Avenue to the White House. Along the way, six thousand American soldiers, sailors, and marines saluted the royal couple as army planes added extra pageantry in the sky. Police and rescue were also employed to tend to the five hundred people who fainted from heat exposure.

On arrival at the White House, the king and queen, after shaking hundreds of diplomatic hands, retired to their rooms, after eagle-eyed American staff removed offensive artwork, like a print depicting the British surrender at the Battle of Saratoga.

Then the couple made their way to the party of the century at the British ambassador's garden, which had just been washed down with a summer rainstorm. Edith Wilson, J. P. Morgan Jr., and members of the Rockefeller and Vanderbilt families were among the guests while across town a Texas congressman named Lyndon Baines Johnson hosted a stag party for those who didn't make the cut.

Back in the White House, the king joined FDR and Eleanor for a dip in the presidential pool, while the queen, whose delicate Scottish skin had been sunburned, cooled herself with special, but annoyingly noisy, air-conditioning units that had been installed for her comfort.

That evening at the White House the State Dining Room was aglow with candlelight and white orchids for the six-course dinner. Toasting the couple, FDR said, "I am persuaded that the greatest single contribution our two countries have been enabled to make to civilization, and to the welfare of peoples throughout the world, is the example we have jointly set by our manner of conducting relations between our nations. It is because neither of us fears aggression on the part of the other that we have entered into no race of armaments." The king responded with a wish "that our great nations may ever in the future walk together along the path of friendship in a world of peace."[10]

Eleanor Roosevelt, earlier that spring, had resigned from the Daughters of the American Revolution when the women's organization denied Black contralto Marian Anderson a venue for a concert, citing "white artists only" contracts. She invited Anderson to be the primary entertainment for the evening, despite letter writers saying it was an insult to the king and queen to be in the same room as a Negro. Moreover, showing the moral verve that was her trademark as "first lady of the world," Eleanor asked Anderson to perform Negro spirituals as well as Schubert's classic, "Ave Maria."[11] (The DAR later reconciled with Anderson, and today the organization is a partner of the Marian Anderson Museum and Historical Society in Philadelphia.)

The king and queen were not scandalized by the Black singer and seemed to Eleanor to have "a keen sense of the difficulties under which a great many people live and labor today." She went on to say, "It is interesting to find one so young with as compassionate an understanding of the conditions which push people to desperation."[12]

While the festivities were off to a splendid start, they were tainted with the inevitable political strain in Washington. One congressman from New York, William Barry, spoke out against the "British propaganda to entangle us with them," while another publicly asked for an immediate pay schedule to commence to get back the money the country loaned Britain for the First World War.

It was with this unease hovering that the royal couple made their visit to the US Capitol where they received congressional handshakes under a portrait of the Cornwallis surrender at Yorktown. One Texan legislator was so taken with Elizabeth's regality that he jokingly proposed trading her for the debt repayment. His colleague from Louisiana kissed her hand. She was the real star and her brightness cut through any of the political apprehension. The young daughter of cabinet secretary summed up Elizabeth's charm when she said, "Oh, Daddy, I have met the fairy queen."[13]

In a truly moving twist of history the royal couple next made a boat trip with the president and First Lady to Mount Vernon to visit the grave of a man who had been regarded by many as a traitor to his king. Bearing a wreath of white lilies, King George VI and Queen Elizabeth stepped into the simple tomb of George and Martha Washington. The king took two steps forward, placed the wreath, took two steps back, and offered

General Washington a simple bow. Elizabeth called the Washington house and gardens "one of the loveliest places" she had ever seen, high praise from a woman who grew up in a Scottish castle and lived in some of the grandest palaces in the world. Elizabeth would have felt an affinity with the home of Washington, because they, in fact, shared a common ancestor in Virginian Augustine Warner who migrated from England in 1650. Warner's daughter Mildred married Washington's grandfather. Warner's other daughter Mary was Elizabeth's ancestress whose family had returned to England before the Revolution.[14] The royal couple also paid their respects at the Tomb of the Unknown Soldier at Arlington National Cemetery.

The next day the king and queen left Washington for New York by train. When they arrived in Sandy Hook, they sailed to Manhattan, almost the same boat ride Nathan Hale took to his death back in 1776. On board, the royal standard flew alongside Old Glory for the first time in history.

While a twenty-one-gun salute honored them, they strained to see the Statue of Liberty in the hazy distance. The heat had not abated since their motorcade inched through the packed streets in Washington. In New York, nearly four million crowded the hot Manhattan sidewalks for the royals on a six-mile route with over thirteen thousand police officers guarding their path. The couple asked the driver to slow down so they could see and hear the children spilling out of Central Park with placard signs and expressions of joy. Their destination that day was the World's Fair in Queens where they saw a copy of the Magna Carta loaned to the fair by the British government as a sign of diplomatic goodwill.

Meanwhile, the First Lady was finishing the final details in Hyde Park in preparation for the royal sleepover. FDR underscored that the weekend would be one of simplicity and relaxation after the frenetic pace of the last few days, which occasionally tested the king's notorious temper and speech impediment. "I'll put the king into an old pair of flannels and just drive him about in my old Ford," the president promised. The film *Hyde Park on Hudson,* starring Bill Murray as a convincing FDR, recounts the preparations and events of this part of the tour and the interesting characters behind the scenes who had a front-row seat to the historic melee.

The Roosevelt home, Springwood, had been the Hudson Valley family seat for over a hundred years in 1939, practically new by English aristocracy standards. But by American standards, the Roosevelts were true-blue Knickerbockers, and the hamlet of Hyde Park has been blue-blooded since King George III ruled over the colony of New York. Today, Springwood is maintained by the National Park Service and the FDR Library contains mementoes of the royal visit as a highlight of his presidency.

Even if Springwood were not the family home and final resting place of one of our most adored presidents, it would have been famous anyway thanks to the events of June 1939. The king and queen stayed in "The Big House" on the property, usually the residence of Sara Delano Roosevelt, the mother, confidante, and most important woman in FDR's life, much to the irritation of his wife, mistresses, and anybody else who got into her imperious path. Sara, according to her grandson James, regarded royalty as being the only rank equal to herself. She considered herself on a par with Queen Mary when she had visited Buckingham Palace in 1934 and viewed the royal visit to Hyde Park as another opportunity to do what she did best—seize control.

One of the few things that did get out of her control was her son's fondness for martinis, which he was expert in making, serving, and drinking with relish. Both Mrs. Roosevelts (the wife and the mother) were horrified to learn that the president wanted to offer the king a drink, not a cup of tea, on his arrival. "My mother does not approve of cocktails and thinks you should have a cup of tea," FDR said as the two men settled into the library before dinner. "My mother would have said the same thing," the king replied. Not surprisingly, the two had martinis. How many is up for historical debate.[15]

The king escorted Sara Roosevelt into dinner, naturally ahead of the other guests, and then after the meal, the king and president were back to man-to-man talks, something the king enjoyed more than he expected. Maybe it was the martinis loosening the British rigidity in him, or perhaps it was the Roosevelt charm. "He never makes one feel shy," the king recalled. "A good a listener as a talker."[16]

The listening and talking continued until 1:30 in the morning at which point the president, acting as a tender uncle said, "Young man, it's time for you to go to bed." But the king could have talked for hours more. He later told the Canadian prime minister, who had joined him at Hyde Park, that he wished his ministers had been as relaxed and open with him as FDR had been, and even more revealingly, he said, "I feel exactly as though a father were giving me his most careful and wise advice."[17]

So touched by his connection with FDR, the king would carry his notes on their conversations with him in his briefcase as a sort of good luck charm. These notes undoubtedly reveal that FDR was not only prepared to go to war to protect Britain but was deeply interested in selling the new Anglo-American alliance to a public still hostile to Britain over the Revolutionary War and still embittered about the debt from World War I.

The great American sell had to start with the great American icon: the hot dog. Much to the consternation of his aristocratic Hyde Park neighbors, including his mother, FDR planned a hot dog picnic for the royal couple that would bring them down to earth and allow everyone from Manhattan to Peoria to see them as embracing an all-American tradition. *If the King of England gets mustard on his shirt like the blue-collar dockworker in Queens, he can't be that bad. He's a just a regular guy too.*

The day started with a church service at St. James Episcopal, a pillar of the community for over one hundred years and where FDR served as senior warden. FDR knew the church as well as his own house, and personally directed, with the rector, not only who would be invited but who would sit where. Moreover, it was FDR, not the rector, who selected the prayers, the hymns, and the sermon to honor the king and queen. The presiding bishop of the Episcopal Church of America, the Right Reverend Henry St. George Tucker, made his case for America's involvement in World War II. "The nations represented at this service must assume a large share of the responsibility for saving the world of our time from the ills that threaten its well-being." On a lighter note, he said, "One sees what happens when the parishioners bring their guests to church . . . if everyone would do this we would fill the church every Sunday."[18]

Waving his cigarette holder in the air with his chin held high, the president took the royal couple on a wild ride to the top of the hill where the picnic was awaiting them. Known for his maverick driving with one hand, especially on the winding paths of his property, the president gave his guests and security detail white knuckles. The queen later reflected that she could not wait to get out of the presidential vehicle, or roller coaster.

Top Cottage, three miles from where the royal were staying, on Dutchess Hill, was the designated venue for the affair, which had been generating the achieved aim of the president—maximum publicity. The newspaper columns and public interest, however, was not about the pros and cons of the war effort, or the newly formed British alliance, but on the rank inelegance of hot dogs.

Hot Dog Gate occupies files at the FDR library containing letters and long dissertations on the use of hot dogs in foreign policy. "Your actions were beneath the leader of a Christian nation," one observer wrote the president, adding that the use of beer was even more reprehensible. Eleanor aired the concerns and placated the nation about the hot dog controversy in her "My Day" column. Hotdogs were the underdogs in the press, but by the end of the weekend could be credited with saving the world from Nazism.[19]

Swift and Company in Poughkeepsie provided the hot dogs, and the picnic would be rounded out with more American summer classics like potato salad and baked beans. The dessert was strawberries from the Dutchess Country estate of Treasury Secretary Henry Morgenthau. Unfortunately, the photograph of the king eating his first hot dog has been lost to time, but the moment was a seminal historical reset. "The king's willingness to eat cardinal American food would signal their final acceptance of Americans as equals," the historian Will Swift writes.

For her part, the queen got a personal primer in the delicacy of hot dog eating. When she asked the president how it was done, he devilishly told her to stuff it into her mouth until it was all gone. Naturally, photographs of her following his instructions do not exist.

The royal family archives contain home movies the king recorded while at the picnic, which are unavailable to the public at present. His use of a recorder demonstrates not only his embrace of technology, but his genuine interest in American life. The entertainment for the afternoon was the performance of Native American folk tales and songs, which the king also recorded. The queen would field a barrage of questions from the young Princess Elizabeth, the future Queen Elizabeth II, and her sister, Princess Margaret, on the festivities. "Our children were so thrilled with the description of the Indian singing and the marvelous clothes—not to mention the Hot Dogs," she wrote in a thirteen-page letter to the Roosevelts.[20]

That evening the guests stood on the banks of the Hudson River as the sun set and sang "Auld Lang Syne," the New Year's Eve elegy to memories past and present. Fifty years after the royal picnic in 1989, staff and locals, many of whom were there on that June day, reunited for a special anniversary celebration. Although the Queen Mother, as she was known by this time, was not present, she reflected on the "idyllic experience" that defined her first American trip.

The British ambassador breathed a sigh of relief at the close of the tour as it was a roaring success and would provide the necessary public relations coup necessary to get America on his side. "Americans feel closer to the Empire than they did a fortnight ago, and this cannot fail to be of immense importance," he said.[21] Two years later, FDR would turn to his new British prime minister visiting the White House and tell him that the tour, especially that fateful hot dog picnic, was the "beginning of the coming together of the two English-speaking races, which would go on after the war."

This new prime minister knew all about it: He was the son of Jennie Jerome. Jennie's American dream had come true. Her Winston would build a bridge that would save the world.

14

BETWEEN US AND WE

Winston Churchill kept a marble sculpture of Jennie's hand on his desk as a reminder of her guiding influence in his life.[1] Now that he was a wartime prime minister, he would need it more than ever. His ascent to the top job had been full of Churchillian drama and bulldog determination, but the hour had finally arrived, and Winston was the man for the hour, if not the century. The king and queen had opposed Winston, deeming him an egomaniac, and too friendly with the Duke and Duchess of Windsor, both opinions being true. However, over time, they would be in his debt and credit his Americanness for saving their lives, and the Crown.

Within months of the historic hot dog picnic, Germany had invaded Poland, signaling the evil aggression that Hitler would unleash on Europe and the world in the coming months and years. "It is the end of the world . . . the end of everything," Ambassador Joseph Kennedy told FDR in a phone conversation as he tried to hold back tears.[2] By April of 1940, Hitler had taken Norway and Denmark, but America, despite FDR's friendly exchanges with Churchill and the royals, still was not all in.

The king and president wrote fervent letters of cooperation back and forth, but words alone would not save Britian from bombs and potential invasion. "The US is not coming in to help us & nothing yet will make them," the king wrote in his diary.[3] FDR had a 1940 election looming, and championing a war, regardless of its rectitude, was not a winning campaign theme.

The queen and Eleanor also exchanged letters, building on the bond they shared in Hyde Park. "I think I can understand a little better what a weight of sorrow and anxiety must be yours," Eleanor wrote, to which Elizabeth responded, "We are all prepared to sacrifice everything in the fight to save freedom . . . our hearts have been lightened by the knowledge that friends in America understand what we are fighting for."[4]

On May 13, Winston went into full Churchill mode by delivering a fiery speech at the House of Commons that could have rallied his most courageous Spencer-Churchill ancestors. "Victory at all costs," he argued. "Victory, however long and hard the road may be." He asked for leaders and citizens alike to put forth their "blood, toil, tears and sweat" to defeat the enemy through fighting, praying, serving, and, most importantly, loving their country.[5]

Later that month, the Netherlands and Belgium fell to the Nazis, while French and British troops were surrounded at Dunkirk, a major turning point of the war. London steeled itself for an imminent invasion. The young Princesses Elizabeth and Margaret recalled the wartime years when they lived at Windsor Castle to avoid the London bombings, but leaving the country was unthinkable. "They will not leave me," the queen said defiantly. "I will not leave the king, and the king will never leave."[6]

In September 1940, six bombs fell on Buckingham Palace, miraculously not harming any life, but destroying a chapel and plumber's workshop. As Nazi bombs descended during the Blitz, the king and queen, dressed in their regal finest, walked through the streets of London, calm and serene. Photographs of the couple offered the images of courage and hope their subjects hankered after as war ravaged their world.

The Americans would muster their own courage and hope in December of 1941. At 1:30 on the afternoon of December 7, FDR's secretary of the navy informed him of the attack at Pearl Harbor, something FDR, as a navy man, took especially hard. Addressing a joint session of Congress, FDR prophesied that this was "a date which will live in infamy." Now it would be Britain's turn to console America.

"We are proud indeed to be fighting at your side against the common enemy," the king telegrammed to FDR. Later that month, Winston set up camp at the White House for a three-week visit. The house was a natural habitat for Winston, who had always said he would have been an American president had he been born in Jennie's hometown of New York. His presence rankled Eleanor, who blamed the prime minister for keeping her husband up so late. Like the king, Winston relished smoking and drinking with FDR until the small hours of the morning. However, Winston preferred brandy to martinis. According to their son, Elliott Roosevelt, his mother would hint that the men should turn in for the night, but Winston would ignore her and keep puffing away.

When Winston spoke to a joint session of Congress, he invoked the memory of Jennie, and, as ever, touted himself. "I cannot help reflecting that if my father had been American and my mother British, instead of the other way around, I might have got here on my own," he said. It must have been the brandy or maybe it was Churchill's God-given gift for oratory, but by the end of his speech, the crowd was stunned into silence and then erupted into rousing applause.[7]

Displaying her fortitude, Eleanor crossed the Atlantic in 1942 to show her solidarity with her British friends and offer support for the Allies. While she interacted with Churchill because she had to, there was still no love lost between the two. Eleanor felt far more comfortable with the king and queen, who led her around London to see firsthand the destruction. They walked into St. Paul's Cathedral, where, forty years later, Lady Diana Spencer would marry Elizabeth's grandson the Prince of Wales. During the war years, the cathedral's dean and staff slept on-site to extinguish fires that may have destroyed sacred church icons. The high altar had already been damaged from a bomb, a horrific reminder of the evil tyranny of Nazism. A church plaque to an American-born pilot named Billy Fiske touched the First Lady. It read HE DIED THAT ENGLAND MAY LIVE. More poignantly, Eleanor learned that a bust of George Washington by Jean-Antoine Houdon, given to the cathedral in 1921 to commemorate an American hero and former British soldier, had been moved from the cathedral for safety. Today, the bust rests peacefully in the cathedral's crypt.[8]

In April of 1945, FDR was visiting Warm Springs, Georgia, with his longtime love Lucy Mercer Rutherford, a relationship encouraged by his daughter, Anna, who understood the solace Lucy brought to FDR during the most difficult time of his public life.

He collapsed in Lucy's presence on April 12 and never recovered consciousness, despite a shot in the heart of adrenaline. He was gone, just as the war was ending. Churchill and FDR's brandy and cigar friendship produced the defining victory of the twentieth century—the defeat of the Nazis and the end of World War II. The friendship between the United States and the United Kingdom would never be the same. Two centuries of animus had blossomed into a new era of alliance. Sadly, FDR would not live long enough to see the full flowering of this victory and this new era of cooperation.

"I was overpowered by a sense of deep and personal loss," Churchill said, on hearing the news of FDR's death. The king, writing to Churchill, said, "I have lost a friend, but to you who have known him for so long and so intimately during this war the sudden loss to yourself personally, must be overwhelming."[9]

Churchill and the king could not attend the state funeral, but an unprecedented court mourning ensued of the American president. The teenage Princess Elizabeth, showing the love of country that she would display as Queen Elizabeth II, wore her military uniform to the memorial service at St. Paul's Cathedral, standing by her father, in naval uniform, and her mother, top to toe in black. Putting aside their stiff upper lips, the royal family held back tears during "The Battle Hymn of the Republic" and, more poignantly, "The Star-Spangled Banner." Addressing the House of Commons, Churchill choked up when he recalled his last communications with the president from Warm Springs. "He never lost faith in Britain," Churchill explained.

On Victory in Europe Day, May 8, just a month after FDR's death, Churchill joined Princess Elizabeth, Princess Margaret, and their parents on the balcony of Buckingham Palace to see the euphoria sweeping across their land. Until the end of their lives, Queen Elizabeth II and Margaret would regale friends and families with their memories of that day—being able to go to street parties, elbowing their way through the enthusiastic crowds. It was one of the best days of their young lives.

Harry S. Truman was the new American president, and Churchill was quick to forge another special relationship. Ever the political operator, he planned for Truman to visit London that summer to get help to rebuild the city after the bombings. Churchill continued as prime minister until the summer of 1945 and then came back to power from 1951 to 1955, enabling him to serve King George VI and Queen Elizabeth II.

It was during Winston's second stint as prime minister that he honored his familial connection to America by accepting an honorary membership in the Society of the Cincinnati, America's oldest and most prestigious lineage fraternity since its founding in 1783.

Headquartered at Anderson House, a Beaux-Arts mansion near Washington's Dupont Circle, the society promotes and educates the public about the nation's founding through its collections, library, and the American Revolution Institute. Membership is exclusively male and requires direct ancestry from commissioned officers of the Continental and French armed forces. Today, the society has nearly five thousand members.[10]

Back in 1947, aware of Winston's American roots through Leonard Jerome, the president general of the society wrote to Churchill's office and offered honorary membership to "the first Englishman ever to be elected." Churchill accepted, but did not receive his medal, a traditional insignia Eagle on a ribbon, until he visited President Truman in January 1952.[11]

The press had a field day with Churchill's post–World War II visit. A cartoonist from the *Baltimore Sun* parodied Winston in his top hat crunching his cigar under the headline MY KINFOLK HELP ME UNDERSTAND BOTH SIDES. In the cartoon, Winston is flanked by a Continental and a Royalist, while Winston himself looks at the viewer amusedly. While the cartoon may have been satirical, it did, at its heart, contain a truth as Winston described the transatlantic history as a struggle between "Us and We."

Addressing the crowd at the Society of the Cincinnati ceremony, which included Vice President Alben Barkley and Chief Justice Frederick Moore Vinson, Churchill, then seventy-seven, said, "I value this honor and let it be a help to all those forces—they are, in my opinion, irresistible forces—which draw our two nations together; not for unworthy purpose of combination or gathering strength, but in order that we may defend the freedom of the world." In the Anderson House collections there is a signed copy of a biography of Lord Randolph Churchill signed by Winston that was given as a gift to the society.[12]

Back in London, Churchill also spearheaded the dedication of the American Memorial Chapel, located behind the high alter in St. Paul's Cathedral, which today houses the Roll of Honor, a 473-page book opened by General Eisenhower that contains the name, rank, and service detail of more than twenty-eight thousand men and women who died while stationed in Great Britain.

Just months before his death in 1963, President Kennedy conferred honorary citizenship on Jennie's son in the Rose Garden of the White House. This was the first time Congress and the president jointly offered this honor to a foreign national, although Winston was not present for the ceremony. The American ambassador to the United Kingdom, David

Bruce, later handed the eighty-eight-year-old his American passport, which duly went into his archives.[13]

Churchill would die two years later, and the so-called Special Relationship term that he coined will take on even deeper meaning when his fellow Spencer kinsman, the future King William V, ascends the throne.

15

NOTHING LIKE A DAME

In June of 1966, scores of well-heeled American ladies, their furs and hats in tow, boarded a plane to London. Before taking off, they posed for a group photo, which today is redolent of 1960s vintage glamour. It hearkens back to a time when people dressed—*really dressed*—for airplane voyages. The trip's purpose was a stop at Sulgrave Manor, the ancestral home of George Washington in Northamptonshire, and, perhaps more importantly for many of them, a tea with Prince William's great-grandfather, seventh Earl Spencer. Known as Jack to his friends, Lord Spencer had been on the Sulgrave Manor board since 1937 and had taken a keen interest in Sulgrave's development. In December of 1949, Lord Spencer and Lord Halifax, who had just been named British ambassador to the United States, stood in the Great Hall of Sulgrave Manor, not far away from the Spencer family seat, Althorp. The occasion was the commemoration of the 150 years since the death of George Washington, whose ancestors had left England's pastoral landscape for the rugged New World centuries before. Against a wintry chill, the Britishers huddled under a portrait of Washington attributed to Gilbert Stuart.[1] Also looking down on the crowd that day were generations of Washington men and their wives represented by the six shields depicted in the Great Hall's windows. These shields showed the coat of arms for Lawrence, the original builder of Sulgrave; his father; his grandfather; his sons, Lawrence and Robert, and his grandson, also called Lawrence.[2]

Lawrence is the name of choice in the Washington family. A Lawrence built Sulgrave Manor beginning in 1540; and a Lawrence, Washington's half brother, named Mount Vernon in 1734. Not far away from the windows, visitors can see the Lion of England and the Tudor Dragon of Wales on the Sulgrave walls, illustrating that despite George Washington's place in history, this is very much a British home.[3]

After Earl Spencer and Lord Halifax welcomed their guests in 1949, they offered toasts to "A Red Rose for the Washingtons." Legend has it that a Washington forbear had given a cottage to a village widow as an act of charity. Her yearly rent was a red rose on the feast day for St. John the Baptist. If generosity of spirit has multigenerational karmic effects, then the story of Sulgrave Manor is a prime example of a house that is blessed.[4]

Sir Reginald Blomfield, the prominent architect, oversaw Sulgrave's transformation from little-known Tudor estate to what the Marquess of Cambridge described as a "shrine for all Americans and a center from which sentiments of friendship and goodwill between the British and American people will forever radiate."[5]

The magic of Sulgrave's history is indeed a Cinderella tale. From its original purchase by Lawrence Washington for the unroyal sum of 324 pounds, it had been deserted by 1659 after the sale to Lawrence Makepeace in 1610. According to Lord Lee of Fareham, who like Lord Spencer was one of many aristocrats to help Cinderella find her golden carriage, Sulgrave led "an uneventful, but dignified existence" as a "frowsy and neglected" property that had "degenerated into a common farmhouse."[6] So insignificant was Sulgrave that it was not worthy of a mention in the country estate catalog, *Murray's Handbook for Travellers in Northamptonshire and Rutland*, in 1878. The author Washington Irving, while researching his 1855 biography of Washington, visited Sulgrave during its neglected days, and described it rather blandly: "I visited Sulgrave a few years since. It was in a quiet, rural neighborhood where the farmhouses were quaint and antiquated. A part only of the manor house remains and was inhabited by a farmer."[7]

Indeed, the house and its 213 acres had been let by farmers for 200 pounds per annum. The only regal feature that Irving would have noticed, among the decay and nettles, was the gable on the entrance way still emblazoned with the Washington coat of arms—the inspiration for the stars and stripes on the American flag.[8]

Although Jack would be known as the Spencer most closely associated with Sulgrave, he was not the first. Back in 1913, his father, sixth Earl Spencer, served on Sulgrave's Committee of Management, as the Brits and Americans celebrated one hundred years since the signing of the Treaty of Ghent in 1814. This treaty ended the War of 1812, during which the White House was destroyed and Francis Scott Key wrote his iconic ballad.[9]

This commemoration was a transatlantic source of partnership, and the first major thawing of frostiness between the two countries. In 1911, then-president Theodore Roosevelt was the honorary chairman of the American Peace Centenary Commission of which Andrew Carnegie was the chairman. The following year American and British representatives, including Lord Rothschild and the author Sir Arthur Conan Doyle, met in London to decide the best ways to mark this anniversary. They decided on three concrete objectives: to erect a statue of George Washington in London, to promote Anglo-American dialogue, and to purchase and restore Sulgrave Manor. Lord Spencer, the elder, was a key leader in this final goal due to his family's personal and proximal connection to the Washington family.[10]

Lord Spencer and his colleagues tasked with Sulgrave Manor estimated it would cost 25,000–30,000 pounds, between three and four million in today's currency, to take Sulgrave from neglected farmhouse to a home benefitting minor nobility. This project was not only supported by the aristocracy in Britain but by the royal family itself.

A 1914 invitation from King George V reads: "His Majesty and The Prince of Wales having given their gracious approval and generous contributions to the effort being made in England and America under the auspices of The Sulgrave Institutions of the two countries to secure the money needed for the restoration, preservation, and maintenance of the ancestral home of George Washington." This fundraising appeal featured two angelic figures reaching across an ocean grasping each other's hands with the words "Setting Up a Symbol."[11]

That June, an Anglo-American Peace Centenary Ball took place in London, supported by the king, the Prince of Wales, and their circles in the highest echelons of British society. Princes, dukes, earls, lord and ladies all lined up to support Sulgrave Manor, but the house's biggest champions would be dames—American ones. Enter Katherine Cox of Virginia, the head of the National Society of the Colonial Dames of America, a similar lineage organization to the Society of the Cincinnati but comprised exclusively of women.[12]

Inaugurated in 1891, the "Dames," as they call themselves, are descendants of men from the thirteen original colonies "who shaped the foundation upon which the nation was built." Some of these men were colonial governors, Founding Fathers, or leaders who made significant pre-Revolution era civic contributions. Headquartered in Washington, DC, the Dames still strive "to preserve the records and relics of the Colonial period of American history, and by these objects, to teach the meaning of patriotism."[13]

The Manor House at Sulgrave and its surrounding ten acres were purchased for £8,000, some $1.5 million in today's currency, by the British government, with the approval of the American ambassador to the United Kingdom, Walter Hines Page. They sensed the groundswell of new Anglo-American support and formed an international committee to honor the Treaty of Ghent in general, and the little-known Sulgrave Manor, in particular.

Addressing the Colonial Dames gathered in Washington, DC, Cox pitched Sulgrave Manor as a long-term project for her organization. Their first contribution was a portrait of George Washington, a copy of Charles Willson Peale's 1772 painting, in the attire of a colonel of the provincial forces.[14]

Known as *George Washington, Colonel Commanding Virginia Colonial Troops*, the picture shows a gentle George, looking up with his hand inside his coat, happy and content as a British subject. Within just a few short years of this portrait's completion, George would be leading troops in rebellion.

That summer of 1914, Mrs. T. Harrison Garrett represented the Dames at a ceremony in which the Duke of Teck, acting on behalf of the royal family, presented the keys of the house to Ambassador Page. While on the property, Garrett looked for the right place for the portrait, and noted the vast restoration needed for the house, far more than the British donors or the Dames had expected.

Ironically, in 1914, the celebration of one war's end was interrupted by the start of another. World War I, which America would enter in 1917, would interrupt the Treaty of Ghent memorials, and fundraising for Sulgrave Manor. The copy of the Peale portrait would stay Stateside until it was safe to travel to England.[15]

After the Armistice in 1918, Lord Burnham of the *Daily Telegraph* organized a campaign that raised $25,000 in 1919 with a larger goal of building a museum on-site, and an educational center. Ruth Moore Lee, the Viscountess of Fareham, encouraged her sister in New York, Faith Moore, a member of the Colonial Dames, to obtain the Gilbert Stuart portrait of Washington for the house, which was unveiled at a 1921 ceremony with the American ambassador to the United Kingdom, George Brinton Harvey, and his wife, a member of the Daughters of the American Revolution. This portrait, unlike the Peale copy, shows a mature Washington, after the war had hardened his features, but fortified his character. The two pictures were studies in historical contrasts.[16]

Viscountess Lee, as the former Ruth Moore was known, was, like Fanny Work, a rich New Yorker who married an Englishman, Arthur Lee. The couple would ultimately acquire the sixteenth-century estate Chequers, and give the house to the British government. Chequers is now the getaway retreat of the British prime minister, a sort of English Camp

David where visiting dignitaries can have more relaxed discussions with government officialdom. Lord and Lady Lee were some of Sulgrave's most prominent supporters, as was Mr. J. P. Morgan, who donated an historically accurate armchair to the bedchamber.[17]

As restorations on the house continued and the collection of artifacts grew, so, too, did the attention and care to the Sulgrave garden and orchard, something that would have pleased the nature-lover in George Washington, whose gardens at Mount Vernon still attract admirers. White-and-red roses of England; damask roses; the Nelly Custis rose, named for George's step granddaughter; and modern David Austin roses are just a few varieties of blooms that once surrounded the house.[18]

The Sulgrave parish church, just a short walk away from the house, dates from 1564 and is where Lawrence Washington and his family worshipped and are buried. As was the custom of the day, Lawrence marked the entrance to the church with the year and the initials of the monarch ER (Elizabeth Regina) to show his devotion to God and Queen Elizabeth I. The effigies of the Washington forbears rest peacefully inside the church where today's worshippers can sit on the Washington family pew, restored with the backing of Sir Charles Wakefield, later Lord Wakefield. In 1930, the church was installed with a new organ, another contribution from the Dames.[19] In 1922, influenced by his ambitions and historically minded wife Helen, former president William Howard Taft, then serving as chief justice of the Supreme Court, stopped by Northamptonshire. Not coincidentally, Helen was a Colonial Dame of the Washington, DC, society.[20]

As the sesquicentennial in 1926 approached, a fundraising appeal, steered by the Dames with support of English friends, went out with postcards that read "Will you contribute $1 for the perpetual care and maintenance of this historic home?" The Endowment Fund raised some $100,000 in 1920s currency from twenty-seven thousand donors.[21] Mrs. Gilmer Speed Adams, one of the many pilgrims to Sulgrave Manor in the late 1920s, found it difficult to find the place in the middle of the English countryside. She put up signs directing visitors down the right roads, making sure the placards had a COURTESY OF THE NATIONAL SOCIETY OF THE COLONIAL DAMES OF AMERICA tagline. The efforts of the Dames were so well regarded that a contingent of them traveling to London in 1925 were received by King George V and Queen Mary at Buckingham Palace.[22]

By the following summer, Sulgrave Manor had made such an impression stateside that a full-size replica of the house was erected at the Philadelphia Sesquicentennial Exposition commemorating the country's 150th birthday. The Sulgrave replica won the gold medal for best exhibit.

The economic downturn of the late 1920s did not impact the upward trajectory of Sulgrave. The Dames, through the sale of postcards and admissions, enabled more staff hires, and more caretakers and gardeners at the property. The plumbing was updated, a driveway and parking lot were built, and the estate's barn was turned into a museum of all things "Washingtonia," including a velvet coat belonging to the general himself. Coinciding with the interest provoked by the sesquicentennial, Anglophile pilgrims on their way to see Stratford-upon-Avon, the birthplace and burial site of William Shakespeare, wanted a new detour on their trip: the Washington family home they had been hearing about. England was now our friend. Churchill had given the Special Relationship its oratory resonance, but Sulgrave Manor would give it a visual life of its own.

Lord Spencer was Sulgrave's fairy godfather, and his involvement was not coincidental. The Washington and Spencer families are connected by land and shared experiences. Lord Spencer was a cantankerous fellow, but had a soft spot for architecture, antiques, and family history. He would have known that his Spencer ancestors were fond of their Washington neighbors and were kind to them when they fell on hard times. Washington and Spencer ancestors rest in peace side by side under the ancient roof of St. Mary the Virgin with St. John Church in nearby Great Brington. As the chairman of the board of Sulgrave Manor, he was simply continuing that legacy of neighborliness.[23]

Born in 1892, Jack was educated at Trinity College, Cambridge, and served in the British Army during World War I, during which a German bullet hit his kneecap, leaving him for dead in no-man's-land. If not for a fellow officer rescuing him, he would have bled to death on the field. His grandson, the ninth Earl Spencer, describes Jack thusly: "Grandfather was a figure of awe; his moustache bristled, his stomach bulged under outsized trousers, and he had the uncompromising air of a man who had no time whatsoever for fools."[24]

In 1922, Jack married Lady Cynthia Hamilton, whose portraits bear a striking resemblance to Diana. Although Cynthia died in 1972 when Diana was a young girl, she had a lasting impact on her, and according to Diana's biographer Andrew Morton, Diana believed Lady Cynthia was her spirit guide. "Saintly" was the word used most often to describe her.[25]

Both Jack and Cynthia were living embodiments of noblesse oblige—giving their time, money, and talents to their community and commendable causes. Jack was a revered, if not formidable, figure in Northamptonshire and reveled in the art and architecture of Althorp, the Spencer family home.

"The house soon became the passion of my grandfather's life," Earl Spencer reflected. "He had the mind of a curator, and he loved nothing more than hand rinsing the china or dusting the books in the library."[26]

By the time Lord Spencer took the helm of Sulgrave Manor, nearly ten thousand people a year were visiting the property, and the numbers were increasing yearly. Thanks to the restorations, and donations of period furniture and paintings to the house collection organized by the Dames and British aristocrats, Sulgrave Manor had the patina of the gentleman's house it once was. "Gifts to the gardens and furnishings for the house give the impression that the Washington family is living here," noted the minutes of a 1935 Dames progress report on Sulgrave.

These improvements came in time for the 1932 bicentennial of Washington's birth. The 1603 bed hangings and chair covers donated by Lady Sandwich to the hyacinth bulbs given by Lady Victoria Hicks-Beach all conspired to resurrect George Washington as a man for the twentieth century, even in the eyes of the countrymen he fought against.[27]

On July 2, 1937, in honor of the coronation of King George VI and Queen Elizabeth, Lord and Lady Spencer hosted a garden party at Althorp for 275 people, including the Sulgrave board, who took home a check for the ongoing restorations. That fall Queen Elizabeth stayed as a guest at Althorp. While in Northampton, she was taken to Sulgrave for the first time by her Spencer hosts. The queen gave Sulgrave a snuff box, which is still on display today.[28]

As World War II dawned, the American flag and Union Jack that flew outside Sulgrave were packed up for protection, and Sulgrave Manor's doors were closed for tours. Lord Halifax, the British ambassador to the United States, joined Lord Spencer on the board during the war years, another example of Sulgrave's political and cultural import. The house survived the war, and in celebration, the board was presented with Sulgrave's 1538 deed signed by Washington's ancestor Lawrence Washington. The house and its ongoing lecture series and educational programs tempered resentments from the British people that the Americans had not entered the war soon enough. Using Sulgrave as a bridge builder, Prime Minister Clement Attlee made a transatlantic broadcast from the Great Hall of the house, which can be viewed today on YouTube.[29]

This was a time of great challenge for Earl Spencer, who was preoccupied by his own house repairs. His devotion to Althorp and its vast collection was tested by tedious maintenance issues, staff expenditures, and the overall financial burden of the sixteenth century property. For a time, Jack considered giving Althorp to the National Trust as most of his time was spent with a bucket in hand catching rainwater from one leaky roof to another. His financial woes were somewhat mitigated by the sale of the family's London home, Spencer House, which ultimately was purchased by Lord Rothschild.[30] In his spare time, Jack tended to everything at Sulgrave from installing an oak garden bench, to exterminating wood worms in the parlor, to restoring the Washington church's belltower.[31]

Working in concert with the Dames was great fun for Lord and Lady Spencer, and by 1966, the Dames, were making that first glamorous trek to London to meet the man who had become their hero. This tea is known as "Dames Day," and has become a beloved tradition. While furs and hats may not be necessary these days, the pilgrimage is still a way of celebrating a decades-long friendship.

Earl Spencer, having served Sulgrave for decades, did not live long enough to see the bicentennial celebrations in 1976. He had died the year before, but a tree was planted in his honor on the property, and the bicentennial bust of George Washington by Avard Fairbanks was secured under his leadership. Lord Spencer was the last in his family to serve Sulgrave, but his contributions have had multigenerational effects.

On the other side of the pond, 1976 was a banner year for America, the climax being Queen Elizabeth II's state visit at the invitation of President Gerald Ford. She and Prince Philip barnstormed the Northeast just as her parents did decades before and would be greeted by an equal level of euphoria, but this time Elizabeth would go where no monarch had gone before—Philadelphia, the cradle of American liberty. Dazzling in a pink gown and diamonds, Elizabeth was heralded by trumpets played by cadets from Valley Forge Military Academy as she made her way up the steps of the Philadelphia Museum of Art. The queen had arrived in Philadelphia on Her Majesty's Yacht, *Britannia*, where she would stay that evening. "You know, this is one of the finest symbols of any country in the world," she said, as she took in the Liberty Bell. She stopped to talk to eager Americans who lined the streets, like one nun, Sister Rose Margaret, who told the queen she was a Camden, New Jersey, girl, but her parents were from England. "Really?" the queen said. "God bless you."[32]

If her parents' trip in 1939 had been to reset the way Americans saw World War II, then this visit was a reset of the way the monarchy viewed America. Presenting her new friends in Philadelphia with a Bicentennial Bell, she said she was grateful, not resentful of our shared history.

She stood as a "direct descendant of King George III. He was the last Crowned Sovereign to rule in this country, and it is therefore with a particular personal interest that I view those events which took place 200 years ago . . . We lost the American Colonies because we lacked that statesmanship to know the right time, and the manner of yielding, what is impossible to keep. But the lesson was learnt in the next century and a half we kept more closely to the principles of Magna Carta which have been the common heritage of both countries. This was the outcome of experience learned the hard way in 1776. Without that great act in the cause of liberty performed in Independence Hall two hundred years ago, we could never have transformed an Empire into a Commonwealth. Ultimately peace brought a renewal of friendship which has continued and grown over the years and has played a vital part in world affairs. Together we have fought in two world wars in the defense of our common heritage of freedom. Together we have striven to keep the peace so dearly won. Together, as friends and allies, we can face the uncertainties of the future, and this is something for which we in Britain can also celebrate the Fourth of July."[33]

16

ELM COURT

By 1981, Newport, Rhode Island, was the de facto base for William's American family since they had established themselves there in 1896. Elm Court on Bellevue Avenue is home of the descendants of Frank Work, who purchased the 1853 Italianate mansion for $115,000 in late nineteenth-century currency. The *New York Times* described it as one of the "best known villas" in the area, long before it had a royal connection.[1]

Newport's Bellevue Avenue could not be a more fitting place for royalty, British or American. Newport is, as author Elizabeth Drexel Lehr describes it, "the very Holy of Holies, the playground of the great ones of the earth from which all intruders were ruthlessly excluded by a set of cast iron rules."[2]

The city was founded in the 1600s by Puritans whose austerity is in sharp contrast to the lavish displays of wealth that their community has come to embody. By 1884, Newport was the home base for the Naval War College, and the sea is integral to Rhode Islanders who love their "Ocean State" and revel in the sailing, yachting, and chic resorts that surround them.

But before the Gilded Age, Newport was a middle-class summer getaway of no real distinction. There were a few notable figures in town like Julia Ward Howe, Henry Wadsworth Longfellow, and the literary giants Henry James and Edith Wharton, but they lived quietly, and in subdued luxury. Author Greg King describes this era of Newport as having "an intellectual milieu of quiet probity." Saratoga Springs was the first fashionable summer spot for Manhattan elites of the day, but it would soon be supplanted.[3]

Two Carolines elevated Newport from bookish beach town to a destination of decadence: Caroline Perry Belmont, and the Gilded Age's queen, Caroline Astor. Mrs. Belmont's home, By-the-Sea, was the first of the large-scale homes on Bellevue Avenue. A Rhode Island native, Mrs. Belmont understood the benefits of the ocean breezes and coastline beauty of this mostly unknown city.

Her husband, August Belmont, was a successful financier, close friend of Leonard Jerome, and the namesake of the Belmont Stakes thanks to his enthusiastic patronage of the horse racing industry. Designed by Mrs. Belmont's first cousin, their new three-story summer home was, like most of its architectural predecessors, Italianate in design with a French mansard roof, semicircular portico, and requisite veranda for enjoying the ocean views.

With By-the-Sea completed, the Belmont power couple used it for Gilded Age entertainment, which established Newport as a new social mecca with ten-course French dinners prepared by their small army of servants. Instead of escaping New York society, the Belmonts were bringing New York to Newport.[4]

Social writer Cleveland Amory in his *The Last Resorts* describes Mrs. Belmont in her Newport glory:

> Mrs. Belmont had elegant French manners, beautiful jewels, and was a pioneer resorter. When she deserted her beautiful country seat at the once fashionable Staten Island and built "By-the-Sea" at Newport, the event marked the beginning of a new era.

When the always-in-the-know Ward McAllister, who had a Newport farm, caught wind of this social shift, he filled in his "Mystic Rose,"

Caroline Astor, who was never to be outdone where social trends were concerned. In 1881, Mrs. Astor got her own 1852 villa on Bellevue, a rather modest home she then got to work making not so modest. Commissioning Richard Morris Hunt, she added rooms, and Gilded Age magic to augment rooms, enlarge walls, and inspire envy in visitors.

The home would be known as Beechwood, and an invitation to it was a sign of social primacy. Every July 1, Mrs. Astor's ball in her baroque ballroom, refined by Stanford White, was the place to be. Beechwood was purchased by tech billionaire Larry Ellison in 2010 and has been closed to public since that time. Major renovations, the addition of huge boulders around the property, not to mention Mr. Ellison's less-than-charming personality, have placed Beechwood in lower tier status for the past two decades. While Mrs. Belmont's By-the-Sea would be destroyed in 1946, Beechwood is still standing. The fact that Newport and Mrs. Astor play prominent roles in the Julian Fellowes series *The Gilded Age* just adds to the fascination.[5]

In 1888, green with envy, Alva Vanderbilt got a blank check from her husband Willie to build "the very best living accommodation that money could provide," reportedly as a penance for his infidelity.

Seeing herself as a queen to not only rival, but eclipse Mrs. Astor, Alva used Versailles as a source of inspiration for her project. Not by accident, she gobbled up six hundred acres on Bellevue, also employing Richard Morris Hunt to build her Newport castle. To keep an air of mystery, she erected fences and trained dogs to keep out nosy neighbors and reporters. She was a lady who loved control, and she would decide when her plans would be revealed.

Huge porticos, monumental pillars, and some five hundred thousand feet of marble would conspire to create the aptly named Marble House. If Mr. Vanderbilt was paying for being an unfaithful husband, he would pay very dearly indeed.

On August 19, 1892, Alva was ready to make her debut as Newport queen. "The sight was one never before seen in Newport," reported the

New York Times of the splendid housewarming party. "The grand portico was ablaze of lights and liveried attendants were on hand from carriage to cloakroom." Although Marble House made Alva an even greater social success, it did little to help her floundering marriage to Willie or her cruel treatment of her daughter, Consuelo, over whom she ruled like a military dictator. Unlike Frank Work, who actively opposed Fanny's marriage to a British aristocrat, fearing it would bring her unhappiness (which it ultimately did), Alva insisted on it, twisting Consuelo's arm into a union with the Duke of Marlborough, with her daughter's happiness bearing zero consideration. By the time Alva moved into Marble House, she was already onto her next victim: the son of August and Caroline Belmont, Oliver, whom she would marry in 1896.

The Vanderbilt divorce shocked and entranced New York society, much like the drama of Fanny's scandals. Both Fanny and Alva would carve out unconventional lives as divorced women, defying their class and times with marked fortitude, if not brazenness. Banished from Marble House, Alva's Newport home with Oliver was called Belcourt, also on Bellevue, where she was a fixture of notoriety. Sometimes in the middle of a society luncheon, Alva would invite her guests to listen to the incessant tour guides camped on Bellevue with their megaphones. "Here you see before you the new home of a lady who is much in the public eye, a society lady who has just been through the divorce courts. She used to dwell in the marble halls with Mr. Vanderbilt. Now she lives over the stables with Mr. Belmont."

Bringing her guests closer to the windows for a better view "of that dreadful man with the megaphone," Alva would encourage them to have a listen. "He's going to tell all the tourists about our staircase. It really is too funny for words."[6]

Henry James declared these marble mansions "white elephants," and decried the desecration of the understated elegance of the city he knew.[7] The most famous "white elephant" in Newport is the one most associated with its reputation as an enclave of the rich: The Breakers, home of

Willie Vanderbilt's brother, Cornelius Vanderbilt II, and his wife, Alice. Motivated by rivalry with Alva, the couple created what outranks any private summer residence in the world. Two million dollars was spent on the massive wrought-iron iron gate alone, which still greets guests at Ochre Point Avenue. The gate is adorned with the fleurs-de-lis, acorn leaves, and the imperious monogram of CV.

With its seventy rooms, including an Italian Renaissance state dining room that would rival the Vatican's, The Breakers is the largest of Newport's cottages, and was built primarily for score keeping and entertaining. When the new Newport denizens were not promenading down the Cliff Walk, the oceanside trail with breathtaking views of the ocean and The Breakers, they were joining Fanny in carriage-riding adventures, or socializing at the most exclusive club in town—the Newport Casino Club; there they would gossip through the night about tomorrow's party, such as the August 1885 debutante ball for Gertrude Vanderbilt, daughter of Willie and Alice, who would become the patroness of the Whitney Museum in New York. "Into those six or seven weeks were crowded balls, dinners, parties of every description, each striving to eclipse the other," one observer noted cynically about the Newport summer.[8]

It was into this brutal system of one-upmanship that Elm Court was bought by Frank Work and developed into a major player on Bellevue Avenue with the full participation of Fanny and her daughter, Cynthia.

In 1902, Fanny brilliantly executed Cynthia's debut at Elm Court, despite her recent custody battle with Jim Burke Roche. Jim was evidently banished from Elm Court for Cynthia's debutante ball; the father of the deb is nowhere mentioned in society coverage. "Miss Roche has been one of the most popular belles of the summer," the *New York Times* read on September 2. "Many novel and beautiful floral pieces were sent to Elm Court. One was a large sedan chair filled with lilies of the valley. The reception room, where Miss Roche received [guests] with her mother, was the perfect floral bower." The article described the other flowers as an "elaborate" riot of blue and white.

The makeshift ballroom on the lawn for the affair measured 40 x 70 with a 20 x 20 extension for the eighty dinner guests. The B List attendees came for "the cotillion" dancing and supper later in the evening. The party favors were card cases for the gents and hogskin purses for the ladies.

The evening and hostesses were so colorful they managed to knock a luncheon for Grand Duke Boris Vladimir of Russia given by Mrs. Cornelius Vanderbilt Jr. to the bottom of the social column. Fanny Burke Roche may have been breaking Mrs. Astor's publicity rule, but in Newport social warfare, she and Cynthia were the clear winners.[9]

By 1904, *Good Housekeeping* had noted that young Cynthia was not only a member of the Four Hundred, but was a skilled automobilist, tennis player, and horsewoman, something that was sure to make her horsey family proud.[10]

As the daughter of an American socialite and British peer, Cynthia Burke Roche lived a life of an American aristocrat, and established herself as a doyenne in Newport, where she had made her debut under her mother's tutelage and continued Fanny's legacy as a keen horsewoman and superb hostess. Born in London before her parent's divorce, she became a naturalized American citizen in 1908. Never without her signature parasol, Cynthia was the epitome of a Newport lady when she inherited Elm Court after Fanny's death in 1947.

Cynthia was trained to marry well and did—twice. Her first marriage was to Arthur Burden, the grandson of Henry Burden of the Burden Iron Works fortune, and a fellow fixture of Gilded Age society in New York and Newport.

Cynthia's best friend was Natica Rives, and the two girls married the Burden brothers. They, along with Reginald and Alfred Vanderbilt, and their wives, had formed a notable group of bright young things who frequented all the right parties. "Both Miss Roche and Miss Rives were girls of exceptional charm and vivacity and had few rivals for popularity at the dances and other entertainments of those days," the *New York Times* explained. But their charmed lives took a turn for the worst when

Natica killed herself in her mother-in-law's Fifth Avenue apartment three months after her wedding.[11]

Arthur would die at age forty-two in 1921 from an equestrian injury, leaving behind Cynthia and their young daughter Eileen. The following year she married Guy Fairfax Cary in an Elm Court ceremony surrounded by seventy guests, including Vincent Astor and Consuelo Vanderbilt, and eleven thousand Columbia roses. Wearing a white georgette gown with a blue hat, Cynthia was given away by her brother Francis. Her new husband was the great-grandson of the ninth Lord Fairfax, after whom Fairfax County in Virginia is named. The couple were passionate students of antiques and, thanks to family money, became renowned collectors. They filled their five-story New York townhouse with their finds, and the Redwood Library in Newport is the home of the Cynthia Cary Collection today.[12]

Cynthia and Guy had two children they named after themselves. When Guy made Cynthia a widow for the second time, she retired to Elm Court where she remained a glamorous dowager. By 1964, Cynthia had sold their New York townhouse to the Dalton School, one of Manhattan's most exclusive institutions. At the time of her death two years later, her estate was worth $700,000 in 1960s currency, nearly $7 million today.[13] Elm Court was then inherited by her son, Guy, who maintained the estate until his death in 2004.

Her daughter, Cynthia Cary, was born in 1924 and was educated at the Chapin School in New York City. It was at Elm Court that she, too, shone as a debutante and bride. In the summer of 1947, she married Charles Bingham Penrose Van Pelt at the Trinity Protestant Episcopal Church. Her husband was an alum of Groton, Harvard, and the University of Pennsylvania Law School who served in US Army Military Intelligence in the Pacific during World War II, while Cynthia was a nurse's aide for the war effort. The Van Pelts had three children: Guy, Abby, and Peter, who grew up near Philadelphia hearing about their Fermoy connection, and the glittering life of their great-grandmother,

Fanny. They would see her many portraits in Elm Court when they visited Newport for family functions.[14]

In 1981, the phone rang at Elm Court. On the line from London was Edmund, Lord Fermoy, Maurice's son who had assumed the title on his father's death in 1955. Lord Fermoy wanted the American branch of the Fermoy family to know that his cousin, Lady Diana Spencer, was to marry the Prince of Wales. Diana was the second youngest child of Frances Shand Kydd, daughter of Maurice and granddaughter of Fanny, for whom she was named. Although it was not discussed in the media, the new Princess of Wales was deeply connected to America, a place she had never visited. In fact, Diana barely knew about her American kin in Newport, but they certainly knew about her.

A wave of enthusiasm ran through Elm Court that spring. Lord Fermoy invited the Americans over for the wedding festivities, but only a select number would be invited to the ceremony and would stay at Clarence House as the guest of the Queen Mother.[15] As Diana's wedding approached at the end of July, Newport's high season was aflutter with local gossip.

Abby Van Pelt, Diana's American cousin, was one of those Yankee relatives who could barely contain her enthusiasm, although she had not made the cut for guest list. This minor detail did not stop her from being in London for the wedding of the century.

"It was like being at a Super Bowl," Abby told a reporter as she took in the air of excitement that engulfed the city and Britain, which had been burdened with years of economic downturn and cultural unrest in the 1970s. Then, along came a fresh breeze in the form of Diana, who had just turned twenty on July 1 of that year. Although she was barely out of her teens, this young woman would be an overnight goddess. Diana's hairstyle, pearl choker, and "Shy Di" downward gaze would beguile young women like Abby, who clamored for any bits of information about the bride and the wedding preparations.

Lord Fermoy hosted a picnic for the American cousins, where Abby got to meet Lady Diana's Spencer family; her sisters Lady Sarah and Lady Jane, and the heir apparent to the Spencer estate, Viscount Althorp, then a seventeen-year-old Charles Spencer.[16]

As no trip to London is complete without a stop at Harrods, the chic department store, Abby made her way there for some retail therapy between sightseeing. As she perused the scarf counter, the salesgirl whispered, "She was just in." "I thought it was wonderful that there wasn't a need to identify Diana other than by 'she,'" Abby explained.[17]

On July 29, 1981, Abby watched Diana's horse-drawn carriage from her hotel's rooftop and thought of her time in Chillicothe where she had learned about their mutual, and humble, roots. With a Ross County Historical Society archivist as her guide, she meandered the streets, houses, and haunts that were a part of Frank Work's youth. "This is such a pretty city, and I am amazed at the number of handsome old houses you have here. It was exciting seeing places where my forbears lived," Abby explained to a local reporter.[18]

When Uncle Guy died without heirs, Elm Court was passed to Guy Van Pelt, Abby's brother, who has called Elm Court home for two decades. His family, which includes his wife Mary, and twin daughters Mary and Cynthia, is the sixth generation to live at Elm Court, which is both a warm family home, and a reminder of its splendid past. Elm Court is at once regal and hospitable but deeply inspired by its American heritage and the people who have lived in it. A portrait of Thomas Jefferson greets visitors in the entryway, as does another of Edmund Burke in the dining room, where a giant painting of Fanny establishes her as Elm Court's reigning matriarch.

Surrounded by hedges, the nearly four acres on which Elm Court sit are punctuated by American beech trees. The lily pond of yesteryear has been removed, but the lawn where so many society fetes have been enjoyed is still lush and green with the same greenhouse and cutting gardens which boast a riot of colorful dahlias.

Fanny's presence is everywhere, from her giant portrait in the dining room to the architectural touches she added with Stanford White and Ogden Codman Jr. Van Pelt has restored parts of the house, but it mostly stands true to the way Frank and Fanny wanted it. Indeed, there are references to their passion for horses throughout. A Currier and Ives print shows Frank driving a team of horses in a race, and a whole wall is dedicated to family members on horseback. Photos of Maurice and Frank as young lads in uniform, and as men in their elder years, adorn the top of the piano. Their carriage house was mostly destroyed by a fire, but some of the horse stalls are just the way they were when Fanny would pull up her horses at the house's main entrance. Her spirit lives on in Mary, now sixteen, an accomplished equestrienne, whose countless ribbons are on proud display at Elm Court. Similarly, Fanny would have relished seeing Cynthia, a promising ballerina who has performed at La Scala. A sign across the street on Bellevue mentions the house's connection to the royal family, but mostly, Elm Court is like the family inside—privately dignified.[19]

17

"FIX YOUR EYES UPON THE REAL"

In 1978, Lady Diana Spencer, the daughter of eighth Earl Spencer, left pastoral Northamptonshire for the cosmopolitan streets of South Kensington in London. Her single girl's flat at 60 Coleherne Court was purchased for some 50,000 pounds, about 323,000 today, thanks to a trust from a woman she never met—her American great-grandmother, Frances Burke Roche.[1]

Before she was the most famous woman of the twentieth century, Diana epitomized the "Sloane Ranger" of the late 1970s and early '80s—a young woman of an upper-class background who favored Barbour jackets, Laura Ashley florals, and a traditional outlook on a changing social and cultural order. It was at this Coleherne Court flat that the cult of Diana was born.

It was fitting that she started her adult life in a home that was, in effect, purchased by Fanny because the two led strikingly similar lives with strikingly vivid personalities. Both were spoiled, glamorous, scandalous, and headstrong. "I never descend from my own pedestal one fraction without hurting my own pride," Fanny wrote in her 1910 diary. But both had a softness, an enchanting charm that attracted admirers and ravenous media attention. One was born in America but was lured to the British Isles through marriage. The other was born in England but likely would have made America her home had she lived. Both were products of high society but rebelled against establishment strictures. Frances and Diana suffered through acrimonious marriages, divorces, and mental illness that, as we will learn, had become all too familiar in the Burke Roche family. Both lived passionately, although one would die an old lady, and the other would meet her end tragically young. "I think families should look after their members," Fanny wrote. "Stand by to see that no one gets off the sensible path of right living with all its hideous trouble, disaster, disgrace and loss."[2]

Diana Frances Spencer's path started July 1, 1961, at Park House, the home of her maternal grandfather, Maurice Burke Roche, Fanny's son, fourth Lord Fermoy. Diana's mother, Frances Burke Roche, was Maurice's third child, and was named for her Granny Fanny, who stayed close to Maurice and his children until her death in 1947. When Frances was a teenager, the tall and striking blonde had her requisite coming out party, like the women before her, and was expected to marry young and marry up. This she did exceedingly well. At her debutante party, she locked eyes with John, Viscount Althorp, then in his late twenties, and the heir to the Spencer estate, Althorp.

Viscount Althorp, known as Johnnie, had been educated at Eton and the Royal Military Academy Sandhurst. Coming of age during World War II, Johnnie was a captain in the Royal Scots Greys and landed in France the day after D-Day. He furthered his training in agriculture in anticipation of his life's work: looking after a vast estate and the responsibilities of landed gentry. At eighteen, Frances did not have much education or life experience, but she had what was necessary—good looks and good genes to pass to the next Spencer heir.

Despite their age difference, Viscount Althorp moved quickly in courtship, and the two were married at Westminster Abbey in 1954 with Queen Elizabeth II in attendance. Her American granny, the other Frances Burke Roche, had died several years before, but the American side of the family was represented by Diana's cousins once removed, Cynthia Van Pelt Russell and her brother, Guy Cary.

The Althorps had two daughters before Diana—Sarah and Jane—but failed to produce the necessary male "heir and spare," as Consuelo Vanderbilt, Duchess of Marlborough, put it. Like Georgiana Spencer, and countless women in the aristocracy before, Frances was under intense pressure to accomplish something completely out of her control. She had to produce a son to keep the titles and property in the immediate family. Only producing girls would have necessitated Earl Spencer passing the title and property to a next of kin at the time of his death. Her frustration came to an end, or so Frances thought, in January 1960, when she gave birth to one John Spencer. Sadly, the boy died the same day.

"The word *entail* is as much a part of aristocratic vocabulary as money is to a banker," explains royal author Lady Colin Campbell. "What it means is that everything is held from generation to generation by the person currently in possession of the title. It is a way of getting around the inheritance and tax laws, of keeping the estate, the house, and everything within it . . . Only in special circumstances can an entail be broken, and even then breaking it is never easy or inexpensive."[3]

When Diana came along the following year, her birth, after two girls, an infant death, and years of waiting, was considered a disappointment. Although she was a healthy and beautiful child, Diana carried within her deep feelings of rejection that would haunt her with devastating effects throughout her life.

By the time Frances gave birth to Charles, who would become the ninth and present Earl Spencer, the marriage was on the rocks, but this was the early 1960s when divorce, especially in the upper classes, was unthinkable. Like her grandmother during her marriage to Jim Burke Roche, this Frances felt trapped in a high society nightmare with no exit. To an outsider, Diana's mother had it all—a country manor house with several servants, four children, and access to the highest echelons of London society—but she found this life boring, and her husband dull.

After a raucous row at a party, Frances finally left Viscount Althorp, taking Diana and little Charles with her to a flat in Sloane Square while her other children were at boarding school. With echoes of the demise of her grandparent's marriage, Frances was stunned when Viscount Althorp refused to send the children back to her in London after a Christmas visit, prompting immediate divorce proceedings.

Although she was still a child, Diana was old enough to grasp the negativity between her parents and understand her home life would never be the same. It was around this time that two of her most striking personality traits came to the fore: her stubbornness and her compassion. According to her nanny, Diana would revolt by locking maids in the loo, throw clothes out the windows at Park House, and babble defiantly when shushed. Despite this acting out, Diana demonstrated an adult poise in the way she looked after her little brother. She would tuck him into bed, help him tidy his room, and mother him like one of her dolls.

In April of 1968, Diana got a foreshadowing of her life in the future when her family's personal problems became newspaper copy. A Mrs. Janet Shand Kydd sued her husband Peter for divorce, naming Frances as his mistress. Indeed, Frances had fallen in love with Peter but never expected to lose her children. It was easily assumed in divorces at the time that the mother would receive custodial rights of the children, especially a mother as elegant and highborn as Frances. But luck was not on her side. Not only did Viscount Althorp come out swinging to keep the children at Park House, but he also got Frances's own mother, Ruth, Lady Fermoy, to take his side. Frances was toast.[4]

But why did Lady Fermoy stoop to such a betrayal? Two words: royal connections. Ruth wanted the children raised at Park House, near the royal family, not with her daughter's new wallpaper merchant lover, whom she would later marry, forfeiting the Spencer title to become Mrs. Shand Kydd.

As this family chaos encircled her, Diana escaped into Barbara Cartland novels and her favorite sports—swimming and dancing, her lifelong passions. As Princess of Wales, she would often zigzag the palace pool, or dance onstage to Billy Joel's "Uptown Girl," much to the embarrassment of her husband.

Diana had athletic talents, but her deficiency as a student was seen early on at Riddlesworth Hall, where she was known as a "creature of the heart, not the mind."[5] At a young age, she realized her ability to get—and enjoy—attention, which she achieved through a meticulous care for her clothes, a rarity in a child. When she was obliged to weed the school's garden for misbehavior, which was often, she would do so in a carefully selected hat, something not lost on her headmistress.

From Riddlesworth, Diana headed to her mother's alma mater, West Heath, where her domineering personality, redolent of Fanny's, was remembered by her peers. "She could be really nasty," one classmate recalls. "That look, which everyone now thinks is so sweet. If everyone had been at West Heath, they'd know it's anything but sweet. She used to make the younger girls tremble with that look."[6]

In June 1975, Diana's family life had another upheaval. That summer, her grandfather, Jack, seventh Earl Spencer died, thereby making Diana's father eighth Earl Spencer, and her brother Charles, the new Viscount Althorp. Diana's new home would be Althorp, and she relished the proximity to her Spencer ancestors. She had always had a curiosity and interest in her family, particularly the women in the Spencer line. Diana was surrounded by familial inspiration in the form of portraits of ancestors by Joshua Reynolds, Thomas Gainsborough, and other paintings by Anthony van Dyck and Peter Paul Rubens. She grew up with stories about Spencer heroines Georgiana, Duchess of Devonshire, and Sarah Churchill, Duchess of Marlborough, who became a close confidante of Queen Anne. Of course, there was Winston from the Spencer-Churchill line, but what really captivated Diana were the family matriarchs.

The first Lady Diana Spencer was friendly with Georgiana, Duchess of Devonshire, and became the Duchess of Bedford. She was known as "Dear Little Di," and sadly died at the age of twenty-five. Di was the favorite granddaughter of Sarah, Duchess of Marlborough, who tried to engineer a marriage with Frederick, Prince of Wales, at the time. Throughout her life, Diana would think about these strong and independent antecedents during moments of personal crisis. *Remember you are a Spencer*, she would often tell herself.[7]

The new Lady Diana Spencer was fourteen and had reached her full height of nearly six feet with shoes, an advantage if one is a clotheshorse, but not a dancer. Diana's dreams of pursuing professional ballet were dashed when she shot up like a gazelle. Her new goal, which she would pursue with laser focus, would be to become a princess.

Following in the footsteps of the first Lady Diana Spencer, Lady Sarah Spencer, Diana's older sister, set her cap for Charles, Prince of Wales, the most eligible bachelor in the world in 1977. Sarah, fiery and confident, wanted to succeed where her ancestress had missed the mark—she would bag the big prize and become the next queen of the United Kingdom, fulfilling a centuries-long Spencer ambition. But Diana had a plan of her own, although she had been earmarked for Charles's brother Prince Andrew as he and Diana were closer in age. In fact, Diana had earned the nickname "Duch" as a child in anticipation of her one day becoming a royal duchess. She was also fond of the Disney film *The Aristocats*, whose main feline is named "Duchess." The "Duch" moniker stuck well into Diana's adulthood, even after she became Princess of Wales.

That fall of 1977, Sarah, the new girlfriend of Prince Charles, invited the prince to stay at Althorp and join their hunting party, which included the sixteen-year-old Duch. Duch came face-to-face with her future husband in the Nobottle Field, and the exchange between the two was nothing more than cursory.[8]

The following month, Diana failed her exams, and with no prospect of university ahead of her, was thrust into the world. Thanks to Granny Fanny's trust, she had money of her own and could move to London where she occupied her time with odd jobs, including cleaning for her sister and looking after the baby of an American executive in London. She eventually settled into a job with Young England, a kindergarten where she could indulge her affinity with children. But, like most young women of her time, she had her eyes on the altar and could not get the man she met in the field that day out of her mind. Charles was once a fairytale figure in her girlish imagination, but after meeting him, she made him her target. "She is the sort of person who knows exactly what she wants, then waits until she can get it. If she'd been a wild animal, she'd have made an excellent hunter."[9]

Open season for Diana started when Sarah's romance with Charles fizzled, and Diana's sister, Lady Jane, married Queen Elizabeth's courtier Robert Fellowes. Jane and Robert, as key figures in the royal court, were given a grace-and-favor apartment at Kensington Palace, and would be invited to holiday with the royal family at their Scottish estate, Balmoral. Lady Jane included Sarah and Diana in the stays in Scotland and at the family's Sandringham estate near Park House where they had spent their early years. The girls were only too happy to get away from Althorp as it had been infiltrated by their new stepmother, Raine, whom they despised. Raine, the new Countess Spencer, was the daughter of Diana's favorite novelist Barbara Cartland, who had married her father and took over the running of the Althorp with alacrity during the earl's convalescence from a stroke. Raine, an imperious and highly capable woman, suffered the hostility of the Spencer children for most of her life, but forged an unlikely friendship with Diana in the final years of hers.

Sarah had blown her chances of becoming the Princess of Wales when she, in a rather fiery redhead moment, told a reporter that if the prince proposed she would turn him down. "I would only marry for love," she famously, and stupidly, said. "I don't care if it's a dustman or the king of England." Taking her at her word, Charles moved on to Anna "Whiplash" Wallace, known for her whiplash tongue that she would unleash, all too frequently, in moments of irritation. She, too, proved too much drama for the highly sensitive prince.

Diana, while a failure at school, was an ace in the art of seduction and manipulation. From a distance, she followed the success and ultimate failures of Charles's girlfriends and learned how to appear to be the sweet and unassuming bride he needed. In essence, however, Diana was just as defiant and fiery as Sarah and Alice. Two people, Lord Mountbatten and Diana's grandmother, Lady Fermoy, and one major event helped her entice and bag her prince.

From the time Prince Charles was a young man, he leaned heavily on the advice and friendship of Lord Mountbatten, his beloved "Uncle Dickie." His relationship with his father, Prince Philip, had been strained, and Uncle Dickie became his true confidante, apart from his grandmother, Queen Elizabeth the Queen Mother. Born in 1900, first Earl Mountbatten of Burma was a Royal Navy officer in the First and Second World Wars who had been an honorary member of the royal family. It was he who encouraged Charles to enter the navy himself and vetted potential brides for the future king. One of those possible brides was his granddaughter Amanda Knatchbull, whose friendship with the prince never ignited into anything other than a great friendship. It was Uncle Dickie who encouraged Charles to find a girl as Diana appeared to be: young, virginal, and compliant. Tragically, he never got a chance to see his surrogate son walk down the aisle. On August 27, 1979, his fishing boat off the coast of County Sligo, Ireland, was bombed by the IRA, killing Lord Mountbatten, his grandson, another family member, and a young boy from the crew. The other members of party were seriously injured. Charles, and the world, were gutted.[10]

When Diana was invited to Balmoral the following summer, she went in for the kill. She provided a listening ear to a prince still in the throes of grief. Even at eighteen, she communicated sympathy, something in which Charles revels, despite being one of the most privileged people on earth. "It was just the right tactic to use with Prince Charles, because he really is very soft-hearted," one observer of their courtship explained.[11]

It was sympathy that also drew Charles to his first great love, a match that Uncle Dickie discouraged. Charles had met Camilla Shand in 1975, and was smitten with this woman, who was about the same age, and had a mutual love of English country life. Like Diana, Camilla had no academic achievements or career ambitions. She was from an upper-class family, not as grand as the Spencer clan, but respectable. In her late teens, she had made her debut and set sights on a dashing army officer named Andrew Parker Bowles. Like Diana, when she set her mind on a man, she got him. After her marriage, she and her husband maintained their closeness with the Prince of Wales, who is the godfather of their son, Tom. Those who know Camilla say she is down-to-earth, uncomplicated, and loves nothing more than a walk in the garden with her dogs. This cozy, maternal quality in both women is what Charles found so appealing.

That summer of 1980, Diana was weaving her web. After the trip to Balmoral, she leaned on her grandmother, Ruth, Lady Fermoy, Queen Elizabeth the Queen Mother's lady-in-waiting, to get an invite to Birkhall, the Queen Mother's house on the Balmoral estate. Ruth and Elizabeth were keen to get their grandchildren together, and this would be yet another opportunity for Diana to shine. "Getting Prince Charles was a piece of cake for her," explained a schoolmate. "She has always been extremely manipulative. She had to keep her head and make all the right moves, whether towards or away from him didn't matter. She was pulling the strings, don't kid yourself. And she had help—from her family."[12]

By that autumn, Charles was toast. She was the official girlfriend. "She went after him with single-minded determination," the prince's valet recalled. "In all my years, I've never seen anyone as tricky or determined as she was. She was like a jellyfish. You couldn't see her coming but, my God, the effect of the sting. Looking back, I can see he didn't have a chance."[13]

One of the things Diana deftly concealed from the prince was her indifference to the country. She preferred the city, and loved shopping at

Harrods and going to pop concerts and smart cafés in London. Charles loved his hands in the soil of his garden, stalking deer in Scotland, and fly fishing, which he did with Diana. She, ever the actress, pretended to be in heaven. In truth, she was bored to tears.

It was around this time that Charles bought his pride and joy—Highgrove, his Georgian house in Gloucestshire, not far from the Parker Bowles home. It had nine bedrooms, four receiving rooms, and its gardens have been a passion project for Charles for decades. It was here that he and Diana spent much of their courtship, away from the ever-increasing media interest. Diana, at this point, was an unknown, but that was soon to change.

Both she and her grandmother Frances Burke Roche were in the middle of, and, to some extent, the victims of radically shifting media landscapes that fed on the private lives of fascinating women. In the Gilded Age days of Fanny, she and her fellow socialites were hunted by *Town Topics*, the nineteenth century's version of Gawker, wherein society figures were in perpetual fear of having their dirty linen aired. The paper's owner, Colonel William D'Alton Mann, was a Civil War veteran from the Seventh Michigan Cavalry, which he led in the Battle of Gettysburg. He moved into the newspaper business after his war days but maintained his take-no-prisoners approach in his coverage of high society. He enlisted into his new army butlers, servants, messengers, and all manner of spies to spill the tea on their employers and friends. Soon society coverage went from benign stories of guest lists and table settings to tabloid tawdriness. Colonel Mann shamelessly trafficked in scandal and the miseries of the rich and powerful. Although everybody read *Town Topics*, nobody admitted to it. "I am really doing it for the sake of the country," Mann explained, cloaking his evil deeds with patriotic intentions.

Fanny's divorces were the perfect fodder for Colonel Mann's ink cannons. Whereas some of his columns were merely mean-spirited, such as those reporting that Alva Vanderbilt dyed her hair and wore diamonds to cover her ugly hands, his coverage of marriages going bust, illegitimate children, and family feuds spared no nasty detail. This media feeding frenzy nearly brought Fanny to the brink and foreshadowed the culture of tabloid journalism to come.[14]

So too did her great-granddaughter Diana Spencer fall under the microscope of the modern mudslinger: *Private Eye*, the subject of numerous lawsuits for its scandal-mongering and ferocious reporting of public figures since its founding in 1961. By the early 1980s, Prince Charles and his quest to find a bride offered *Private Eye* readers the ingredients for the perfect story: privilege, sex, and glamour. It had, for example, made the claim that Anna Wallace, the prince's former flame had, to put it decorously, a social disease. Now, the fresh-faced Diana was the new prey. As she dashed around London, photographers and reporters clamored for the latest juicy morsel about her past, or lack thereof. In the post–sexual revolution era, it was deemed impossible for a nineteen-year-old to be a virgin. Thus, Fleet Street sleaze fueled a grotesque interest in Diana's sexual history.

When stories hit the papers of a possible assignation with Charles on the royal train, Frances Shand Kydd, demonstrating the Fermoy Irish spirit, came out in robust defense of her daughter. "May I ask the editors of Fleet Street," Frances wrote in a letter published in *The Times*, "whether they consider it necessary or fair to harass my daughter daily, from dawn until well after dusk? Is it fair to ask any human being, regardless of circumstances to be treated this way?" Her mother's plea fell on deaf ears. As 1980 wore on, so too did the public fascination with Diana accelerate. This media storm put pressure on Charles. If he dragged his feet, her reputation would continue to be trampled by the gutter press.[15]

Lord Fermoy, perhaps encouraged by Frances, defended his niece's honor by telling royal reporter James Whitaker that Diana had never had a lover. While the frank comment was regarded as vulgar by some, it had the desired effect of shutting down the scuttlebutt of Diana's suitability as a bride.

In the end, the press both hurt and helped Diana. This would be the constant for the rest of her life: a love-hate relationship with the media, which simultaneously haunted and canonized her. This media pressure, along with the urging of his family, and an increasingly impatient public, resulted in the announcement of her engagement to the Prince of Wales on February 24, 1981. That winter day, she walked arm in arm with the man of her dreams sporting a suit picked out at Harrods by Frances, and a dazzling sapphire and diamond engagement ring that became a permanent part of her collection. It would later be given to the current Princess of Wales by William when they were engaged in 2010.

As Lord Fermoy phoned "the Americans" at Elm Court, few in the media were aware of Lady Diana's relatives across the pond, and even fewer gave them any column inches. *The Washington Post*'s Henry Mitchell published a pre-wedding revelation that she was eligible to join the Daughters of the American Revolution, a slightly catty dig at her new in-laws. "Now the princess's essential American connection is her great-great-grandfather, Frank Work, of Chillicothe, Ohio and later of New York; and his wife, Ellen Wood Work. Now this Mrs. Work was a daughter of John Wood of Shepardstown, W. Va., and Ellen Strong of Philadelphia," Mitchell wrote. "Ellen Strong—we are about to hit pay dirt here—was the daughter of Joseph Strong of Coventry, Conn., and Rebecca Young of Philadelphia. This Mr. Strong, who was a graduate of Yale in 1788, himself had 25 percent well-documented forbears who lived in New England in the period between 1623 and 1650."[16]

Americans were up at the crack of dawn on the morning of July 29, 1981, to watch Diana, having shed puppy fat and whittled her waist to nothingness, sail down the aisle, a vision of bridal perfection. Her gown was so voluminous and her train so dramatic that it could be seen from far away by the throngs of well-wishers lining the streets of London, among them her American cousin, Abby Van Pelt, who got a glimpse of Diana that day. Another woman watching Diana come down the aisle was

Camilla Parker Bowles, who, thanks to her friendship with the Prince of Wales, was seated inside St. Paul's. Distrustful of Camilla from the start, Diana did manage to have her excluded from the wedding breakfast.

Holding her veil in place was the Spencer Tiara, strategically chosen to represent the powerful Spencer dynasty. Diana could have had her pick of jewels, but she stuck with her family, of whom she was always proud—the family of Georgiana, Winston, and now the most famous woman on earth. In Diana, the Spencer family had achieved their goal of being as close to the throne as possible and producing a royal bloodline. For the Burke Roche family, Diana carried with them the unknown story of their matriarch Frances. Even Frank Work, for all his Anglophobia, would have gotten a kick out of seeing Diana Walk down the aisle of St. Paul's, light years away from his dusty streets in Chillicothe. Frank's great-great-granddaughter was now Her Royal Highness The Princess of Wales, the future queen of the United Kingdom.

Diana was the first Princess of Wales since Princess May of Teck assumed the title in 1910. This gave Diana the perfect canvass to create an image of modern royalty. This she did in a magical way, leaning on fashion editors to help her select a wardrobe, hairstyle, and exquisite jewelry collection that was simultaneously regal and relatable.

The public could not get enough of the new bride and princess as she stooped down to talk to small children or sat at the bedside of the elderly with a charisma and naturalness that the other members of the royal family did not emanate as readily. While out on her first engagements, she would refuse an umbrella if the people she was greeting were getting soaked. This connection with the man on the street coupled with her youth and beauty was manna from heaven for newspapers.

"All the Spencers have strong personalities," said Barbara Cartland, the author and the mother of Diana's stepmother, Raine, Countess Spencer. "Diana has magnetism. Everywhere she goes people find that irresistible attraction which makes them want to know her, and where women are concerned, copy her."[17]

Diana felt the love of an adoring public, but her marriage was doomed from the start. In fact, the honeymoon stage of her union did not make it past the honeymoon. The images of the couple relaxed and smiling in Scotland were mere façades to maintain the national enthusiasm. Behind closed doors, it soon became clear to Charles that the girl of his engagement and the woman he married were two different people. His new wife hated the country, was uninterested in any books other than ones written by Danielle Steel, and, most troubling, was given to wild mood swings and volcanic outbursts. Diana's troubled childhood and eating disorders, provoked by the manic media attention, imploded her personality.

While Charles escaped to Highgrove, Diana preferred the more urban environs of Kensington Palace, which would be her home base for the rest of her life, even after her eventual divorce. The couple and their families hoped that the strain of the media interest would wane, and Charles and Diana would ultimately settle into domestic bliss, and Diana's personal problems would fade as she matured.

A major ray of hope in this direction appeared in the fall of 1981, just a few months after the wedding, when the palace announced that the Princess of Wales was expecting a baby. What should have been the happiest time of Diana's life turned out to be the darkest. According to her biographer Andrew Morton and Diana herself, she was in the throes of bulimia—overeating several times a day and then vomiting. This had the desired effect of keeping the princess as slim as she was on her wedding day, but wreaked havoc on her already fragile psyche.

Although Diana inherited many gifts from Frances Burke Roche, she also inherited many burdens, and family mental illness was one of them. Fanny, her son Francis, and Edmund, the fifth Lord Fermoy, Maurice's son, would all suffer from depression. "A fearful scene of loneliness and depression comes to all of us at times," Fanny wrote in a letter to Francis in 1913, presumably to ease him out of a blue period.[18] In 1984, Edmund would succumb to suicide,[19] and in 2025, Rosie Roche, at the tender age of twenty, also took her own life. The fact that Rosie and Edmund both died by gunshot wounds, after long battles with depression, make their deaths all the more tragic in their familial connection.[20]

In reading Fanny's diaries, the volatility of her moods is strikingly like those Diana would experience. From the Gotham Hotel in January 1910, Fanny writes, "At 7:00 awake and wept bitter tears of vexation, humiliation, retrospection chiefly over my martyrdom."[21]

By the time of William's birth in the summer of 1982, Diana, already miserable with postpartum depression, believed Charles was in love with Camilla Parker Bowles. Her feelings of worthlessness, felt as an unwanted child at Park House, came roaring back and were as acute as her physical exhaustion. She later admitted to what psychologists call "cutting"—using sharp objects to slash the arms or legs in a desperate cry for help.

"When no one listens to you, or you feel no one is listening to you, all sorts of things start to happen," Diana later recounted in her 1995 Martin Bashir interview. "You have so much pain inside yourself, that you try to hurt yourself on the outside, but it's the wrong attention you are looking for."[22]

"I feel dull. Stupid. Neuralgic. A little sad and down. A little lonely! I pride myself upon my self-control and self-sufficiency and yet," wrote Fanny. "My life is so fearful that I never can contemplate it from any point of view in anything but utter discouragement and despair." While strolling through the daffodils in April of 1906, Fanny lamented, "It was all so lovely, so full of spring promise. I walked on trying to stifle the sorrow in my heart. Why, why always—all through life these sorrows, privations, and miseries. I ask so little! . . . It has all narrowed down to such a little life."

Another diary entry: "Will there ever be better days for me, I wonder? I do not mean pleasant, amusing days. Those belong to youth. But will I ever be able to sleep without dread and shuddering? Can I ever lay my head on the pillow without apprehension, of what the morrow may bring?"[23]

For Diana's part, being an overnight global superstar did nothing to improve her inner turmoil, but the eager crowds she encountered in her public life lifted her spirits. As the royal couple embarked on their international tours, with Prince William in tow, her bulimia was out of control. Images of Diana in public, looking emaciated, caused alarm. But Diana later said that being with people gave her "healing." As Charles and Diana did their "walkabouts" in Australia, for example, fans lining the streets screamed her name and shoved each other out of the way to get a royal handshake. The love she received from the crowds was a welcome substitute for the lack of love in her marriage. Diana, like Fanny, was a social creature and fed off the excitement. "It is the mania for being sociable, entertaining," Fanny called it.[24] Prime Minister Tony Blair would eventually style Diana "The People's Princess" for the warmth she gave and received from people from all walks of life.

Despite the deepening cracks in their new marriage, Charles was doing his best to keep the peace at home. Knowing Diana's love of jewelry, he gave her a diamond necklace with a heart centerpiece shortly after William's birth. In the era of *Dynasty*, big hair, shoulder pads, and fabulous jewels were in vogue, and nobody personified this "more is more" aesthetic than Diana, Princess of Wales, with the possible exceptions of Joan Collins and Ivana Trump. Her pearl choker with a large sapphire became a signature piece, as did her emerald choker with matching earrings.

Her selection of tiaras, including Queen Mary's Lover's Knot Tiara now worn by her daughter-in-law Catherine, Princess of Wales, created the "Dynasty Di" of the magazine covers. This love of, and escape into fashion and jewelry was a favorite Fanny indulgence, especially during her lonelier moments. "Bought very expensive gem piece and pendant," Fanny recorded in her diary. "I bought both pieces in rubies to wear together. Dealers turned and complimented me saying ruby alone worth what I paid for the whole."[25] Today, many of Fanny's jewels are at Elm Court, her Newport home, in the possession of her descendant Guy Van

Pelt, whose twin daughters may one day wear Fanny's rubies. Diana's other daughter-in-law Meghan, Duchess of Sussex, frequently is seen in Diana's Cartier watch and wore her aquamarine cocktail ring to her wedding night party.

It was in 1985 that Diana made her first trip to the United States and brought the full "Dynasty Di" effect with her. Wearing an off-the-shoulder midnight blue gown, she greeted President and Nancy Reagan on the steps of the White House. Her smile and sapphire choker sparkled for the press corps, hungry for photos of the royal couple, as they were decades earlier when King George VI and Queen Elizabeth came to Washington. Mrs. Reagan, a former actress and Hollywood insider, knew of Diana's fondness for dancing and pop music, so she arranged a dance between Diana and John Travolta celebrated in an iconic White House photograph. While in Washington, Charles and Diana also visited the National Cathedral and National Gallery of Art. (Perhaps if Diana's American lineage had been better known, a stop in Newport or Coventry could have been arranged.)

Diana returned to the United States four years later when she came to New York on her first solo visit to America for the debut of the Welsh National Opera's performance at the Brooklyn Academy of Music. Several hundred attendees, including future President Donald Trump and Bianca Jagger, paid $1,000 a head for the performance and dinner where Diana dazzled in a white gown with matching bolero jacket.[26] While in New York, Diana did her bit for the British economy by promoting British teddy bears at FAO Schwarz, but her most daring stop was at Harlem Hospital. Two years earlier, Diana surprised the world when she used her fame to reach out to the AIDS community in England as one of the first people in public life to be seen shaking hands with and embracing AIDS patients during a time when the disease and homosexuality were studiously ignored by polite society. Diana's handshakes without gloves broke through stigmas and ignorance that were shamefully prevalent.

Harlem Hospital was an understaffed and underserved community center that catered to children born with AIDS and cocaine addiction. Before the royal visit, hospital staff, already hard-pressed to attend to their patients, were in a frenzy to get ready. The peeling paint and grimy floors were spiffed up in anticipation. The hospital's communications team briefed everyone on how to address the princess. "No need to bow or curtsy if you are an American," was the standard line. Hospital volunteer Jana Haimsohn said, "What these kids really need is attention. If the publicity around Princess Diana's visit does something . . . good." Haimsohn missed meeting Diana because she sadly had to attend the funeral of a seven-month-old baby who had died of AIDS just days earlier, which gave all the more weight and urgency to the attention Diana's visit would garner.[27]

Once at the hospital, Diana went one step beyond a handshake this time: she picked up and cuddled a young boy with AIDS in a gesture "that probably does more in eliminating people's inappropriate fears about associating with people with AIDS than any education program we could put together," explained Charles Windsor, the hospital's executive director. The news of Diana's cuddle went around the world, and by the time Windsor went through his mail for the week he found a letter from the State of New York saying that he would be getting $250,000 for pediatric AIDS programs.[28]

As a new decade dawned, and Diana moved into her thirties, she was leaving her Dynasty Di days behind her and realizing the global power she wielded to truly make a difference. Just as her Spencer ancestress Georgiana, Duchess of Devonshire, had grasped her political agency, she, too, saw a chapter of hope and fulfillment. With that visit to Harlem, Diana could almost hear the words coming from Fanny. "Do Good. Look up. Fix your eyes upon the real, the good, the true! Live for those things which bring you peace and serenity."[29]

In November 1991, she was at the bedside of Michael Kelly at the Mildmay Mission Hospital in East London. "Now I am known as a man with AIDS, I'm worried someone might throw a brick through my window," he told her. "Unfortunately, you have to live with their ignorance," she replied.[30]

In the Presence of the Princess of Wales became the most sought-after words on a charity fundraising appeal or gala invitation. Diana's star power and openness to new and unconventional causes made her the number one charity worker in the world. "Mother Teresa in a tiara," she was dubbed by cynical observers. With her marriage over in all but name, Diana redefined herself, despite her critics. "I am a humanitarian figure. I always have been and I always will be, "she said flatly.[31]

"Whether narcissism and public approbation do play a part in Diana's motivation, only she can say for sure," royal author Lady Colin Campbell observed in the early 1990s. "But what is indisputable is that she is as committed to her work when the press and television cameras go away as when they are in evidence."[32] And her impact, as evidenced by the aftermath of the Harlem Hospital visit, was indisputable.

As she gained strength from the public and her newfound sense of mission, Diana was beginning to put her eating disorders and emotional troubles behind her. Her charity work had helped her find a voice, and she wanted the world to hear it. She went back to Coleherne Court, metaphorically, as she looked for a way to get her message out. Two of her closest friends from her Coleherne Court days, Carolyn Bartholomew and James Colthurst, were two of her best confidantes. They had heard it all: the bulimia, the cries for help, the hopeless unravelling of her marriage, but they didn't know how to help her. In one of her more dire moments, she told Colthurst she wanted to stand in the middle of Kensington High Street and scream her litany of woes. "As your enemies think you are mad," he reminded her, "that course of action would hardly strengthen your position."[33]

Colthurst had another course of action in mind, one that would reveal her story but also scandalize the royal family. Just as Fanny turned to her diary to vent her real (and perceived) miseries, Diana found an outlet in

Andrew Morton, a royal correspondent who had been writing about her for years. "While I had met Diana at numerous cocktail parties where the royal couple chatted to the media, exchanges had normally been bright, light, and trite, usually about my loud ties," Morton recalled.[34]

Colthurst, however, had developed a much friendlier relationship with Morton, the two often playing tennis and lunching together. With Diana's blessing, Colthurst mooted the idea of Morton writing a book on the Princess of Wales with the participation of the princess herself to expose her life—warts and all. Because Morton was a well-known figure to palace courtiers, he could not interview Diana at Kensington Palace, so the three hatched a plan to have the princess record answers to Morton's questions after which the tapes would be handed off to Morton by Colthurst.

That summer of 1992, *Diana: Her True Story* was published, sending booksellers around the world into a frenzy. Readers were agog at the book's revelations: Diana, the fairy-tale princess, was a suicidal mess, whose glamorous façade hid an entrapment in a cold and unloving royal system. More shocking was the suspicion, later confirmed, that Morton's sources were not only Diana's friends and relations, but Diana herself. The royal family's long held tradition of "never complain, never explain" had been broached in the most egregious way. Diana had certainly galvanized the public—especially women—to sympathize with her, but in the process, she had irretrievably broken any attempt to put her marriage or her relationship with her in-laws back on track.

Also in 1992, Diana's father, eighth Earl Spencer, died, knowing full well the breakdown of Diana's marriage, and her intention to oublicize it in the Morton book. "It is a chance for my own self to surface a little rather than be lost in the system. I rather see it as a lifebelt against being drowned and it is terribly important to me," she wrote to him.[35]

While the book flew off the shelves in America, it was banned at Harrods in London and at mainstream supermarkets like Tesco for its sensational claims. Over two hundred years after America split from the royal family, they still captivated us, and, perhaps in our appetite for royal dirt, we took pleasure in the republican fervor it was stoking. Magazines like *People* discovered that any cover of Diana or any royal story was guaranteed to go gangbusters in sales. Diana, even in death, has remained *People*'s most popular cover girl, a testament to the enduring fascination Americans have for royalty.

November 1992 was a watershed moment for the world: Everything was changing. Bill Clinton was elected president of the United States, upending twelve years of Republican control of the White House. Across the Atlantic, the final nail was falling into a deeply weakened monarchy. Prince Andrew and his wife, Sarah, the Duchess of York were well on their way to divorce, while Princess Anne, the queen's only daughter, had a divorce of her own from Mark Phillips that had been finalized in the spring. The papers should have been reporting on the good works and public projects of the royals, especially Anne; instead, the queen's subjects read one tawdry headline after another. Far from being taxpayer-funded public servants, the queen's children were widely regarded as jokes. It seemed her corgis were the only ones with good public images.

When the Prince and Princess of Wales stepped off the plane in Seoul for their tour of Korea, their body language was palpably fraught. Diana, paradoxically, glittered in pearls and diamonds, but her face was etched with sorrow. On December 9, 1992, the news the world had anticipated, but still regretted hearing, was announced: The Prince and Princess of Wales were separating. It was finally official. In an apt metaphor for what Queen Elizabeth called her "annus horribilis," Windsor Castle, a home for the royal family for centuries, went up in flames. Indeed, the queen, in her deadpan humor, would reflect "1992 is not a year on which I shall look back with undiluted pleasure."[36]

With her separation official, and her life ahead of her uncertain, Diana turned to her touchstone—Althorp—where she could take solace in the spiritual and physical proximity of her Spencer ancestors. In April of 1993, her brother, then the ninth and current Earl Spencer, offered her the use of Althorp's Garden House at a rental price of $12,000 a year, including a cleaner and gardener. Diana was planning to redecorate and move in, making the Garden House her country home, when Lord Spencer withdrew his offer, saying that the press and security arrangements would be too troublesome. This caused a fracture in the brother-sister relationship, causing Lord Spencer to request Diana's return of the Spencer Tiara she had had in her possession since wearing it on her wedding day in 1981.[37]

Diana also sought solace with the House of Fermoy. Her grandmother Ruth, Lady Fermoy, then eighty-five, but still rapier sharp, sided with Prince Charles, and upbraided Diana for her behavior, effectively blaming her for the separation. Diana, still hanging on to bitter memories from her parent's divorce, had never forgotten Lady Fermoy's betrayal of her mother in the Spencer custody hearings. "My mother and grandmother never got on. They clashed violently. My grandmother tries to lacerate me in any way she can. She feeds the royal family with hideous comment about my mother running away and leaving the children," Diana said. Indeed, the Archbishop of Canterbury, Robert Runcie, confirmed that Lady Fermoy regarded Diana "as an actress, a schemer." But finally, before Lady Fermoy's death in July 1993, Diana had a heart-to-heart with her grandmother, and, while Lady Fermoy may not have told Diana what she wanted to hear, at least the cold war between them was thawed.[38]

Diana also turned to her own mother, Frances Shand Kydd, during this pivotal time, to better understand her past as a reflection on her present. Then living in a remote part of Scotland, the twice-divorced Frances was a beloved "Granny Frances" to Diana's sons, although her relationship with Diana was as shaky as her relationship with Ruth. In 1996, Frances would be arrested for drunken driving, and the following year gave an interview to *Hello!*, which Diana counted as the final straw. Frances would eventually convert to Catholicism and dedicate her life to Catholic charities, but at the time of Diana's death, they were not on speaking terms. Frances died in 2004, and Diana's sons represented her at their Granny's funeral.[39]

Diana always maintained a respectful, but not warm, relationship with the ultimate matriarch in her life, Queen Elizabeth. "I just long to hug my mother-in-law and tell her how deeply I understand what goes on inside her. I understand the isolation, misconception, and lies that surround her and feel very strongly her disappointment and confusion," Diana wrote in her own diary. Despite Diana's rebel bent and American roots, she remained a monarchist at heart and was proud of the fact that her son would one day be king. Despite the War of Waleses throughout the 1980s and 1990s, Diana never intended to harm the monarchy, nor did she try to estrange her children from the royal fold.[40]

Although she was as her brother would later describe her "a very British girl," Diana had a love affair with the United States that would endure for the remaining years of her young life. During her marriage, her trips to the White House and New York had been highlights of her tenure as Princess of Wales. Now as a separated woman—and freelance princess—she could travel to the United States as often as she wished. Maybe it was the warmth and affection she received from the American public, or maybe on a subconscious level, she was pulled like a magnet toward the land of her ancestors.

Her friendship with Lucia Flecha de Lima, the wife of a diplomat, gave her an excuse to visit Washington, and the Manhattan gala circuit, always angling for a Diana appearance, allowed her to visit New York where she stayed at her beloved Carlyle Hotel on East 76th Street. In 1995, at the Council of Fashion Designers, Diana proved to the world that she was her own woman by wearing a daringly backless dress, something that would have been forbidden as a royal. While at the Carlyle, Diana amazingly ended up in the same elevator as Michael Jackson and Steve Jobs. When the silence in the lift became awkward, Diana broke into a girlish rendition of "Beat It."

America brought out the best of Diana: the charming, the youthful, and the humanitarian. The neurotic, the paranoid, and the weak part of her character she could leave behind in England. Ironically, on July 4, 1994, at Spencer House, which had been sold by Diana's grandfather Jack to Lord Rothschild, she celebrated Independence Day with American billionaire Teddy Forstmann, with whom she developed one of her post-Charles friendships. Forstmann helped her widen her growing rolodex of influential Americans, such as those she met through him on Martha's Vineyard and at a dinner in Georgetown at the home of *Washington Post* publisher Katharine Graham.[41]

While Diana played the field as a newly single woman, Charles remained true to his first love, Camilla Parker Bowles. In June 1994, perhaps in response to *Diana: Her True Story*, Charles gave a television interview in which he confirmed his friendship with Camilla. In a rare moment of brutal openness, Charles, when pressed by the interview, said he had tried to remain faithful to his marriage until it was "irretrievably broken down, us both having tried." This statement, tantamount to admitting adultery to the world, stunned audiences, who tuned in in their millions.[42] Diana, ever canny, turned up at a gala event the same night in a Christina Stambolian dress with a slit up her thigh, revealing her long legs in black stockings. The newspaper headlines juxtaposed a pensive-looking Charles with a dazzling image of Diana. The message was clear: Game. Set. Match. Diana. The black frock has a life of its own, known to royal watchers as "the revenge dress."

Diana was back in America in early 1995, taking a coach class ticket from Minneapolis to Denver under the pseudonym "Heather Rood" for a ski holiday in Vail. It was the beginning of the year, and she wanted to be in what she called "a great country. It symbolizes hope and the promise of better things to come."[43] She had befriended Colin Powell and Hillary Clinton, whom she admired but deemed "too ambitious." She would later be Mrs. Clinton's guest at a luncheon during which Clinton joked it was "the nicest British invasion the White House had ever had."[44] Henry

Kissinger, always ready to dine with a beautiful woman, presented Diana with a special award at the United Cerebral Palsy Foundation's gala where he called her "a luminous personality as a member of the royal family, but we are honoring the princess in her own right," adding that Diana "aligned herself with the ill, the suffering, and the downtrodden."[45] There were rumors afloat that the ultimate New Yorker, Donald Trump, who had met the princess on her previous trip to the Big Apple when she was married to Charles, was in hot pursuit of the post-divorced Diana, but in an interview in 2017, President Trump denied any relationship. "She was lovely. I liked her and respected her," but flatly refuted claims they were an item.[46]

Diana was making inroads in her own country, too, looking to create a global ambassador role for herself. Tony Blair, in 1994, was a senior Labour Party member of Parliament, introduced to Diana by mutual friends. They had conversations about her future role for Britain before his election as prime minister in 1997. Diana's efforts to officially represent the British government were effectively blocked by the royal family, which gives more weight to the theory that she would have decamped to America eventually.[47]

Diana's coziness with journalists was generally an advantage for her, especially as she navigated her public image after her separation. However, her deception by the BBC reporter Martin Bashir led to yet another bombshell scandal in her life, and one of the sleaziest examples of journalistic malpractice. Bashir played on Diana's paranoia by telling her and her brother, Earl Spencer, with whom she had reconciled and who was now one of her media advisers, that her apartment and telephone calls were being surveilled by British security services. Bashir went so far as to forge documents and bank statements to further his claims, and Diana fell easily into his unscrupulous hands.

Convinced that her husband and the British government were conspiring to spy on and even kill her, she granted Bashir a tell-all interview to come out swinging against them. On Guy Fawkes Night, the

British commemoration of the 1605 attempt by Catholics to blow up the Houses of Parliament and assassinate King James I, Diana's infamous *Panorama* interview was recorded in secret at Kensington Palace. Two weeks later the broadcast blew up the airwaves with some twenty-three million people tuning in. With a feminist perspective, she explained the opposition to her as caused by "confusion and fear . . . I think that every strong woman in history has had to walk down a similar path." One of the most stunning utterances of the princess is when she doubted Charles's readiness to be king and sadly predicted that she would never be queen. She, did, however, say she would be just as happy as "queen of people's hearts," because as she put it, "someone's got to go out there and love people and show it."[48]

The fallout from the interview was seismic. Within weeks of the broadcast, the queen suggested that divorce proceedings commence. After years of public warfare and mudslinging, with plenty of blame to go around on both sides, the Prince and Princess of Wales, the future king and queen, were done. By August of 1996, Diana received a lump sum payment of £17 million, kept her apartment at Kensington Palace, but lost the style "Her Royal Highness." Thereafter, she would be known simply as "Diana, Princess of Wales," a comedown that Diana bitterly resented.[49] The Spencer clan, always sensitive to their proximity to power, took it badly too. When Lord Spencer delivered his eulogy to Diana in 1997, he pointedly rubbed it in. "She needed no royal title to continue to generate her particular brand of magic."[50] The fact that he said this in the presence of the queen made it even more stinging. A young Prince William reportedly told Diana, "Don't worry, Mummy. I will give it (the HRH) back to you one day, when I am king."[51]

Speaking to her brother-in-law Sir Robert Fellowes, the queen's private secretary, said she viewed the divorce as "the beginning of a new chapter." A new chapter as a renegade, much like her American forbears, unfettered by royal dictates, but still respectful of the institution as it was the future of her son, the heir to the throne. When she asked a former driver for Princess Anne to join her new drastically slimmed-down staff, her words summarized this new chapter. "Come and join the rebels," she beckoned him.[52]

This new chapter in Diana's drama needed editing, and she yet again turned to William for advice. Displaying a maturity well beyond his teenaged years, he suggested she clean out her closets to get rid of dresses from her past, effectively doing a clean sweep of her royal wardrobe, and metaphorically, purging her royal life. Seventy-nine of these dresses were earmarked for discarding, including the gown she wore to the White House in 1985. Diana flew to the city she had come to call her second home—New York—the stomping grounds of Fanny Work. There, the dress collection was auctioned at Christie's, bringing in $5.7 million for the Royal Marsden Hospital and its specialized AIDS treatment centers.[53]

In photographs from the auction's receptions, the Princess of Wales glows with a renewed life force. "It had been a long road," her biographer Andrew Morton reflected of this transitional time for her. "For the first time since she was a teenager sharing a bachelor apartment with three girlfriends, the princess was free to be herself . . . She had proved to the world that it was possible to combine glamour with integrity, happiness with compassion, without the necessity of sacrificing her life on the altar of duty and propriety."

In the last year of her life, she spent less and less time in England as her commitments to charities and the royal family were significantly scaled back. Morton estimates that she made twenty overseas trips and only spent twelve weeks at Kensington Palace between her divorce in August 1996 and her death almost exactly a year later. While New York and Washington were frequently on her calendar, in the summer of 1996, Diana took her first trip to the American heartland for a three-day trip to Chicago, focusing on cancer research programs. At a gala dinner at the Field Museum, she wowed Chicagoans in a purple Versace dress, and danced with another media admirer—the late Phil Donahue. The *Chicago*

Tribune, under the headline DI HARD 4: THE TAKING OF CHICAGO, noted that "usually sane sensible people seemed to swoon" in her presence, and "the ones who touched Diana's hand looked like they needed CPR."[54]

Back in Washington, and back in purple—this time a lavender suit, at the side of Elizabeth Dole, then the head of the American Red Cross, for a press conference on the international campaign to ban land mines, a major cause for the princess. In the last months of her life, juxtaposed with images of her at glittering galas, would be footage of her casually dressed cuddling African children whose limbs had been blown off due to the scourge of these weapons of war. Diana's embrace of this cause is credited with bringing more public support to the Ottawa Treaty that has eliminated most of the world's anti-personnel landmines. The treaty has been signed by 164 countries, with the United States being a notable exception.

In 1997, riding high on her success as an international humanitarian, Diana looked like another high society New Yorker, Jackie Onassis. Thanks to the unabashed luxury offered by her new boyfriend, Dodi Al Fayed, the playboy son of Harrods owner Mohamed Al Fayed, Diana stretched languidly on the deck of the Al Fayed yacht, the *Jonikal,* as photographers clicked away with long-lens cameras. The photos were redolent of Jackie's post-assassination days on the yacht of Aristotle Onassis.

Diana had been the guest of the Al Fayed family during that fateful summer, cruising the Mediterranean, occasionally coming ashore for shopping sprees, and, throwing caution to the wind, kissing passionately under the sun. A GUY FOR DI, ran the *People* headline, showing a beaming Diana on the cover, yet again. Meanwhile in cold and gloomy Britain, Prince Charles, as in love with Camilla as ever, planned a fiftieth birthday party for her at Highgrove. Photos of Diana in a leopard-print swimsuit frolicking in the ocean naturally knocked poor Camilla off the tabloids.

Diana and Dodi had a celebration of their own. They lifted their vintage champagne glasses on August 28, 1997, and toasted to the first anniversary of Diana's divorce. According to many observers, the couple, who had just begun their courtship that summer, were deeply in love, and were planning to marry. Father Frank Gelli, a Church of England priest, began a friendship with the Princess of Wales after he wrote her a letter of support in the early 1990s. Over time, she relied on his spiritual guidance as she navigated various relationships and nurtured her "spiritual yearning," as he describes it. That summer of 1997, she called him from the *Jonikal* to catch up. It would be the last time he talked to her. Father Gelli recalls the obvious affection between Dodi and Diana when Diana brought her boyfriend to meet her priest in the final weeks of her life. The fact that she introduced her beau to her priest at all says this was no summer fling, but a serious relationship. Father Gelli also remembers Dodi's fondness for America, where the couple would have likely spent most of their time.[55]

Dodi had bought a "Tell Me Yes" ring from the Alberto Repossi's shop in Monaco. Their plan was to use the Al Fayed money to build a charitable foundation focusing on Diana's causes—cancer, AIDS, land-mines, and women's issues. Their home base would be Julie Andrews's former home in Los Angeles, which Dodi had purchased for $7 million at the time.[56]

While the final days and hours of their lives have been as hotly debated and investigated as Lincoln's assassination, what is certain is that Diana was ever closer to making a new home in the land of her American family. "She loved Americans and loved America," explained her friend Richard Greene. "She felt a sense of freedom in America and was thinking, Why not America? The whole of life was opening up for her."[57] Her friend David Puttnam agreed with Greene that her life would have ended up on American shores. She and Puttnam had serious talks about her purchase of a home on Martha's Vineyard, where she had holidayed with great pleasure.[58]

On August 30, Diana and Dodi made one final stop in Paris before Diana was scheduled to continue home to London. She had become increasingly irritated by the paparazzi swarming around them as they jet-setted around southern Europe and was ready to get home to see her boys. After having her hair styled in the Ritz's salon, she and Dodi tried to dine in the hotel, but were unnerved by the stares of curious fellow diners. They sneaked out the back entrance of the hotel with Dodi's apartment as their destination. Moments before their departure, their driver Henri Paul had soothed his own nerves with a drink (or several) at the hotel's bar. The Mercedes sped off like a bullet into the Paris night, eerily quiet at the end of summer. As paparazzi chased the car relentlessly, Dodi shouted to Paul to accelerate.

At the entrance to the tunnel at the Pont de l'Alma bridge, Paul lost control of the car, sending it crashing into the thirteenth pillar. In a flash, Diana's American dream hit a wall, and her new chapter came to a screeching halt.

18

AMERICAN CROWN

Autumn is making a welcome descent into Manhattan. It is late September 2023, and New Yorkers, always frenetic, are up for an early morning jog in Central Park, not far from the streets Frank and Fanny Work's carriages strolled down and Diana, Princess of Wales, dazzled on her Big Apple excursions. As the joggers pounded the pavement, they likely did not notice the tall man with a British accent among them.

"I decided to join the hordes of New Yorkers doing their morning routine," William, Prince of Wales explained onstage at the Earthshot Prize Innovation Summit later in the day at the Plaza Hotel. "It was wonderful waking up in New York on a sunny morning rather than the rain we had yesterday. It was beautiful getting some fresh air this morning."[1]

The Earthshot Prize Innovation Summit was a project he started in 2020 to gather and award innovators in climate activism and environmental awareness, causes dear to his heart thanks to his father and grandfather's ministrations. The late Prince Philip and King Charles are known for their fervent stewardship of the natural world. Funnily enough, the name of the awards was inspired by an American: President Kennedy, whose 1962 "moonshot" speech challenged the country to send a man to the moon by the end of the decade. William's scheme, worth some 50 million pounds, awards five one-million-pound prizes to climate warriors each year through 2030.

"Growing up in my family gives you a certain sense of history," William explained. "I'm simply the latest in a line that can be traced back generations." Pointing to a tree on the Windsor Castle estate, he said, "This is close to Windsor Castle, which has been home to my family for over 900 years; thirty-nine monarchs have lived here and enjoyed these beautiful surroundings."[2] While William was in New York, he could have said the same thing about his American family.

It had been ten years since William had been in Manhattan, but standing next to former Mayor Michael Bloomberg that fall day he was reminded how popular he remained. "The prince has clearly won over Americans of all stripes, "Bloomberg said. "That is no small feat. America has not seen that kind of bipartisan consensus since 1776. But this time we're all drinking to the king's health."[3]

Just a year before William had assumed the title Prince of Wales and was living proof of the Shakespearean line "uneasy lies the head that wears a crown" from *Henry IV*, part 2. With the late Queen Elizabeth in dire health, William was seen driving family members, including Andrew, the now-former Duke of York; Sophie, Countess of Wessex; and Edward, Earl of Wessex, to Balmoral to pay their final respects to his grandmother, Her Majesty Queen Elizabeth II, who was in her final hours. The queen, after ninety-six years and seven decades on the throne, finally left the world on September 8, 2022. The image of William behind the wheel transporting his family down the winding Scottish roads was the perfect metaphor for his role as family leader and new global statesman: a steady hand on a bumpy ride. His uncle Prince Andrew had been banished from public duties thanks to his connection to sex trafficker Jeffrey Epstein, and as the press was ran roughshod over the royal family for this scandal, William's estrangement from his brother, Prince Harry, also continued to dominate the headlines. And yet it got worse.[4]

Not even a year into his reign, his father King Charles III was diagnosed with cancer in January 2024 only emerging on Easter Sunday, looking old and frail on his way into church services in Windsor. As

William looked at these images of his "Papa," he must have felt the weight of the crown much earlier than he ever expected. As the world reeled from the king's news, his wife Catherine, Princess of Wales, also announced she was undergoing "abdominal surgery" and would remain at home recuperating, leaving her public and the always ravenous Fleet Street journalists hungry for unseemly details.

From January 2024 until late March the world seemed to be engaged in two conversational parlor games: "Where's Kate?" and "What's wrong with Kate?" The online trolls had a field day in indecent chatter posting memes about Catherine's corpse, and Stephen Colbert brazenly made punchlines about infidelity in the Wales's marriage. (Colbert has since issued an apology, but that wasn't enough to stop a slander action from the married woman he accused of adultery with William).

Just as "Kate Watch" reached a crescendo, Catherine posted a photograph of herself on Mother's Day in early March showing her radiantly happy flanked by their children Charlotte, Louis, and George. Within twenty-four hours of the photo's release, major news agencies like Reuters and the AP announced they were rejecting the photo due to dramatic editing and photo manipulation. In other words, the photo specialists thought the photo was a fake.

A tidal wave of doubt and scandal enveloped William and Catherine, who, up until then, were known for never putting a foot wrong. *How could they have acted so stupidly? Didn't they know a photo that had been drastically altered or photoshopped would be scrutinized and caught?* Ultimately, these questions led to a bigger and more pressing question: *What are they hiding?*

The mystery mounted until March 22 when Catherine sat on a bench in a simple sweater and told the world the truth—she too had cancer and had been keeping her secret to protect her children. In a heart-wrenching video message, she thanked the public for their concern but pleaded for privacy as she and her young family navigated this new crisis together.

The first few months of 2024 brought the extraordinary interest in William into sharp focus, and the crises in his life were played out on the world stage—his natural habitat since he was born.

The 7 lb., 1.5 oz child, the second in line to the British throne, cried "lustily." This was one of the few details given by the Buckingham Palace spokesman, shortly after his arrival on the evening of June 21, 1982. "He's in marvelous form," his father, then Charles, Prince of Wales, announced to the media packed outside St. Mary's Hospital in Paddington. One reporter asked Charles if he was the most beautiful baby in the world. "Well, he's not bad," the proud father said.[5]

His name would be a source of contention, among many others, between his parents. His father had his heart set on Arthur, the king of myths and chivalric legend. But Diana, ever the strong arm in the marriage, held out for William, another inspired choice. William the Conqueror was England's first Norman ruler and earned his title by his courageous warfare at the Battle of Hastings. The future King William V would be christened William Arthur Philip Louis, in honor of Charles's choice, his father the Duke of Edinburgh, and his great mentor, Louis Mountbatten.

"Thank heavens he hasn't ears like his father," Queen Elizabeth cracked upon seeing her grandchild.[6] The sense of joy in the family and in the country that summer was palpable. The Falklands War in Argentina had finally ended just a week before William's birth, and the country was slowly awakening from a nightmare of economic malaise. A new decade of prosperity was dawning.

At William's christening were members of two important families whose American connections would make William the first monarch to have a truly American patriot bloodline. His grandfather, eighth Earl Spencer was there, representing the Spencer clan whose connections with George Washington and Sulgrave Manor go back centuries. The ghost of Winston Spencer Churchill was hovering over the Lily Font at Buckingham Palace that day, chomping on a cigar with great enthusiasm.

His grandmother Frances Shand Kydd and great-grandparents Maurice and Ruth, Lord and Lady Fermoy were there representing William's American family via Frances's grandmother Frances Burke Roche, whose roots go back to the heart of the Revolution.[7]

But before William grew into the dashing and beloved statesman we know today, he would have to endure the trials and hard knocks of life that everyone, king or pauper, must meet.

While the world was smiling and happy that summer of 1982, his mother was not. She was a twenty-year-old woman deep in the morass of postpartum depression and self-loathing, despite overnight worldwide adulation. By the time she and Charles took baby William on his first overseas tour of Australia less than a year after his birth, there were questions lurking in the media about her state of health. James Whitaker, a well-known royal reporter for the *Daily Mirror*, had already floated the possibility of Diana's eating disorders, something that was not understood by the public at the time. "Would she snap, would she cry, would she collapse from the heat?" *The Sydney Morning Herald*'s Alison Stuart asked.[8]

While Diana looked wan and tired, she still managed to rally and dazzle the crowds, but the baby William was a close second in the popularity contest. "He loves his koala bear he's got," Diana told an Australian boy. When William landed on a blanket on a lawn in Auckland between his parents, the photographers went wild, and hearts melted around the world. The political cynics were doomed, or as the *London Evening Standard* put it, "this tour has set republicanism back ten years."[9]

The following year Prince Harry, William's brother, arrived, but by this point their parents' marriage had virtually dissolved. When Charles made a regrettable comment about wanting a daughter, Diana imploded emotionally. This was her revelation that her marriage was over. Her memories of being an unwanted child resurfaced. Her mother, Frances

Shand Kydd, showing the Burke Roche feistiness, flatly informed her son-in-law that he should be grateful Harry was born healthy.

This period was the advent of the so-called War of the Waleses, a decade-long mudslinging fest between Charles and Diana during which their most private moments and disputes were played out for Fleet Street, who fed the public hunger for more vitriol. Of course, the two primary casualties of the war were William and Harry, who were developing their own personalities. "Harry's the naughty one, just like me," Diana would often say.[10] "You'll be king, I won't, so I can do what I want," Harry would tell his brother as an excuse to break the rules.

Despite the playfulness between them and the lavish privilege that surrounded them, the boys acutely felt the gulf between their parents, and even at a young age, were aware of the media's harmful intrusion. William took on the protector role in the family, often pushing tissues toward his mother in her many tearful moments.[11] This bred an animus for the media, which still festers inside William today as he protects a family of his own.

In 1991, William, sometimes against his wishes, began making official public appearances, grudgingly cooperating with the media, in anticipation of his future role. On St. David's Day in March, the future Prince of Wales joined his parents for a visit to Wales, and got close to American shores when he sailed through Niagara Falls with Diana and Harry while Prince Charles had engagements in Toronto. The fact that William was a public figure in high demand was made abundantly clear when an injury at school made international headlines. William was hit in the head with a golf club, which required minor surgery, but the media fracas, which pitted Charles and Diana against each other as competing parents, was likely more painful for everyone involved.

William and Harry spent their last holiday with their parents on the yacht of billionaire John Latsis in 1992. The years of tension and acrimony came to a head when Diana visited William at school to tell him that she and Charles were separating. She wanted him to hear the news from her before it was announced in the House of Commons, but William, being wise beyond his years, had long expected the worst.

"Diana saw William as her champion, and he had a natural knack for supporting her when she needed it most. He assumed the role of supportive son and had reached the rewarding age when the child becomes a companion and a friend to his parent," explains William's biographer Robert Jobson, who believes that Diana "continued to load his young mind with her adult troubles." Whether it was him promising to give her back the Her Royal Highness style after he was king, or advising what to do with her wardrobe after her divorce, William assumed this role even if he himself was still essentially a schoolboy.[12]

Charles and Diana put their separation troubles behind them, and presented a united front when William enrolled at Eton in 1995. One of the most prestigious schools in the world, Eton boasts a constellation of alumni since its founding in 1440, including the first Duke of Wellington, who apocryphally claimed that the Battle of Waterloo had been won on the fields of his august alma mater.[13] William would be the first senior member of the royal family to attend and would wear the traditional black morning coat like all the other boys, including the actor Eddie Redmayne, a classmate who has praised William's lack of pretensions while a student. The school's rigorous academic schedule, high standards of excellence, and character-building curriculum no doubt fortified William for the worst day of his life.

By the summer of 1997, William was fifteen, and well on his way to becoming the heartthrob that John F. Kennedy Jr. was in the 1980s. Tall, blond, and with Diana's charisma, William was every young girl's dream. He and Harry had spent the summer with their mother in the south of Europe, frolicking in the ocean on the Al Fayed yacht, and had returned to spend the last days of August with their father and grandparents at Balmoral, the royal family's Scottish castle.

William was fast asleep in the early morning hours of August 31 when the Mercedes carrying Diana and Dodi Al Fayed crashed in Paris. By this point, Diana and Charles had healed their relationship post-divorce and were finding it increasingly easier to co-parent. Charles was awakened around 1:00 A.M. and told the news that Dodi was dead, and Diana was gravely injured. The lights turned on in the dead of night at Balmoral as the queen, Prince Philip, Charles, and their assistants went into crisis mode in their pajamas and dressing gowns. Their worst-case scenario materialized when the next call came in: Diana was dead.

Charles was devastated. He paced the floor and then walked the Scottish estate as the sun came up, pleading with God to help him break the news to his sons. William was the first to hear, and then Harry was told by Charles and William together. William credits his father and grandmother, the late Queen Elizabeth II, for their handling of a catastrophe. William understood the queen was acting as a grandmother first, then a head of state. "At the time, my grandmother wanted to protect her two grandsons," William later reflected. Queen Elizabeth insisted that the family attend their usual church service that Sunday morning as planned. Inside the church, William said he was given "the privacy to mourn, to collect our thoughts." He later told a magazine that the support he was given at the time has helped him on the road to healing. "I am in a better place about it than I have been for a long time, where I can talk about her more openly, talk about her more honestly, and I remember her better, and publicly talk about her better. It is not like most people's grief, because everyone else knows about it, everyone knows the story, everyone knows her."[14]

On September 6, 1997, William, despite his royal title, was every inch a Spencer. As he walked behind his mother's coffin, adorned with white lilies and a card that read "Mummy," William was representing, with his uncle, ninth Earl Spencer, centuries of Spencers who had lived and died for Crown and country. As Winston Churchill's coffin made the same journey through the streets of London in 1965, so, too, did the public see firsthand the power of a family. Unlike Winston, who had died an old and venerable stateman, Diana had died in the full flush of youth, with so much potential unrealized.

The Spencer clan had closed ranks, and Lord Spencer landed a few punches in his eulogy when he promised Diana "on behalf of your blood family" to look after her sons, William and Harry, ostensibly to make sure they maintained her Spencer independent streak and would not be subsumed completely by the royal family. This is something William has never forgotten.[15]

"We feel we at least owe her to stand up for her name and remind everybody of the character and person that she was," William explained in a documentary about Diana twenty years after her death.

Earl Spencer made the decision to bury Diana at Althorp, like the great Spencer she was. Her final resting place is The Oval, a small island in the middle of Althorp's lake accessible only by canoe. She is resting in unfettered peace and privacy, things that were denied her in life as "the most hunted person of the modern age," as Lord Spencer put it in his eulogy.

Spencer has allowed select guests to visit The Oval, like Nelson Mandela, who met Diana in her final year, and of course, her sons and family members who row out to her island grave to see the simple obelisk. Althorp has become a pilgrimage spot for Diana fans, who can see a small collection of her gowns and miscellany from her childhood and life thanks to an exhibition on the estate.

By the time William made a trip to Canada the following March with Harry and his newly single father, "Wills Mania," was born. With his downcast eyes like his mother's, "the adoring hysteria associated with the Beatles in their heyday," ensued, according to William's biographer, Robert Jobson, who covered the trip as a reporter. Jobson was alarmed by the exposure of William, then still fifteen. Mary Kenny of the *Daily Express* echoed his reservations. "Diana was adored all over the world. And this is a halo effect that William and Harry will carry everywhere: that they were Diana's sons. But would Diana, if she were alive today, want her elder son to start carrying out royal duties at such a tender age?"[16]

As conspiracy theories about Diana's death and media interest in her and her sons were at fevered pitch, William and Harry issued a rare public statement asking for privacy, and a sense of calm. Mohammed Al Fayed, Dodi's father, had been strident in his belief that his son and Diana were assassinated with the royal family's complicity. Al Fayed set up a virtual shrine at Harrods, the London department store he ran, to the memory of Diana and Dodi, including photos of the two ill-fated lovers, something shoppers found creepily distasteful. "She would have known that constant reminders of her death can create nothing but pain to those she left behind," the boys said in their statement.

William refused to let his mother's death and the media bedlam distract him from his work at Eton: Not only did he excel in his favorites—geography, history, and English—but he was elected to the Eton Society, which required him to wear a special uniform called the Eton Popper. His responsibilities included ushering school events and shepherding younger students to chapel. Ultimately, William finished with three A-levels: an A in geography, one of his great passions, another in history of art, and a C in biology.

It is customary for British students to take what is known as a "gap year" between high school and university. William decided to use this time in Chile with on expedition with Raleigh International working on his budding interest in environmental projects. He would put his geography skills to work backpacking through the most remote parts of Patagonia on the £8,800 he had raised through a water polo match. He had even raised enough to take a disadvantaged student along for the ride. "I'm always bloody chipping in," his father joked, when asked if he had contributed to the fundraising campaign. "Basically, I wanted to do something constructive," William said of this transitional time in his youth.

It was expected that William would follow his father's footsteps to Cambridge for his university education, but showing an increasingly vivid independence, did his own thing in his own way by choosing

St. Andrews in Scotland, the home of his great-grandmother Ruth, Lady Fermoy. "I do love Scotland—there is plenty of space. I love the hills and the mountains, and I thought St. Andrews had a real community feel to it. I've never lived near the sea, so it will be very different. I just hope I meet people I get on with. I don't care about their background." His bucking of the Oxbridge education shows he was taking a more egalitarian view of his future, and showing his father, and courtiers, most of whom came out of Oxford or Cambridge, that he was his own man. "God help anyone who tried to tell William what to do. He would listen, but he would never be pushed around by the system or anyone who thought they were high up."[17]

Applications to St. Andrews shot up by over forty percent after William's matriculation was announced, mostly from eager young women hoping to compare notes with the prince, but as a public figure since birth, his antennae was always finely tuned for fakes. "People who try to take advantage of me and get a piece of me, I spot it quickly and soon go off them. I'm not stupid."

The university has taken a decidedly American turn in the years during and since William's time on campus. *The Times* reports that one in five students at St. Andrews is now from the United States, mostly from the East Coast, earning the school the sobriquet "mini-Nantucket." The paper says that "over the past two decades St. Andrews has been transformed from a quaint, windswept Scottish university into a globally recognized academic institution, a kind of Ivy-adjacent outpost," where "around every corner you hear an American accent. This is not your average British experience."[18]

William had just started his studies at St. Andrews when worldwide disaster struck, a tragedy much closer to home that he realized. On September 11, 2001, planes flew into the World Trade Center in New York and the Pentagon near Washington, DC. As the globe came to terms with the loss of life, everyone from London to Asia to Africa was an American in spirit. Queen Elizabeth II ordered "The Star-Spangled

Banner" to be played at Buckingham Palace at the Changing of the Guard ceremony. Passersby and traffic came to a somber halt.

Students at St. Andrews wanted to do something to help, and a long-standing campus tradition was born. The "DONT WALK" fashion show was started to raise funds "to respond to the harrowing attacks from thousands of miles away," according to the show's website. "DONT WALK" was named as a call to everyone to not walk past social injustice. It is still walking—and raising funds and awareness—for a different cause each year.[19]

The show holds a special place in the heart of William because it was at the show's inaugural event that he first saw his friend Catherine Middleton as more than a friend. They had first crossed paths at their residence hall where Catherine later admitted she turned "bright red" when she bumped into William one day.

In March of 2002, Catherine, in the now-famous black transparent slip dress, sashayed down the charity runway. William had paid £200 for a ticket to the show and attended with his then-girlfriend Carly Massy-Birch, while Kate, as she was known then, was seeing an older law student. "Wow, Kate looks hot," William said to a buddy that night. The dress had done the trick and set this upper-middle-class girl from Berkshire on the road to being a future queen.

WILLIAM AND HIS UNDIE-GRADUATE FRIEND KATE TO SHARE A STUDENT FLAT, read the cheeky headline in the *Mail on Sunday* that April. It was Kate who is credited with rallying William to stay at university when he mulled over quitting after his first term left him daunted. After taking up new academic coursework in geography, and moving into a flat with Kate and friends, did the wind come back into the prince's sails.

Throughout their time in Edinburgh, William and Kate were photographed in campus haunts, and on family holidays. Even in his early twenties, the media had him already walking down the aisle. "Look, I'm only twenty-two, for God's sake. I'm too young to marry at my age. I don't want to get married until I'm at least twenty-eight or maybe thirty."

While William was averse to marriage at this point in his life, his father certainly was not. William and Harry were at Prince Charles's side in April 2005 when he finally married his longtime love, Camilla Parker Bowles, the woman who had brought such misery to their mother. It had been eight years since their mother's death, and despite the pain of their parents' divorce and the wreckage of the past, William and Harry both understood, now that they were grown men, the happiness that Camilla brought to his life. They, and the public were assured, however, that Camilla would not assume the title of Princess of Wales, but would be known as Her Royal Highness The Duchess of Cornwall. There would only ever be one Princess of Wales in the minds of Britons, and Americans, who still followed the royal family as eagerly as they did in the Diana years.

Two days after this twenty-third birthday William walked down another aisle—the one at Younger Hall at St. Andrews—where his grandmother Queen Elizabeth, grandfather the Duke of Edinburgh, father, and Camilla watched him get his degree with Kate. "I shall be very sad to leave," he recollected of his college days. The vice-chancellor Dr. Brian King reminded the students in his commencement address that St. Andrews was the "top matchmaking university in Britain . . . I say this every year to all new graduates: You may have met your husband or wife . . . so we can rely on you to go forth and multiply."

After graduation, William and Catherine (she told her friends she wished to drop "Kate" around this time) were still an item, and the media mused that Catherine, with a less-than-aristocratic pedigree, was a democratic, almost American, choice for the future king. "Kate . . . a real princess of the people: a non-blueblood. For republicans who prefer to be citizens rather than subjects and who hoped, after Diana's death, that the demise of the monarchy was imminent it's not the happy-ever-after they envisaged. But it might yet be for William," explained *The Independent on Sunday.*

Although Catherine's family was middle class by William's standards, her parents were multimillionaires thanks to their entrepreneurial verve. Michael Middleton and the former Carole Goldsmith met while working for British Airways and married in 1980, two years before their first child, Catherine Elizabeth, was born. Catherine would be joined by Pippa and James, and their constant rotation of birthday parties for friends and relations gave Carole the idea that would launch the family from respectable middle-class into upwardly mobile affluence. In 1987, from her kitchen table, she started Party Pieces, a mail-to-order party-decorations business. By the mid-1990s, the business was worth millions. The Middletons may not have been American, but they certainly lived the American dream. Catherine and her siblings attended the best schools, and brushed shoulders with the highest echelons of society. By the time Catherine graduated from university, the family could afford to put her and her sister Pippa in a flat in the heart of London. Like Diana before her, her myth started as a single woman making her way in the city.[20]

Also like Diana, Catherine was tall, lean, and loved clothes, and she wore them brilliantly. As she dashed around the city, photographers snapped her everywhere. While Diana was overwhelmed by the media attention and succumbed to eating disorders and mental illness in the harsh light of the public gaze, Catherine eased into life as a public figure more readily. "Never complain, never explain," as the royal motto went. Catherine's fortitude and equanimity were down, it has been said, to her solid and stable upbringing by Carole and Michael, both of whom are universally acknowledged as outstanding parents. Catherine had wanted to work in an art gallery or for a fashion firm, but due to the media frenzy around her, worked behind the scenes for her family's business.

Meanwhile in 2006, William was stepping, or marching, into the family business when he entered the Royal Military Academy Sandhurst, the training ground for officers in the British Army. While William would be the most senior member of the royal family to train there, he would also be following the Spencer-Churchill tradition during his forty-four-week course. Sir Winston was a proud alum of

Sandhurst, although it took him three attempts to pass the entrance exam, mainly due to his deficiencies with mathematics. Once there, however, Winston flourished, ultimately graduating twentieth out of a class of 130 in December 1894. "It shows that I could learn quickly the things that matter," Churchill said.[21]

For his part, William learned the rudiments of grenades, pistols, rifles, first aid, and how to polish his boots properly. It was made clear to him and his fellow cadets that no dispensations were to be given to anyone, regardless of their princely rank or family. "We receive people from all backgrounds," explained Lieutenant Colonel Roy Parkinson, a Sandhurst instructor. "It's a team effort here. If someone steps out of line, they're stamped on, whether they're a prince or not."

William placed in the top third for his year, and was commissioned as an army officer in December 2006, becoming a lieutenant in the Blues and Royals Regiment. He "passed out," as it is known in the Sandhurst vernacular, on a crisp winter day with Catherine making her first official public appearance at the Sandhurst ceremony. She made her presence known loud and clear in a scarlet coat as she arrived with her parents, who had come to think of William as a second son. It was a special day in William's budding military career, but as the second in line to the throne, he would be prevented from frontline war zones. Harry, however, who also trained at Sandhurst, would be deployed to Iraq the following year. As the queen reviewed the cadets that day in their blue uniforms, she paused by a few seconds longer in front of William who was wearing her Golden Jubilee Medal. She cheekily said hello to her grandson, and William momentarily broke protocol, and flashed her a smile.

The following year William and Catherine turned twenty-five. The press was still hot on the heels of the princess in waiting. Columnists criticized her work ethic, because all she appeared to do was turn up with William, and work part-time for her parents and Jigsaw, a British fashion company. The media was turning from adulatory to blatantly cruel, mocking her mother's background as an airline hostess. The pressures, and the frivolities of youth, caused the couple to temporarily break up that April. Not one to accept defeat lightly, Catherine hit the town with Pippa, and the two "sizzler sisters" as Fleet Street dubbed them, showed William and the world what he was giving up to find his freedom. Her "sizzle" strategy did the trick. Within months, Catherine was spotted in the royal box two rows behind William at the "Concert for Diana" at Wembley Stadium where they danced to the aptly titled hit "Back for Good" by pop band Take That.

What would Diana think of Catherine? This is a question that has rattled the brain of many royal watchers. Lady Colin Campbell believes that while the competitive spirit in Diana would have been threatened by the beauteous presence of her daughter-in-law, she would have approved "whole-heartedly" of the new Princess of Wales.[22] In 2011, the long courtship was over. Like Diana before her, Catherine had waited for and ultimately won her man. The couple stepped out in front of a throng of reporters at Buckingham Palace in November 2010 to announce their engagement. Catherine wore a stunning blue day dress that highlighted the her narrow waist. It also matched perfectly the sapphire and diamond ring that had been Diana's. "It's very, very special," she said, beaming. The couple revealed they had formally agreed to marriage while on holiday in Kenya near Lake Alice. William had been secretly lugging the ring around his backpack, waiting for the right moment to pop the question. "I knew if this thing disappeared, I would be in a lot of trouble . . . It went really, really well and I am so pleased she said yes."[23]

A few months later, the couple returned to the place where their journey together began—the University of St. Andrews—to celebrate the school's 600th anniversary. Not long thereafter, on April 29, 2011, they married at Westminster Abbey in front of a global audience, just as William's parents had three decades before. Catherine, wearing a gown by Sarah Burton for the house of Alexander McQueen, sailed down the aisle on the arm of her father with the trumpets of the rapturous hymn "I Was Glad." Catherine wore a tiara by Cartier that had been given to Queen Elizabeth on her eighteenth birthday by her mother, who had received it as a gift from her husband, King George VI, in 1936. It was a "something borrowed" for the third generation. William and Catherine would thereafter be known as Their Royal Highnesses The Duke and Duchess of Cambridge, but to the down-to-earth couple, they were just man and wife.

That summer William and Catherine hit the ground running, taking their royal show on the road to shore up support for the monarchy in Canada, where Catherine showed she was a born natural, after years as a royal girlfriend. Then they made their way to the promised land—the country of William's ancestors. They arrived in Los Angeles, and according to the British ambassador at the time, Sir Nigel Sheinwald, crossed paths with a wide swath of American society, from the glitterati at the Beverly Hilton to those unfortunates on the margins of society on skid row. After mingling with Hollywood royalty like Nicole Kidman, Jennifer Lopez, and Barbra Streisand, they—rather democratically for a royal duke and duchess—boarded British Airways flights back to London.[24]

Catherine settled into her life as a new royal superstar with her typical no-fuss way of working, while William continued his career as a helicopter pilot for the Royal Air Force. The cozy nest of two became three (plus dog Lupo) in the summer of 2013 when Catherine gave birth to their son, and the heir to the throne, Prince George, whose arrival was eerily similar to William's at the same hospital. When the couple emerged with the baby in their arms, William joked self-deprecatingly about the newborn having more hair than he did. "He's got a good pair of lungs, that's for sure," he said. The threesome set up shop in Nottingham Cottage, a two-bedroom house near Kensington Palace, where their royal apartments were being readied.

They announced their son would be named George Alexander Louis. King George III and George Washington must have been happy to hear the future king would share their name. The little prince was given a forty-one-gun salute by the King's Troop Royal Horse Artillery in Green Park. The Spencer clan at Althorp delighted in the news of George's birth. Earl Spencer recalled that "my father always told us that Diana was born on a blisteringly hot day at Sandringham in July 1961. It's another very happy summer's day, half a century on."

By the time Princess Charlotte Elizabeth Diana arrived in May 2015, William's family had taken a more regal lifestyle. The queen had lent him Anmer Hall, a country estate for weekends in Norfolk, and their Kensington Palace apartment had been renovated to the tune of twelve million pounds. The four-story space has twenty rooms and costs the taxpayer nearly five million pounds to maintain. Apartment 1A remains his London base today, and is where William and Catherine receive special guests, like President and Michelle Obama, who stopped by to see Prince George on the hobby horse he had been given on behalf of the American people.

With Prince Louis's arrival in 2018, the family was a house of five, and "Pops," as William is known by his children, said he had become more "emotional" with the addition of children in his life. The previous year his tears were not far from the surface when, for the first time, he spoke of his mother on the twentieth anniversary of her death. "Not only is this the first time we've spoken so openly and at length about our mother, it is also the last time," he said, as he introduced the documentary *Diana, Our Mother: Her Life and Legacy* with Harry, who had taken his place at Nottingham Cottage. "We feel we at least owe her twenty years on, to stand up for her name and remind everybody of the character and person that she was. Do our duty as sons protecting her . . . I still feel emptiness on Mother's Day."[25]

William spoke openly about his two-decades-long struggle with grief. As he did his princely duties and went abroad on behalf of his grandmother, especially to war-torn parts of the world, it was clear he was tapping into a sense of compassion that had been honed by his own profound sadness. The stalwart Catherine and his three children were the penultimate elixirs.

His brother Harry had turned to drugs and alcohol to self-medicate his grief. Unlike William, who had found a wife and family, Harry was still a lonely bachelor at Not Cot, as it is sometimes called. But in 2016, he met a beautiful American divorcée, Meghan Markle, and his life, and his relationship with his brother, would be irretrievably altered. Catherine and William, while happy for Harry, were on their guard. Markle was an actress, a dodgy profession in aristocratic circles, and, by her own admission, ambitious. "Personally, I love a great love story," she told a reporter for *Vanity Fair*, with her face naturally on the cover, shortly before she and Harry became engaged.[26] Prince Charles, for his part, welcomed his future daughter-in-law warmly, and was relieved to see both his sons settling into happy families of their own after the animus between him and Diana had overshadowed their childhoods.

In November 2017, Harry and Meghan announced their engagement, and the wedding date was duly set for May 2018. The country and world went ballistic for what they thought would be a modernized royal family with the entrance of a divorced American bride. But there were early warning signs: "What Meghan wants, Meghan gets," Harry told flummoxed staff at the palace. Harry had allegedly tussled with the queen's friend and dresser Angela Kelly when she did not allow Meghan to wear the tiara she wanted for her wedding. Meghan ultimately wore Queen Mary's 1932 bandeau tiara, after William reportedly banned her from using any of Diana's jewelry.[27]

Tensions had been running high between William and Harry, according to William's biographer, because he had advised Harry to slow down in his courtship of Meghan, and not rush into marriage so quickly. Ever the Spencer, Harry did not take kindly to being lectured, even by his older brother. Regardless, William agreed to serve as his best man.

The sun shone brightly on Windsor on May 19, 2018, as Harry and Meghan became the Duke and Duchess of Sussex as American and British flags waved in unison in the packed crowds around St. George's Chapel. Meghan was the first American since Wallis Simpson to marry into the family, but this American divorcee was treated with cheers, not jeers. Because Meghan identified as biracial with an African American mother, her marriage signaled a reset in race relations in Britian and in the royal family whose critics had long harbored resentment for its connections to slavery, dating back to the colonial era. This was a new chapter in the royal family in which its historical past, with all its political glories and errors, was coming full circle.

Unlike Maurice and Francis Burke Roche, the two brothers had bad blood brewing between them, and it quickly spilled into the relationship between Meghan and Catherine. Within months of their sunny nuptials, the couple was besieged with bad publicity. First it emerged in the *Daily Telegraph* that Meghan brought Catherine to tears in the lead up to the wedding.[28]

"We've got four different personalities, and we've got the same passions to make a difference, but different opinions . . . we're stuck together for the rest of our lives," William said at a public engagement with his wife, brother, and new sister-in-law. The "different opinions" may have been a reference to Meghan's political activism, which is forbidden in the royal family. Indeed, family members do not even vote. Their support of any political cause or candidate is against the framework of Britain's constitutional monarchy. With the rising tide of Trumpism, Brexit, and a host of hot-button issues in the culture, the royal family maintained its "don't ask, don't tell" political inscrutability. This was difficult for Meghan, whose American sense of democracy and openness naturally chafed under these restrictions. During an event, William squirmed in his seat when Megahn praised the #MeToo and #TimesUp movements, which were deemed too political for royal women to wade into.[29]

The media had dubbed Harry and Meghan and William and Catherine the "Fab Four," like the Beatles, but this new foursome would also break up in the most disastrous way. Less than a year after the wedding, Harry and Meghan announced that they were splitting from the court of William and creating their own court with their own aides. William and Harry had shared aides and communications officers for years, but this decision on the part of Harry and his new bride sent a loud and clear message of independence.

Not only did the brothers not want to share staff, but they evidently did not want to share space. While Harry and Meghan lived at Not Cot after their wedding, they were within walking distance of William's home at Kensington Palace. They quickly decided to decamp to Frogmore Cottage in Windsor Great Park, placing them miles away from the brother and sister-in-law from whom they were becoming increasingly estranged.

Team Sussex was hit with another media blitzkrieg with allegations of bullying by Meghan. Staff gossip about Meghan's diva demands and antics made their way to William. One said Meghan "governed by fear," with others who had left her staff consoling each other as "The Sussex Survivors' Squad." According to his memoir, *Spare*, Harry said that William confronted him about Meghan, and a physical altercation ensued. By May 2019, a year into her royal role, four of Meghan's staff members had departed in quick succession. An investigation of the bullying claims was conducted by the palace, but its findings have not been released, nor have the names of the staff members involved.[30]

By early 2020, the War of the Brothers had hit rock bottom. Harry and Meghan saw no way out, but, well, out altogether. They released a statement that January saying they, and their baby son Archie, would be leaving as working members of the royal family.

"After many months of reflection and internal discussions, we have chosen to make a transition this year in starting to carve out a progressive new role within this institution," they said. "We intend to step back as 'senior' members of the royal family and work to become financially independent, while continuing to fully support Her Majesty The Queen.

It is with your encouragement, particularly over the last few years, that we feel prepared to make this adjustment. We now plan to balance our time between the United Kingdom and North America, continuing to honour our duty to The Queen, the Commonwealth, and our patronages. This geographic balance will enable us to raise our son with an appreciation for the royal tradition into which he was born, while also providing our family with the space to focus on the next chapter, including the launch of our new charitable entity. We look forward to sharing the full details of this exciting next step in due course, as we continue to collaborate with Her Majesty The Queen, The Prince of Wales, The Duke of Cambridge and all relevant parties."[31]

The only problem was they were not collaborating with Queen Elizabeth or any "relevant parties." In fact, when William arrived for an emergency meeting with Harry, the queen, and Prince Charles on January 14, he could barely control his anger at Harry's bombshell decision. Queen Elizabeth released a counter statement soon thereafter that left no doubt that she—not Harry—was in charge.

"Although we would have preferred them to remain full-time working Members of the Royal Family, we respect and understand their wish to live a more independent life as a family while remaining a valued part of my family," she said in a statement released by Buckingham Palace.

"It has therefore been agreed that there will be a period of transition in which the Sussexes will spend time in Canada and the UK. These are complex matters for my family to resolve, and there is some more work to be done, but I have asked for final decisions to be reached in coming days."[32]

Far from settling into the Commonwealth country of Canada as they had led the family to believe, the couple and their baby headed for California, Meghan's home state, where they lived in a borrowed house from Hollywood star Tyler Perry, before finding a home of their own. This new house in Montecito would be central command in their war against the royal family as they unleashed their army of journalists and surrogates to paint the family as racist, unfeeling, and in league with the British media. William was at the center of the storm. "We're very much *not* a racist family," William said with gritted teeth after a 2021 televised interview with Oprah Winfrey during which Harry and Meghan affirmed what their surrogates had been saying. "No, I haven't spoken to him yet, but I will do," William said, almost threateningly, referring to Harry. The most shocking allegation in the interview was that there was discomfort in the family about having a grandchild, Archie, who could be dark-skinned, and that Archie would not be given a princely title as a result. This allegation resurfaced a centuries-long wound in Britian, and around the world, about slavery and race relations writ large. The Oprah interview came less than a year after the killing of George Floyd, and the collective consciousness of the world was as raw as ever.

When William and Catherine visited the West Indies to represent the queen during her Golden Jubilee year in 2022, race—not the royals—took center stage, with *The Guardian* describing the visit as "the perfect storm." It was supposed to be, the reporter explained, "a chance to present the modern face of the British monarchy to a region where republican sentiment is on the rise. But it really didn't turn out that way."

Upon arrival in Belize, protesters greeted them with rage, not the warm welcome they are used to. In Jamaica, the prime minister told them the country would be "moving on" to become a republic, and a government committee in the Bahamas urged the royals to issue "a full and formal apology for their crimes against humanity."

In an optical public relations disaster, photographs of the royal couple shaking hands with Jamaican children through wire fences landed with a giant thud. Equally tone-deaf were images of the couple, dressed in white, in an open-top Land Rover in a military parade, that harkened for many the colonial past.

"My grandparents could trace generations back to slavery, but they died believing Jamaica was fully independent. Imagine, sixty years later and it's still an extension of the British empire," one observer said, summing up the views of many. "They should recognise that members of the royal family from Charles II to William IV were involved with and supported slavery and the slave trade, and that this is part of their past," another local said.[33]

More dirty laundry, especially William's, was to come. A Netflix series documented Harry and Meghan's "freedom flight" from the tyranny of the royal family and British media, while Harry's 2023 memoir, *Spare*, detailed his troubled relationship with his brother. Harry's contention that William was "trapped" in his royal role may have been the most stinging. "My brother can't leave that system, but I have," Harry explained.

Harry and Meghan continue to live in the United States and have made the occasional trip back to London. In September 2025, Harry had tea with King Charles after months of estrangement, but friends of the brothers see no rapprochement in the offing for William and Harry. In a strange twist to the future king's American story, his brother has expressed an interest in becoming an American citizen.

"I have considered it, yeah," he said on ABC's *Good Morning America* in 2024. Asked what might stop him applying, he said: "I have no idea. It's a thought that has crossed my mind but it's not a high priority for me right now," he added.[34]

Becoming a citizen would require Harry to renounce his princely rank as the naturalization oath of the United States contains the words *I absolutely and entirely renounce and abjure all allegiance and fidelity to any foreign prince, potentate, state, or sovereignty, of whom or which I have heretofore been a subject or citizen.* If Harry were to take this oath, he and his wife would devolve from the Duke and Duchess of Sussex to Mr. and Mrs. Henry Windsor, or whatever they decided their surname would be. The titles of their children, Archie and Lilibet, would be determined by King Charles, or King William.

The public relations debacle has only strengthened William's resolve to repair the damage done to his family's reputation, especially as Harry's revelations came fast and furiously after the fallout from Prince Andrew's fall from grace. In another gut-wrenching television interview with Emily Maitlis, Andrew unconvincingly tried to distance himself from pedophile Jeffrey Epstein, and allegations he slept with one of Epstein's underage victims. The interview, and the public outcry, put Andrew out of commission for any public duties, but the damage had been done. According to William's biographer, William and Andrew have never been close, despite their mutual military service, and William has "little sympathy" for Andrew. "His only concern is the serious damage the allegation has had on the institution he was born to lead."[35]

In July of the same year, William grudgingly reunited with Harry at Kensington Palace to mark what would have been Diana's sixtieth birthday. They unveiled a statue of the princess in Kensington Gardens. This was a watershed moment for William, as he took the reins of his family amid disgrace and turmoil. Looking to his mother for inspiration, and perhaps some help from above, William turned to one of her favorite causes—homelessness—at the end of 2021. Diana was always keen for William to see unhoused people as being just like everyone else, but without the privileges. "She wanted to make sure that I understood that life happens very much outside of palace walls, and this is what's going on. This is the real world here."

As William handed out his first Earthshot Awards that year, he reflected on the future, perhaps a way to escape the present and the past. "We are alive in the most consequential time in human history . . . the actions we choose or choose not to take in the next yen years will determine the fate of the planet for the next thousand."[36]

The queen's passing in September 2022 brought William one step closer to his destiny. As he knelt before his father, the new King Charles III that spring day the following year, he was a man fortified by his

American links. He had the courage of Benajah Strong, the grit of Frank Work, the panache of Frances, and the dignified kindness of his great-grandfather, Maurice, Lord Fermoy.

As the new Prince of Wales, with his Catherine by his side, he remained in dignified silence as the slings and arrows from Harry's camp continued. Now in remission, Catherine has returned to public duties. King Charles is well into his seventies and is receiving treatments for his unidentified but incurable form of cancer.

In November 2025, Charles's brother Prince Andrew finally was given the royal ax when his princely title was removed, a decision William is believed to have fully supported. The newly minted Andrew Mountbatten-Windsor, and his ex-wife, the former Sarah, Duchess of York, now simply Sarah Ferguson, are also giving up their royal residence at Royal Lodge, their family home for decades. Buckingham Palace's statement read: "His Majesty has today initiated a formal process to remove the Style, Titles and Honours of Prince Andrew. Prince Andrew will now be known as Andrew Mountbatten Windsor.

"Formal notice has now been served to surrender the lease and he will move to alternative private accommodation. These censures are deemed necessary, notwithstanding the fact that he continues to deny the allegations against him."

Fans of William see Andrew's ultimate humiliation as a harbinger of things to come for Harry and Meghan. Observers believe that William has more mettle than his father, and that when he is king, he will be less forgiving, and more decisive in removing the Duke of Sussex title from his wayward brother.

But just as William was acting with military precision, he also was opening his heart in the tenderest of ways as he talked to a woman whose husband had committed suicide on World Mental Health Day. Rhian Mannings in south Wales lost her one-year-old son, George, in 2012 to an undiagnosed illness. Five days later, her husband Paul killed himself. Mannings said Paul blamed himself for their son's death.

Kensington Palace released a video of William chatting with Mannings for the Royal Foundation of the Prince and Princess of Wales. As they talked, William held back tears, and cupped his hands over his mouth, clearly shaken and choked up by her story. Mannings has since used her experience to launch a charity aimed at supporting parents who suffer the loss of a child or young adult, something that must resonate deeply with William based on Diana's experiences and the trail of mental health problems in her family.

On September 17, 2025, ironically Constitution Day in the United States, William stood by waiting for Marine One as it landed magnificently on the lawn of Windsor Castle. As a helicopter pilot, this occasion was of great interest to him. With Catherine at his side, he greeted the helicopter's master, the president of the United States, and his First Lady. The two shook hands as if they were old friends. This was the first time they had seen each other since their first meeting at Notre Dame, nearly a year earlier.

In a beautiful metaphor, the Prince of Wales walked the president toward the monarchy, as his father the king waited with Queen Camilla at the castle's entrance. As a future king who is one-sixteenth American, with a patriot bloodline, William is doing in life, what he did that windswept day in September, bringing America to its mother country as it celebrates its 250th birthday. Two hundred and fifty years since America cast off its king, it is embracing a future one, one of its own.

At a banquet that evening, William and Catherine appeared in all their regality for a state banquet for the American president. "We're like two notes in one chord, or two verses of the same poem, each beautiful on its own," the president said, before offering a toast to His Majesty King Charles III. "But really meant to be played together. The bond of kinship and identity between America and the United Kingdom is priceless and eternal."

With William seated opposite him, the president looked at King Charles and praised the "remarkable son" he had raised. He then turned toward William and said, "I think you're going to have an unbelievable success in the future."[37]

Sadly, by March 2026, British-American relations were at their lowest point since Benajah Strong joined the Connecticut militia in the run up to the American Revolution. When America and Israel struck Iran, the British government, led by Starmer, initially denied US forces access to British bases, prompting public rebukes of Starmer by Trump. Most notably, he mocked Starmer as "no Winston Churchill." While the two world leaders have talked by phone and are privately making amends, relations have become so fraught that by late March, there is suspicion that King Charles may cancel or postpone his April trip to the US in celebration of its 250th. Within days of the chatter, it was announced that King Charles would indeed come to American shores to address Congress, the first monarch since his mother Queen Elizabeth II did so in 1991.

With Benajah Strong and Nathan Hale's courage, Frank Work's grit, Fanny's panache, and Maurice's humble nobility, William is indeed ready to be the global leader the world desperately needs now. His relationship with America, America's relationship with Britain because of him, is indeed special. As King Charles put it that night at Windsor Castle, "special does not begin to do it justice."[38]

BIBLIOGRAPHY

Barr, Lockwood. *Dr. Joseph Strong, 1770–1812: Philadelphia Physician*. Yale Journal of Biology and Medicine, 1941.

Barrow, Thomas. *Connecticut Joins the Revolution*. Pequot Press, 1967.

Brown, Tina. *The Diana Chronicles*. Anchor Books, 2007.

Burke Roche, Frances. "The Private Diaries of Frances Burke Roche." Unpublished manuscript.

Burke Roche, Mary. *Call Me Maurice: The Life and Times of Lord Fermoy, 1885–1955*. ELSP, 2009.

Campbell, Lady Colin. *Diana in Private: The Princess Nobody Knows*. St. Martin's Press, 1992.

Campbell, Lady Colin. *The Real Diana*. Macmillan, 1998.

Clark, Ellen McCallister. "Cincinnatus on Downing Street: Winston Churchill Joins the Society." https://www.societyofthecincinnati.org/cincinnatus-on-downing-street-winston-churchill-joins-the-society/.

Cooper, Anderson, and Katherine Howe. *Astor: The Rise and Fall of an American Fortune*. HarperCollins, 2023.

Cooper, Anderson, and Katherine Howe. *Vanderbilt: The Rise and Fall of an American Dynasty*. HarperCollins, 2021.

Cornwallis-West, Mrs. George. *The Reminiscences of Lady Randolph Churchill*. New Nostalgia Books, 1908.

Foreman, Amanda. *Georgiana: Duchess of Devonshire*. Random House, 1998.

Gray, Charlotte. *Passionate Mothers, Powerful Sons: The Lives of Jennie Jerome Churchill and Sara Delano Roosevelt*. Simon & Schuster, 2023.

Jobson, Robert. *William at 40: The Making of a Modern Monarch*. Ad Lib Publishers, 2022.

Johnston, Henry. *The Record of Connecticut Men of the Military and Naval Service During the War of the Revolution, 1775–1783*. Genealogical Publishing Company, 2009.

Junor, Penny. *Prince William: The Man who will be King*. Pegasus Books, 2012.

Kehoe, Elisabeth. *The Titled Americans: Three American Sisters and the British Aristocratic World into Which They Married*. Grove Press, 2004.

King, Greg. *A Season of Splendor: The Court of Mrs. Astor in Gilded Age New York*. John Wiley & Sons, 2009.

McCullough, David. *1776*. Simon & Schuster, 2005.

Naden, Gavan and Riddington, Maxine. *Lilac Days*. HarperCollins Publishers, 2005.

Phelps, M. William. *Nathan Hale: The Life and Death of America's First Spy*. ForeEdge Books, 2008.

Purcell, Richard Joseph. *Connecticut in Transition, 1775–1818*. American Historical Association, 1918.

Roberts, Andrew. *The Last King of America: The Misunderstood Reign of George III*. Viking, 2021.

Roberts, Gary Boyd, and William Addams Reitwasner. *American Ancestors and Cousins of the Princess of Wales*. Genealogical Publishing Company, 1984.

Rose, Alexander. *Washington's Spies: The Story of America's First Spy Ring*. Bantam Books, 2014.

Spencer, Charles. *The Spencers: A Personal History of an English Family*. St. Martin's Press, 1999.

Sulgrave Manor Archive, *A History of the National Society Colonial Dames of America and Sulgrave Manor, 1914–1977, Volume One*.

Sullivan, Aaron. *The Disaffected: Britain's Occupation of Philadelphia During the American Revolution*. University of Pennsylvania Press, 2019.

Swift, Will. *The Roosevelts and the Royals: Franklin, Eleanor, the King and Queen of England, and the Friendship That Changed the World*. John Wiley & Sons, 2019.

Unger, Harlow Giles. *Dr. Benjamin Rush: The Founding Father Who Healed a Nation*. Da Capo Press, 2019.

Cornwallis-West, Mrs. George. *The Reminiscences of Lady Randolph Churchill*. Century Company, 1908.

NOTES

Chapter 1: Liege Man of Life and Limb

1   *The New York Times*, December 7, 2024.

2   Roberts and Reitwasner, *American Ancestors and Cousins of the Princess of Wales*, 27.

Chapter 2: A Tale of Two Georges

1   Public remarks of Queen Elizabeth II, July 6, 1976, Philadelphia, PA.

2   Spencer, *The Spencers*, 35–36.

3   Spencer, 30–32.

4   Roberts, *The Last King of America*, 55–57.

5   Roberts, 58.

6   Roberts, 60.

7   Roberts, 8, 80–90.

8   "Royal Residences: Buckingham Palace," royal.uk/royal-residences -buckingham-palace.

9   National Humanities Center.org Toolbox Library: Primary Resources in US History & Literature, "The Colonies, 1690–1715."

10   Roberts, 95.

11   Roberts, 112.

12   Chernow, *Washington: A Life*, 137.

13   Roberts, 162–67.

14   Roberts, 211.

15   Letter from Benjamin Franklin to Thomas Cushing, June 10, 1771, National Archives. Letter to Thomas Cushing from Benjamin Franklin, June 10, 1771, National Archives, founders.archives.gov.

16   Roberts, 238–239.

17 Lord North. Roberts, 238.

18 Transcript of *A Summary View of the Rights of British America*, Monticello archives. Roberts, 244.

19 Letter from John Adams to Benjamin Rush, March 19, 1812, National Archives.org, foundersarchive.gov.

Chapter 3: Food for Worms

1 Author's tour of Coventry with the town historian John Holmy, April 2025.

2 Connecticut Historical Society, *Rolls and Lists of Connecticut Men in the Revolution: 1775–1783*, 90; Johnston, *The Record of Connecticut Men of the Military and Naval Service During the War of the Revolution, 1775–1783*, (Genealogical Publishing Company, 2009), 7.

3 Phelps, 12.

4 Roberts and Reitwasner, *American Ancestors and Cousins of the Princess of Wales*, 27.

5 Purcell, *Connecticut in Transition, 1775–1818*, 7–17.

6 Barrow, *Connecticut Joins the Revolution*, 40.

7 Scheide, "The Lexington Alarm," 53.

8 Author's tour of Coventry with John Holmy, April, 2025.

9 Phelps, *Nathan Hale*, 64–66.

10 *The Times of London*, December 23, 2021.

11 Roberts, *The Last King of America*, 307–8.

12 Phelps, 11.

13 Phelps, 3.

14 Phelps, 3.

15 Phelps, 13.

16 Phelps, 16–21.

17 Phelps, 20.

18 Phelps. 74.

19 Rose, 6.

20 Ibid.

21 Phelps, 58.

22 Phelps, 79.

23 Phelps, 83.

24 Army Journal of Nathan Hale, November 28, 1775. Connecticut Historical Society.

25 Congress Establishes First Committee on Spies, June 5, 1776, DVIDShub.net.

26 Phelps, 130.

27 ConnecticutHistory.org.

28 Rose, *Washington's Spies*, 2, 198.

29 Author interview with Phelps, April 2025.

30 Phelps, 158.

31 Phelps, 158.

32 Phelps, 159.

33 Phelps, 164–67, 170–79.

34 Phelps, 184–86.

35 Phelps, 192–193.

36 McCullough.

37 Author tour of Nathan Hale Homestead, April 2025.

38 Roberts, 454.

39 Ibid.

40 Rose, 274–275.

41 Rose, 278–80.

42 Author visit to grave of Benajah Strong, April 2025.

Chapter 4: Yankee Doodle Duchess

1 Spencer, *The Spencers*, 142.

2 Foreman, *Georgiana: Duchess of Devonshire*, 3.

3 Foreman, 3.

4 Foreman, 4–7.

5 Foreman, 14–19.

6 Foreman, 38–39.

7 Foreman, 54–55.

8 Foreman, 57.

9 Foreman, 215.

10 Foreman, 149.

11 *Morning Herald and Daily Advertiser*, (UK), January 19, 1781.

12 Foreman, 89.

13 Foreman, 139.

14 Thomas Rowlandson, *The Two Patriotic Duchesses on Their Canvass*, April 3, 1784, British Museum, catalog no. 6494.

15   Foreman, 180.

16   Foreman, 205.

17   Foreman, 211.

18   Foreman, 212.

19   Foreman, 218.

20   Foreman, 220.

21   Letter from Thomas Jefferson to John Jay, July 19, 1789. National Archives, Washington, D.C.

22   Foreman, 271.

23   Foreman, 259–60.

24   Foreman, 286.

25   Foreman, 314.

26   Foreman, 313–14.

27   Foreman, 313–14.

28   Foreman, 315.

29   Foreman, 370.

30   Foreman, 371.

31   Roberts, *The Last King of America*, 653.

32   Roberts, 655.

33   Roberts, 656.

34   Foreman, 348.

Chapter 5: Philadelphia Freedom

1   Barr, *Dr. Joseph Strong: 1770–1812*, 430.

2   Barr, 432.

3   Barr, 433.

4   Sullivan, *The Disaffected*.

5   Unger, *Dr. Benjamin Rush*, 3.

6   Unger, 6.

7   Unger, 21.

8   Unger, 29.

9   Unger, 36.

10   Unger, 173–74.

11   Barr, 443.

12   Unger, 60, 75.

13   Unger, 103.

14   Barr, 437.

15   "'Mad' Anthony Wayne," Historical Society of Pennsylvania, March 26,
     2014, hsp.org/blogs/archival-adventures-in-small-repositories/mad
     -anthony-wayne.

16   Barr, 438.

17   Barr, 439.

18   Barr, 430.

19   Barr, 441.

20   Unger, 139.

21   Unger, 148.

22   John Adams to Abigail Adams, December 1, 1793, Adams Family
     Papers, Massachusetts Historical Society, Boston.

23   Barr, 444.

24   Barr, 445.

25   Peck, *Or Perish in the Attempt*, 52.

26   Barr, 447.

27   Barr, 448.

28   Barr, 429.

29   Unger, 249.

30   Unger, 246.

31   Letter to John Adams from Thomas Jefferson, May 27, 1813. National
     Archives, Washington, D.C.

32   Barr, 449.

Chapter 6: The Dean of Madison Square

1   Cooper and Howe, *Vanderbilt*, 16–17.

2   *Chillicothe Gazette*, June 25, 1904.

3   Cooper and Howe, 36.

4   Cooper and Howe, 21.

5   *Chillicothe Gazette*, November 1, 2005.

6   *Chillicothe Gazette*, May 22, 1936.

7   Burke Roche, "The Private Diaries of Frances Burke Roche."

8   *Omaha Sunday Bee News*, October 25, 1931.

9   *Chillicothe Gazette*, November 1, 2005.

10   *Chillicothe Gazette*, December 14, 1894.

11   *Chillicothe Gazette*, March 21, 1911.

12   King, *A Season of Splendor*, 88.

13   *Chillicothe Gazette*, March 21, 1911.

14   *Chillicothe Gazette*, January 30, 1906.

15   *Evening World*, September 3, 1920.

16   *Chillicothe Gazette*, March 21, 1911.

17   *Chillicothe Gazette*, April 18, 1981.

Chapter 7: Cash for Class

1   Cooper and Howe, *Astor*, 70.

2   Cooper and Howe, 70.

3   Cooper and Howe, 75.

4   Cooper and Howe, 76–77.

5   Cooper and Howe, 83.

6   Burke Roche, "The Private Diaries of Frances Burke Roche."

7   Ibid.

8   Ibid.

9   Burke Roche, *Call Me Maurice*, 43.

10   Burke Roche, *Call Me Maurice*, 42.

11   Burke Roche, "The Private Diaries of Frances Burke Roche."

12   Melissa Aaron, nationaltrust.org.uk.

13   *Chillicothe Gazette*, November 1, 2005.

14   Burke Roche, *Call Me Maurice*, 21–22.

15   *The New York Times*, July 17, 1897.

16   *The New York Sun*, September 26, 1880.

17   *New York Tribune*, September 25, 1880.

18   Burke Roche, *Call Me Maurice*, 45.

19   Kehoe, *The Titled Americans*, xvii.

20   Burke Roche, *Call Me Maurice*, 46.

21   Burke Roche, 47.

Chapter 8: The Mother of the Special Relationship

1   Kehoe, *The Titled Americans*, 2–3.

2   Kehoe, 13.

3   Kehoe, 19–20.

4   Kehoe, 35–39.

5   Kehoe, 40.

6 Kehoe, 46.

7 Kehoe, 48.

8 Kehoe, 67.

9 Cornwallis-West, *The Reminiscences of Lady Randolph Churchill*, 47–48.

10 Kehoe, 60.

11 Cornwallis-West, 60–61.

12 Kehoe, 85.

13 Kehoe, 150.

14 Gray, *Passionate Mothers, Powerful Sons*, 148.

Chapter 9: "Not with the Crowd to Be Spent"

1 *The New York Times*, July 16, 1906.

2 Burke Roche, *Call Me Maurice*, 62.

3 *The New York Times*, July 16, 1906.

4 *The New York Times*, July 16, 1906; *New York Times*, November 13, 1901; *Depew (NY) Herald*, November 1, 1906; *New York Times*, September 9, 1907.

5 *The New York Times*, May 10, 1903.

6 *Philadelphia Inquirer*, September 21, 1902.

7 Burke Roche, "The Private Diaries of Frances Burke Roche."

8 *The Post-Standard, Syracuse*, NY, February 22, 1910.

9 Burke Roche, "The Private Diaries of Frances Burke Roche."

10 Ibid.

11 Ibid.

12 Wharton, *The Age of Innocence*, 108–11.

13 Burke Roche, "The Private Diaries of Frances Burke Roche."

14 *Chillicothe Gazette*, October 14, 1907; January 25, 1908; April 21, 1909; *The New York Times*, April 24, 1908.

15 Burke Roche, "The Private Diaries of Frances Burke Roche."

16 *The New York Times*, October 19, 1909.

17 *Chillicothe Gazette*, March 11, 1908.

18 *The Daily Scioto Gazette*, March 11, 1908.

19 *The New York Times*, April 24, 1908.

20 Burke Roche, "The Private Diaries of Frances Burke Roche."

21 *Chillicothe Gazette*, March 21, 1911.

22 Gray, *Passionate Mothers, Powerful Sons*, 182–83.

23 Gray, 185.

24 Gray, 198.

Chapter 10: Winston Takes Manhattan

1 Gray, *Passionate Mothers, Powerful Sons*, 176.

2 Gray, 177.

3 Gray, 233.

4 Gray, 235.

5 Gray, 236.

6 Gray, 245.

7 Gray, 268.

8 *Daily Express* (UK), May 27, 1912.

9 Unpublished diplomatic memoir of Ambassador Joseph P. Kennedy. John F. Kennedy Presidential Library and Museum.

10 Gray, 307.

11 Gray, 310–13.

Chapter 11: Dear Boy

1 Burke Roche, *Call Me Maurice*. January 1, 2009, ELSP, Hong Kong.

2 Burke Roche, 164.

3 Burke Roche, 187.

4 Burke Roche, 167.

5 *New York Tribune*, November 14, 1920; *New York Herald*, September 12, 1920.

6 Burke Roche, 114.

7 *Evening World*, May 10, 1911; *New York Times*, April 23, 1911.

8 Burke Roche, 119.

9 *New York Herald*, November 2, 1920.

10 *The Sentinel* (NC), November 16, 1923.

11 Burke Roche, 278.

12 *New York Herald*, February 13, 1921.

Chapter 12: Bachelor King of Hearts

1 *Daily News* (New York, New York.), December 4, 1927.

2 *New York Herald*, February 13, 1921.

3   Burke Roche, *Call Me Maurice*, 111.

4   Burke Roche, 111.

5   *Sunday Express* (Buffalo, New York), November 18, 1923.

6   *New York Daily Sunday News*, June 20, 1926.

7   *Enquirer* (OH), January 4, 1931.

8   *New York Daily News*, December 28, 1929.

9   Burke Roche, 285–87.

10   Burke Roche, 341.

11   Burke Roche, 353–54.

12   Burke Roche, 361.

13   *New York Daily News*, September 6, 1931.

14   *Buffalo Courier Express*, September 6, 1931.

15   Burke Roche, 372–82.

16   Burke Roche, 380.

17   Burke Roche, 384.

18   Burke Roche, 388.

19   *The New York Times*, January 27, 1947.

20   *Daily Telegraph* (UK), July 9, 1955.

Chapter 13: Hot Dogs and Martinis

1   Swift, *The Roosevelts and the Royals*, 103.

2   "The British Royal Visit," Franklin D. Roosevelt Presidential Library and Museum, fdrlibrary.org/royal-visit.

3   Swift, 77.

4   *Washington Herald*, August 28, 1935.

5   Swift, 100, 110.

6   Swift, 70. Sulgrave Manor archive.

7   Franklin D. Roosevelt to King George VI, September 17, 1938, Franklin D. Roosevelt Presidential Library and Museum, Hyde Park, NY.

8   Swift, 110.

9   Swift, 113.

10   Swift, 119.

11   "Marian Anderson and the DAR," Daughters of the American Revolution, https://www.dar.org/national-society/marian-anderson/marian-anderson-and-dar.

12 Swift, 122.

13 *Cincinnati Inquirer*, June 10, 1939.

14 Elizabeth's Virginian ancestry. Royal Family Archive.

15 Swift, 135.

16 Swift, 137.

17 Swift, 137.

18 St. James Episcopal Church archive, Hyde Park, NY.

19 Letters from the public to Mrs. Roosevelt, June 1939, Franklin D. Roosevelt Presidential Library and Museum, Hyde Park, NY.

20 Letter from Queen Elizabeth, the Queen Mother, to Mrs. Roosevelt, June 11, 1940, Franklin D. Roosevelt Presidential Library and Museum, Hyde Park, NY.

21 Ambassador Lindsay to Lord Halifax, Foreign Office cable, June 20, 1939.

Chapter 14: Between Us and We

1 Gray, *Passionate Mothers, Powerful Sons*, 351.

2 Franklin D. Roosevelt Presidential Library and Museum, Hyde Park, NY.

3 Swift, *The Roosevelts and the Royals*, 156.

4 Letter from Mrs. Roosevelt to Queen Elizabeth, May 1, 1940, Diplomatic Correspondence; Letter from Queen Elizabeth to Mrs. Roosevelt, June 11, 1940, Diplomatic Correspondence.

5 Winston Churchill address to House of Commons, May 13, 1940.

6 Swift, 161.

7 Churchill address to Joint Session of Congress, December 26, 1941.

8 Swift, 194–95.

9 Swift, 261.

10 The Society of the Cincinnati, societyofthecincinnati.org.

11 Clark, "Cincinnatus on Downing Street."

12 The Society of the Cincinnati archives.

13 *Richmond Times-Dispatch*, April 11, 1963.

Chapter 15: Nothing Like a Dame

1 Sulgrave Manor Archive, *A History of the National Society of the Colonial Dames of America and Sulgrave Manor, 1914–1977*, 42.

2 Smith, *Sulgrave Manor and the Washingtons, 1242*. Macmillan, 1933.

3   Smith, 1456.

4   Sulgrave Manor Archive, *A History of the National Society of the Colonial Dames of America and Sulgrave Manor, 1914–1977*, 42.

5   Great American Treasures, https://www.greatamericantreasures.org/.

6   Smith, 206, 233.

7   Smith, 994.

8   Mount Vernon Ladies Association archives on Washington family coat of arms. Sulgrave Manor Archive.

9   Smith, Sulgrave Manor and the Washingtons.

10   Smith, 2809.

11   Sulgrave Manor Archive, *A History of the National Society of the Colonial Dames of America and Sulgrave Manor, 1914–1977*, 5.

12   Sulgrave Manor Archive, *A History of the National Society of the Colonial Dames of America and Sulgrave Manor, 1914–1977*, 42.

13   National Society of the Colonial Dames of America, nscda.org.

14   Sulgrave Manor Archive, *A History of the National Society of the Colonial Dames of America and Sulgrave Manor, 1914–1977*, 6.

15   Mount Vernon Ladies Association archives.

16   Sulgrave Manor Archive, *A History of the National Society of the Colonial Dames of America and Sulgrave Manor, 1914–1977*, 8.

17   Smith, 1747.

18   Smith, 2247.

19   Smith, 2557, 2556.

20   *Illustrated London News*, June 30, 1922.

21   Sulgrave Manor Archive, *A History of the National Society of the Colonial Dames of America and Sulgrave Manor, 1914–1977*, 24.

22   Sulgrave Manor Archive, *A History of the National Society of the Colonial Dames of America and Sulgrave Manor, 1914–1977*, 20.

23   Spencer, *The Spencers*, 306–7.

24   Spencer, 306.

25   Spencer, 314.

26   Spencer, 311.

27   Sulgrave Manor Archive, *A History of the National Society of the Colonial Dames of America and Sulgrave Manor, 1914–1977*, 32.

28   Sulgrave Manor Archive, *A History of the National Society of the Colonial Dames of America and Sulgrave Manor, 1914–1977*, 36.

29   "Attlee and Wife at Sulgrave Manor (1940–1949)," YouTube, https://www.youtube.com/watch?v=RUzdOH640tw.

30   Spencer, *The Spencers*, 312–13.

31   Smith, *Sulgrave Manor and the Washingtons*, 2643.

32   *Philadelphia Inquirer*, July 7–8, 1976.

33   Public remarks of Queen Elizabeth II, July 6, 1976, Philadelphia, PA.

Chapter 16: Elm Court

1   *The New York Times*, May 3, 1896.

2   King, *A Season of Splendor*, 299.

3   King, 300.

4   King, 300.

5   King, 300–303.

6   King, 303–17.

7   King, 326.

8   King, 319–26.

9   *New York Times*, September 2, 1902.

10   *Good Housekeeping*, 1904, 343.

11   *The New York Times*, December 19, 1966; June 16, 1921.

12   *The New York Times*, July 25, 1922.

13   *The New York Times*, December 31, 1966.

14   *The New York Times*, August 30, 1942; August 4, 1947; November 30, 2019.

15   *Chillicothe Gazette*, October 29, 1981.

16   Ibid.

17   Ibid.

18   Ibid.

19   Author's tour of Elm Court, August 2025.

Chapter 17: "Fix Your Eyes Upon the Real"

1   Brown, *The Diana Chronicles*, 68.

2   Burke Roche, "The Private Diaries of Frances Burke Roche."

3   Campbell, *The Real Diana*, 4.

4   Campbell, 21.

5   Campbell, 32.

6   Campbell, 31.

7   Spencer, *The Spencers*, 90–91.

8   Campbell, 46.

9   Campbell, 61.

10   Campbell, 65.

11   Campbell, 68.

12   Campbell, 81.

13   Campbell, 83

14   King, *A Season of Splendor*, 407–15.

15   Mrs. Frances Shand Kydd, letter to the editor, *Times* (UK), December, 1980.

16   *Washington Post*, July 10, 1981.

17   Campbell, 140.

18   Burke Roche, "The Private Diaries of Frances Burke Roche."

19   *The New York Times*, August 20, 1984.

20   *People*, July 22, 2025.

21   Burke Roche, "The Private Diaries of Frances Burke Roche."

22   Interview with Diana, Princess of Wales by Martin Bashir, *Panorama*, November 20, 1995.

23   Burke Roche, "The Private Diaries of Frances Burke Roche."

24   Ibid.

25   Ibid.

26   *Newsday*, February 3, 1989.

27   Ibid.

28   *Newsday*, February 5, 1989.

29   Burke Roche, "The Private Diaries of Frances Burke Roche."

30   Diana & HIV: we remember our patron 20 years on, National AIDS Trust, https://nat.org.uk/views/diana-hiv-we-remember-our-patron-20-years-on/.

31   Interview of Diana, Princess of Wales, Angola, 1997.

32   Campbell, 199.

33   Morton, 28.

34   Morton, 31.

35   Morton, 52.

36   Queen Elizabeth II's public remarks on the fortieth anniversary of her accession, 1992.

37   Morton, 83.

38   Morton, 97.

39   *Washington Post*, June 3, 2004.

40   Morton, 106–107.

41   Morton, 125.

42   Interview with the Prince of Wales, ITV, June 1994.

43   Morton, 234.

44   Hillary Clinton public remarks on the White House visit of Diana, Princess of Wales, June 1997.

45   Morton, 140.

46   President Trump interview with Piers Morgan, *Good Morning Britain*, May 2016.

47   Morton, 142.

48   Interview with Diana, Princess of Wales by Martin Bashir, *Panorama*, November 20, 1995.

49   Morton, 212

50   Eulogy of Charles, Earl Spencer at the funeral of Diana, Princess of Wales, September 6, 1997.

51   Morton, 212.

52   Morton, 209.

53   Morton, 213.

54   *Chicago Tribune*, June 5, 1996.

55   Author interview with Father Frank Gelli, August 2025.

56   Morton, 230.

57   Morton, 235.

58   Morton, 235.

Chapter 18: American Crown

1   *Runner's World*, September 20, 2023.

2   Jobson, *William at 40*, xxi–xxii.

3   *Page Six*, September 19, 2023.

4   *Newsweek*, September 8, 2022.

5   Jobson, 1.

6   Jobson, 4.

7   Jobson, 7.

8   Jobson, 12.

9   Jobson, 15.

10   Jobson, 29.

11   Jobson, 37.

12   *Daily Express* (UK), March 24, 2022.

13   Eton College Collections, etoncollege.com.

14   *British GQ*, July 2017.

15   Eulogy of Charles, Earl Spencer at at the funeral of Diana, Princess of Wales, September 6, 1997.

16   Jobson, 63–64.

17   Jobson, 73.

18   *Times* (UK), May 23, 2025.

19   https://www.dontwalk.co.uk/.

20   Jobson, 98–99.

21   International Churchill Society, winstonchurchill.org.

22   Lady Colin Campbell YouTube channel; Jobson, 177.

23   BBC interview with Prince William and Catherine Middleton, November 16, 2010.

24   *Guardian* (UK), July 10, 2011.

25   *Diana, Our Mother: Her Life and Legacy*, ITV, July 24, 2017.

26   *Vanity Fair*, October 2017.

27   Jobson, 226.

28   *Telegraph* (UK), January 13, 2023.

29   Royal Foundation Forum, February 28, 2018.

30   *Guardian* (UK), January 4, 2023.

31   Statement from The Duke and Duchess of Sussex, January 8, 2020.

32   Statement from Her Majesty The Queen, January 18, 2020.

33   *Guardian* (UK), March 25, 2022.

34   *Good Morning America*, February 16, 2024.

35   Jobson, 256.

36   Royal Foundation of the Prince and Princess of Wales, September 17, 2021.

37   Remarks by President Trump, State Banquet, Windsor Castle, September 17, 2025.

38   Remarks by His Majesty the King, State Banquet, Windsor Castle, September 17, 2025.

INDEX